Leaving China

World Social Change

Series Editor: Mark Selden

Leaving China

Media, Migration, and Transnational Imagination

Wanning Sun

ROWMAN & LITTLEFIELD PUBLISHERS, INC.
Lanham • Boulder • New York • Oxford

ROWMAN & LITTLEFIELD PUBLISHERS, INC.

Published in the United States of America
by Rowman & Littlefield Publishers, Inc.
A Member of the Rowman & Littlefield Publishing Group
4720 Boston Way, Lanham, Maryland 20706
www.rowmanlittlefield.com

12 Hid's Copse Road
Cumnor Hill, Oxford OX2 9JJ, England

British Library Cataloguing in Publication Information Available

Library of Congress Cataloging-in-Publication Data

Sun, Wanning, 1963–
    Leaving China : media, migration, and transnational imagination / Wanning Sun.
        p. cm.—(World social change)
    Includes bibliographical references and index.
    ISBN 0-7425-1796-9 (alk. paper)—ISBN 0-7425-1797-7 (pbk. : alk. paper)
    1. Mass media—China. 2. China—Emigration and immigration. 3. Migration,
Internal—China. 4. Chinese—Foreign countries—Communication. I. Title. II.
Series.

P92.C5 S86 2002
    302.23'0951—dc21

                                                                    2002001948

Printed in the United States of America

♾™ The paper used in this publication meets the minimum requirements of
American National Standard for Information Sciences—Permanence of Paper
for Printed Library Materials, ANSI/NISO Z39.48–1992.

Contents

Preface

The completion of this manuscript coincided with a few newsworthy events involving China on the global stage: Beijing won the bid to host the Olympic Games in 2008; China became a member of the World Trade Organization; and Rupert Murdoch's Phoenix TV finally entered the Chinese market. While these are newsworthy stories for the Western press—after all, they signify the triumph of global media culture and transnational capitalism—empirical questions about what these events mean to ordinary Chinese people are seldom considered, either in journalistic or in academic terms. How, for instance, do Chinese villagers relate to global spaces such as the World Trade Center and global places such as New York, while watching the globally transmitted images of the September 11 tragedies? Will these attacks on the United States—on a day that is supposed to have changed the world—alter the ways in which urban Chinese residents fantasize about going to America? And how will those former mainland Chinese now living in diaspora feel about being Chinese while viewing the 2008 Games on television? Although this book does not directly address these issues, it aims to provide some clues as to where the answers to these and a range of related questions may lie.

The Chinese mediascape at the beginning of the twenty-first century presents a tableau that features both the mobility of people and the movement of media images. More than ever before, people leave their village homes to go to the city, head for the prosperous south, or go overseas. Narratives of social change in contemporary China are inevitably linked to the motifs of departure, arrival, and return. Similarly, Chinese media products are also in flux, as Chinese productions are consumed offshore, and foreign images enter the

Chinese mediascape. As Arjun Appadurai, the cultural theorist of modernity and postnationalism, says succinctly, when images and people are both in circulation, the ways in which modern subjectivity is constructed become unpredictable. In this book, by constructing a narrative about the trajectories of Chinese people and Chinese images since the early 1990s, I am attempting to understand and account for this unpredictability. I seek to describe a number of key moments in the arena of cultural production and consumption whereby tension, contradiction, and ambivalence mark the variegated process of evolution in the transnational imagination of nationals of the People's Republic of China.

A number of people whose intellectual strength and integrity I admire—they know who they are—have advised me at various times that I should simply follow my heart when it comes to deciding which research projects to pursue. This book is evidence that I have taken their advice. Since I left China more than a decade ago, the feelings associated with departure and arrival, and with leaving and returning, have always colored my experience—both intellectual and emotional. Perhaps writing a book about these issues is simply a way of trying to understand and articulate—and hence come to terms with—the reality of being a Chinese migrant who has ended up as a media and cultural studies academic in the West. This is not to say that my thinking on these issues can be put to rest with the completion of this book. A few months ago my parents, who live in China, came to visit me in Western Australia. I initially puzzled and subsequently astonished them by inadvertently describing my recent China trip as *chuguo* (going overseas), rather than *huiguo* (returning home from overseas). On seeing the slightly put-out expressions on their faces—who could blame them for feeling hurt when they see that their daughter no longer considers China her home?—I realized that the business of negotiating the tension between here and there, now and then, is a lifelong career, as long as the mind stays active and curious.

This book is also the outcome of many years' consumption of Chinese media, including press, films, television dramas, and, recently, Internet materials. I take seriously John Hartley's (author of *Uses of Television*) urging to television academics to "go on, watch more television." I am, when it comes to watching TV, closer to the status of a confirmed addict than to that of an occasional abuser. Through this intimate relationship with the small screen, I have come to appreciate the importance of treating media representations as significant cultural texts through which the lived experience of individuals is mediated and made public and visible. This experience of immersing myself in the fictitious world of the screen also teaches me that human affect, desire, and feelings are crucial, yet somewhat elusive, social experiences, which we must take into account in seeking to understand the social transformations and transitions of a given society. Similarly, the experience of consuming media—the diverse ways in which people see a film, watch a show on television, or visit a website on the Internet—mundane and trivial as they may be to some, nevertheless hold significant answers to the ways in which modern subjectivity is (trans)formed. For this reason, I am thankful to the many participants in my ethnographic audience research (many of whom prefer to remain anonymous)—particularly, Liu Jingyuan, Huang Cheng, and Gao Xiangzhu, with whom I spent many pleasurable hours, watching TV, eating, talking, and telling stories about being Chinese.

Parts of this book are revised from articles published over the last couple of years. Although they have been substantially developed and rewritten here, I would like to acknowledge these journals for giving me permission to draw on these materials. They come from "A Tale of Two Chinese Villages: Television, Women and Modernity," *Asian Journal of Communication* (Asia Media and Information Center) 11, no. 2 (2001): 18–38; "To Go or Not to Go to America: Cinema and the Desiring City," *Hybridities: Cultures, Identities and Theories* (Oxford University Press) 1, no. 2 (2001): 1–21; "A Chinese in the New World: Television Dramas, Global Cities, and Travels to Modernity," *Inter-Asia Cultural Studies* (Routledge, Taylor & Francis) 4, no. 1 (2001): 25–44; "Media Events or Media Stories? Time, Space and Chinese (Trans)nationalism," *International Journal of Cultural Studies* (Sage Publications) 2, no. 1 (2000): 81–94; and "Internet, Memory, and the Chinese Diaspora—The Case of Nanjing Massacre Websites," *New Formations* (Lawrence & Wishart) 40 (2000): 30–48. An early version of the first section of chapter 8 also appeared as "Semiotic Over-Determination or Indoctritainment: Television, Citizenship, and the Olympic Games" in the Routledge-Curzon volume *Media in China*.

Individual chapters in the book have at different stages benefited from advice and feedback from a number of people, including Justine Lloyd, Stephanie Hemelryk Donald, Harriet Evans, Yao Souchou, David S. G. Goodman, Michael Keane, Helen Wilson, Peter Mares, Glen Lewis, and Norbert Ruebsaat. Elizabeth Jacka, John Sinclair, and Chua Beng-huat offered useful advice on the early stage of preparing the manuscript proposal. Special thanks to James Donald for putting friendly pressure on me to get the book published, and many friends—most particularly, Justine Lloyd, Mark Gibson, Vera Mackie, John Fitzgerald, and Steve Mickler, from whose thoughts and ideas I have often benefited. My liaison with the China Provincial Research Centre at UTS-UNSW over the past five years has given me opportunities to go to China regularly, so I am indebted to both David S. G. Goodman and Hans Hendrishcke for their support. Michael Cunningham provided technical support in reproducing visual images, and Jane Mummery was unfailingly competent in her copyediting assistance. Pi Dawei from *Beijing Review* kindly supplied the artwork for the front cover. Thanks, of course, go to Susan McEachern at Rowman & Littlefield for her advice and support.

The person to whom I am most indebted to is Mark Selden, whom Rowman & Littlefield had the genius to appoint as a series editor. I have yet to meet Mark in person, but judging from the many editions of "track changes" he has left on electronic copies of all my chapters, and the tons of e-mail correspondence we shared, I have come to be convinced that he indeed does exist and is not simply a cyberian figment of my imagination. To this day, I remain amazed by the breadth of his intellectual curiosity, his capacity to understand and accommodate difference across disciplines, and, above all, his unfailingly fair and frank feedback. I am just downright lucky to have him as an editor.

I have the good fortune of being married to Jim Beattie, whose support and understanding for my work manifest themselves in too many ways to enumerate here. This book is dedicated to him, and to my parents in China, for always being "there."

Introduction:
Leaving China

On May 10, 1999, some eighty Chinese students gathered outside the U.S. embassy in Tokyo to protest NATO's bombing of the Chinese embassy in Belgrade. Waving Chinese flags and photos of Chinese journalists killed in the bombing, these Chinese students from various universities in Tokyo also handed the U.S. Embassy a letter of protest against the United States and NATO.[1] Meanwhile, anti-American sentiment soared in urban China. For three days, university students staged anti-American riots outside the U.S. embassy in Beijing, forcing it to close down. A few days after those riots, the protest took an interesting turn: The students gathered outside the embassy again, this time with another demand, that the United States immediately reopen its visa office.[2]

The Americans are not the only ones the Chinese students love to hate. In August 2001, Feng Jinhua, a Chinese national who has lived in Japan for many years and currently works as a professional there, was arrested for painting "you deserve to die" (*gai si*) on the Yasukuni Shrine (the shrine commemorating Japan's war dead, including eleven men convicted as war criminals at the Tokyo Tribunal) to protest the Japanese prime minister's official visit to the shrine on August 13, 2001.[3] Meanwhile, growing numbers of Chinese have found their way to Japan as tourists, students, and prospective immigrants. In 2000, Japan, for the first time, allowed Chinese to visit Japan on tourist visas, requiring each to deposit 50,000 yuan (over U.S.$6,000) as a guarantee of their return to China.[4] Around the end of 1999, Kyoto immigration officers took twenty-eight Chinese nationals into custody on suspicion of illegally entering and staying in Japan by passing themselves off as relatives of two Japanese women who lived in China before the China–Japan

1

War. The incident followed the relaxation of Japan's immigration rules, allowing relatives of former Japanese settlers in China to migrate.[5]

Despite repeated examples of anger directed particularly toward the U.S. and Japanese governments, and despite the sometimes less than hospitable reception of the host nations, the trend of going abroad—temporarily or permanently, as students or visitors, legal and otherwise—seems unstoppable. For millions of Chinese who have never set foot on foreign soil, the world out there remains a place of perpetual fascination. As a popular Chinese song puts it: "the outside world is indeed fantastic" (*waimian de shijie heng jingcai*). Acting out these fantasies sometimes can prove costly. In June 2000, fifty-eight Chinese nationals, each paying a "snakehead" an average of U.S.$22,700 to go abroad, were found dead in the back of a refrigerator truck at the southern English port of Dover, trying to enter Britain illegally. The Chinese official media release expressed its sympathy to the relatives of these want-to-be migrants, but blamed the "snakeheads," and to a lesser extent, some Western nations' asylum-granting system, for the tragedy.[6]

These vignettes reveal a scenario of danger, poignancy, unpredictability, and even irony, which marks the transnational imagination of Chinese nationals. What lends potency to the dangerous fantasies entertained by those prospective illegal immigrants who are prepared to risk everything, including their lives, in order to leave China? Will the desire to improve one's lifestyle and fortunes through migration—in the case of Chinese nationals wanting to go to Japan—fragment or dislodge a memory of China's former enemy? And how do we account for the obvious ambivalence in the Chinese students' imagination of the United States and Japan, countries that they want to go to, yet hate with passion? What is the position of the Chinese government in these variegated transnational practices, and to what extent are the media responsive to, and constitutive of, such uneven, unequal, and sometimes schizophrenic processes?

The impulse to find some answers to these intriguing questions is the driving force behind the writing of this book. In choosing to call it *Leaving China*, I hope to record my observations mostly from the vantage point of Australia—albeit an antipodean position—of various ways in which China has been "left." The first of these "leavings" was by way of outbound migration—including temporary and permanent ones. Since the start of economic reforms in the late 1970s, successive waves of scholars, students, and business people have left the country to go to various corners of the world, with the United States, Canada, the United Kingdom, Japan, and Australia being their most popular destinations. While some of these students have stayed on and settled in their host countries, others have chosen to return; many have become perennial travelers, repeatedly traversing the territorial and cultural spaces of both homeland and host country. At the turn of the new century, traveling abroad continues, with increasing numbers of young Chinese going overseas for self-funded undergraduate study. According to the official figures released by the Chinese Ministry of Education, since the start of economic reform, 370,000 Chinese students—self-funded and state-funded— have gone overseas, with a return rate of one in three. Out of the sampled groups, roughly 40 percent went to the United States, 22 percent to Japan, and 6 percent to Australia, followed by Canada, France, and U.K.[7] This seems like a conservative figure and clearly does not include the family members who have gone overseas to be with the students. Even Japan, a country known to the Chinese for its exceptionally stringent immigration policy, now allegedly hosts 200,000 mainland Chinese, not including the 50,000 who have overstayed their visas and are living in Japan illegally.[8] In June 2001, the spokesperson of the Chinese Ministry of Education announced that the Chinese government does not approve of sending Chinese students abroad for primary and secondary education, a belated recognition of the growing numbers of students going abroad at earlier ages. Although the government thinks that it has done the right thing to allow hundreds of thousands of students for tertiary and postgraduate education for the past two decades, it cites the loss of Chinese culture and premature exposure to unhealthy Western influence as the main reasons for discouraging Chinese nationals from going abroad for primary and secondary education.[9] Apart from outbound Chinese going abroad to study (*liuxuesheng*), hundreds of thousands of Chinese now annually cross the national borders for purposes of tourism, business, and visiting friends and families. The borders between Hong Kong, Taiwan, Macao, and the mainland have become increasingly porous; Singapore, Malaysia, and Thailand (dubbed *xing ma tai*) have been the favorite tourist destinations for China's affluent urban residents and "new rich"; and sizable numbers of people enter the United States, Canada, Australia, and some parts of Europe regularly for personal and business reasons.

The concept of departures and arrivals, like that of borders, can be reconfigured to include both imaginary and real travels. In addition, the leaving of one's *homeland*—denoting the crossing of a national border—should not be considered a distinct species of event from that of leaving one's *hometown*. Both can more usefully be seen as subspecies of the wider notion of leaving *home*. Leaving one's hometown therefore entails a parallel process of mobility to leaving one's homeland, and, within China, this mostly takes the trajectory of rural to urban, north to south, hinterland to coast, and coast to international. The interconnectedness between, and hence the need to link, these two types of movement lies in the fact that, first, they may represent different stages of movement in the life of one individual; and second, both migrant groups need to negotiate a similar set of tensions and challenges brought about by their (sometimes voluntary) displacement.

Leaving China considers not only the movement—both actual and prospective—of people within or beyond China, but also the ways in which media images, media formats, and media practices themselves travel. Alongside the movement of people within and across national borders, we see an increasingly deterritorialized flow of media images, as well as the adoption of new media formats and practices. For instance, the project of the Chinese state to promote patriotism offshore would not have taken off without the Chinese Central Television (CCTV hereafter) now covering its satellite footprints in many parts of America, Europe, and Oceania. While Chinese newspapers may still be physically restricted to largely domestic circulation, their electronic versions—including both provincial and local publications—are nevertheless accessible via the Internet to those living outside China. At the end of 2000, the Ministry of Information under the State Council in China granted sina.com, a leading Internet media and service company for Chinese communities worldwide, permission to publish online news, making sina.com the first private Internet company in China to receive official approval to publish news and information on the Web. Official Chinese news organizations such as the New China News Agency (Xinhua) and CCTV provide both print and online versions and participate in the staging of media events that may be of national and global interest. Also, documentaries about Chinese living overseas, produced by migrants themselves, are broadcast on national television in China, while television dramas originally screened nationally in China find their way within weeks into video stores in Chinatowns in major world cities; websites maintained by Chinese communities in America, Europe, and Australasia link three continents through a regular feed of cultural products from the PRC "motherland"; and Star TV brings endless channels of Chinese television to the homes of those former PRC citizens around the world who can afford to have a satellite dish on their roof. A transnational imagination is also evident in screen productions emanating from the PRC, which increasingly feature foreigners, foreign locations, and Chinese in foreign settings. For instance, less than a decade since the making of the famous *Beijing Native in New York*, Zheng Xiaolong and his wife—both having lived in the United States as *liuxuesheng*—took their crew to St. Louis, in the heart of the United States, and produced *Treatment* (2000) (*Guasha*), the first Chinese joint production shot in a foreign location, marking the entry of Chinese film production into transnational spaces. For another example, in 2001 CCTV completed the production of *A Modern Family* (*modeng jiating*), a drama series about three children in a family who are involved in interracial marriages or love affairs. Shot in China, Korea, Malaysia, and Australia and involving actors and crew of the four countries, this drama of transnational romance is also scheduled to be screened on Malaysian and Korean television.[10]

Finally, "leaving China" refers to the vicarious travels of millions of Chinese media consumers borne aloft by their imaginations. That is, the book also explores the ways in which the forces of globalization have had an impact on media production and consumption in China in the reform era and the ways they have shaped the formation and transformation of a Chinese transnational imagination. When the movement of people and the flow of images are brought together, rendering unpredictable what Appadurai calls the "self-imagining as an everyday social project,"[11] the meanings of place, space, community, and nation become unstable and contestable. Although some people's lives have been changed for the better by travel, others' have been severely disadvantaged by it. Some have chosen to travel; others have had migration thrust upon them. Some people's travel has facilitated the process of their transnational imagination, others' has hindered it. This book explores the ways in which the movement of both images and people within and across the national borders of the PRC have had an impact on the "work of the imagination"[12] and also considers the nature of the relationship between these two kinds of movement. I am interested in both those who travel and those who may or may not travel, but nevertheless participate in the production and consumption of images and narratives of travel, hence contributing to the formation of transnational subjectivities. For instance, during the last decade or so, narratives of Chinese going to cities within China or going abroad—either literally or in their imaginations—have frequently been the subject matter of cinema, television dramas, novels, and popular journalism, gradually but definitely transforming the social imagination of space and place among Chinese audiences.

CHINESE TRANSNATIONALISM

A project that is concerned with departures and arrivals[13] must recognize that, quite often, the traveler's imaginary construction of foreign and unknown places precedes her or his actual arrival in these places; sometimes, it replaces actual travel altogether. Given this, it is crucial not only to attend to the transnational subjectivity that develops within those who actually migrate, but also to recognize and explore this phenomenon within those who have not, will not, or cannot leave. Bizarre, stupid, or tragic as they may sound, the recurring media stories of some Chinese nationals willing to pay their lifetime saving—and many times more—and endure untold humiliations and risk death or being caught in order to be smuggled to more affluent countries serve as sobering reminders of the danger and the power of transnational imagination. In this book, the investigation of the formation of a transnational imagination involves a number of things.

First, it calls for a fine-grained analysis of the significant narrative forms and discursive strategies used in representing transnational space. This includes looking at how those who are immobile fantasize about faraway or unknown places, and how those who have resettled remember experiences of familiar places about their lives prior to geographical displacement. These acts of fantasy and remembrance take place in a proliferation of spaces—mediatized or actual—all of which have an impact on the formation of transnational spatial imagination. For instance, the China Central Radio's *Lunch Hour* (*wu jian yi xiao shi*) runs *Winds from Abroad* (*hai wai lai feng*) on Sunday. Featuring conversations with mainland Chinese now studying or working overseas, the show is popular with domestic audiences for its capacity to "transport" the audience to unfamiliar places.

Second, studying transnational imagination means asking the question as to what mobility—of people, capital, and images—does to localities through individuals' constructions of a sense of place. Some Chinese mainlanders now living in America challenge the "hegemonic" Chinese translation of American cities, suggesting, for instance, that "Washington" could be called *hua sheng tun* ("peanut village"), not *hua sheng dun* ("prosperous fortress"). Facetious and frivolous as this may be, it seems to suggest—albeit in a small way—the demise of a cargo-cult mentality about "America." Canberra, the capital of Australia, though officially translated into *kanpeila*, is now often referred to by the mainland Chinese-language newspapers in Australia as *kanjing*, resonating with Beijing, the capital of the PRC. Could this be read as a signifier of an imperialistic desire—however inchoate—of some people from the Middle Kingdom? Of particular relevance to the investigation of the construction of a sense of place is the need to examine the changing styles of imagining "the city"—both the "international global city" that acts as a magnet for Third World migrants and the "internal global city" to which Third World rural "migrants" gravitate within their own country.

Third, the inquiry into the formation of a transnational imagination necessitates looking at the ways in which individuals engage or identify with the imagination of people in other places, especially in other national spaces. This includes those many Chinese who have not been overseas, but who identify with the experiences and thoughts of those who have. It also includes Chinese who have left China to live in transnational spaces, and who continue to engage with the imagination of those who have remained "at home." Beijing Television Station's multiple-episode sitcom *Liumei Fangke* (Chinese Tenants in an American House, 1997), for instance, is hilarious to both the domestic audiences and diasporic audiences seeking fun (*zao le*) from "chewing the fat" (*tiao kan*) precisely because it cleverly appropriates a political language reminiscent of the socialist era in China to talk about the lives of a bunch of Chinese living in contemporary America. Fourth, building on, and closely related to, the first three concerns, this investigation into transnational imagination entails looking into the ways in which various forces—economic, social, and political—come to facilitate or inhibit the formation of a particular kind of transnational subjectivity. In other words, I want to show that the formation of transnational imagination is an uneven, unequal, and disjunctive process. The proliferation of media images of the "successful man" (*chengong renshi*) is contiguous with the omission and the marginalization of other social groups, such as laid-off factory workers and rural migrants.[14] My inquiry into the lives of a group of rural women migrants in Anhui now working in Shanghai, for example, suggests that since leaving the village, many have had less time, energy, and opportunities to consume transnational images from media and participate in the act of imagining.

Chinese transnationalism has been studied at a number of levels: the cultural politics of Chinese societies across several geographical entities;[15] the circulation, financing, distribution, and marketing of Chinese cultural products in the age of transnational capitalism;[16] and the production of transnational subjectivities via the representation and consumption of Chinese national, cultural, ethnic, and gender identities of both individuals and communities in mainland and diasporic contexts.[17] This book focuses on this last dimension, but does not exclude the first two. In doing so, it highlights the moment at which the entire nation started to travel to new places—real or imaginary, literally or vicariously. While some want to leave their home(land) for good, others imagine a possible return. It is the variegated nature of this transnational imagining—be it through physical traveling, through identifying with travelers in the everyday consumption of media images, or through other enabling media practices such as the use of videos and the Internet—that is the object of investigation for this book.

My investigation is premised on the following assumption: that the tension between the global and the local is a universal problematic of disjuncture between global late capitalism and the resurgence of nativism. Anthony Smith has identified the tension as one between global culture, which is memoryless and deterritorialized, and national culture, which is time-bound and location-specific.[18] My book takes this tension as its point of departure and seeks to examine a number of ways in which the movement of both people and images reworks and rearticulates the self, spatial imagination, and cultural memory, in both China and certain diasporic Chinese groups worldwide. This tension is particularly pronounced in the case of cultural flow into and out of the PRC. This, as I consistently argue throughout the book, is because unlike elsewhere, the formation and transformation of Chinese transnational consciousness is punctuated, at each crucial moment, by the towering presence of a strong state. It is also burdened by a tenacious national memory of imperialist subjugation and a revolutionary history of resistance to imperialism.

By focusing on a number of ways in which transnational Chinese subjectivities are produced as a result of growing mobility within China and outbound migration to the West in the reform era, this project addresses the issue of mobility per se, and, in doing so, bridges the customary divide between internal migration studies and diasporic studies. In addition, by looking at the impact of mobility on the imagination, it points to a range of ways in which cultural identities and subjectivities are renegotiated. Through a historically grounded and geographically specific analysis of an array of transnational cultural practices, this investigation aims to make possible a new understanding of the relationship between cultural flow and subjectivity formation in a number of contexts. For instance, it addresses the following questions: What goes on in the minds of Chinese in diaspora when they watch videos of television dramas taped from Chinese television? How do images of foreigners and world cities affect the imagination of television viewers in remote Chinese villages? How do the televised images of overseas Chinese cheering for Chinese athletes at the Sydney Olympic Stadium speak to audiences back in China?

In searching for an apt description of the form of Chinese transnationalism apropos of former PRC nationals who are no longer living in China, I have found some of the existing theorizations on diaspora useful as points of reference, but ultimately wanting. Tu Weiming's notion of Cultural China, consisting of the "three symbolic universes,"[19] for instance, does not sufficiently recognize the pluralism within and the movement between them. It would also be inappropriate to lump this group under the general umbrella of the "Chinese diaspora," assuming a deterritorialized and mobile transnational Chinese subjectivity.[20] In an interesting article called "What Is This Thing Called the Chinese Diaspora?" Stephan Chan observes, "Chineseness doesn't need a country, a kingdom, or a state; it is a condition and that condition is sustained by its place in a community anywhere."[21] If this condition called "Chineseness" is the defining quality of the Chinese diaspora, then the departures and arrivals I have described in this book of a more recent Chinese community consisting of former PRC nationals are yet to qualify as "diasporic," since they still need to speak to the Chinese state and nation.

These former PRC nationals cannot forget their country, their kingdom, or the state; neither do their country and the Chinese state want to forget them. On the other hand, they strategically "haggle" with China and carve out a space of being Chinese in relation to the "motherland" and the Chinese state, as well as to the new worlds in which they find themselves. In fact, it is precisely in their negotiated and fraught interactions—mediated in some instances and direct in other—with China that their identities are constantly (re)defined. In trying to carve out a unique space inhabited by this group of people, I find Naficy's concept of the "cultural exile"—both voluntary and involuntary, both political and cultural—useful. His distinction between exile and diaspora—the former still identifies with the motherland, while the latter identifies with the expatriate communities outside the motherland—is also useful.[22] However, I am reluctant to adopt the category of exile without qualification, since I want to argue that political banishment—a concept central to exile—applies only to a small handful of political dissidents. In addition, the relationship between the Chinese state and many of its "wandering sons and daughters" (*hai wan you zi*), an official way of describing its citizens who have gone abroad, is still marked with engagement and entanglement. I am for this reason tempted to describe this transitional—and transnational—position as *paradiasporic*, if I may coin an expression. Under the rubric of this general understanding, I nevertheless see fit to mobilize, at different places, a variety of terms, including *exile* and *diaspora*, and *expatriate* and *migrant* to describe the people in this community. Throughout this book, I try not to delineate between "China" and the "diaspora," instead arguing that media production and consumption in the age of globalization and convergence have created an electronic community of the Chinese nation, consisting of both PRC nationals and former PRC nationals who left China in recent years. I shall argue consistently that this community, living both inside and outside China, but inhabiting an increasingly connected mediatized symbolic space, is made possible not in spite of, but precisely because of, the power of the Chinese state and the strength of a collective memory of the Chinese nation.

POSITIONS AND METHODS

My approach, unlike some other recent theorizations of Chinese modernity and globalization, insists on considering the centrality of the question of the Chinese state in order to understand some less "flexible,"[23] less deterritorialized, but nevertheless transnational, cultural practices. In addition, I argue for an engagement with, and reworking of, issues of territoriality, national history, and cultural memory, in order to consider a more temporal dimension of cultural transaction. This dimension is not so much concerned with the spatial flow of cultural products across the borders between China, Hong Kong, and Taiwan, as with the tension and negotiation between a relatively cohesive memory of a Chinese nation and the contemporary reality of globalization, migration, and displacement. Finally, this fresh perspective demonstrates both the usefulness of, and the potential risk in, using travel as a metaphor in studying contemporary China. Although the project is, in part, an examination of the ways in which the Chinese state seeks to retain its power over the social imagination of the Chinese people, the locus of such an investigation can no longer be limited to the national space of the PRC and must extend to wherever its people and images travel to. What emerges from this methodological intervention is an understanding of cultural and media production and consumption in the PRC that takes account of the forces of globalization not just in terms of capital and structure, but also in terms of people and meanings of media images.

Combining fine-grained cultural analysis with in-depth interviews with television and video audiences and Internet users, I consider cultural production and consumption, including analyses of transnational uses of the Internet, television, video, and films, in a synthesis of a number of disparate disciplinary areas: diasporic Chinese studies, China studies, and media studies. In doing so, I aim, first, to look at media production and consumption in China and by Chinese in terms of flow rather than structure; second, to study the impact of globalization on Chinese media within a "cultural studies," rather than a "political economy," framework; third, to consider the role of the Chinese state and history in the formation of transnational subjectivities in the era of globalization; and fourth, to examine the cultural consumption practices of a more recent and less-studied community in diasporic Chinese studies—those former PRC nationals who have left China during the last two decades.

Framing my study within such parameters means undoing the customary dichotomy between the study of the nation-state and what happens within it, and the study of the "postnational political order"[24]—what happens when refugees, activists, students, and laborers leave the nation. As a student of media and cultural studies, my ambiguous cultural position in relation to "China" is at once that of an outsider and an insider, having been a PRC national first and having become an overseas Chinese later. This position of disciplinary and cultural promiscuity allows me to claim the space of "the renter"[25] in methodological terms, actively learning from other territories and remaining open to possibilities of coalition and appropriation. It is perhaps this position, at once marginal and unstable, which encourages me to identify with the strategy of displacement.[26] Such a position not only recognizes the political and personal tensions of individual researchers, but also, and more important, actively works to "displace and disorder" difference that is created by the boundaries separating disciplines.[27]

The strategy of displacement is also crucial in my attempt at productive engagement with theorizations of place, space, and power in media and cultural studies, feminist studies, and cultural geography, all of which are firmly rooted in the intellectual history of the West. The most obvious example of the need for such an interrogative stance comes from the theorization of virtuality, where it is generally agreed that postmodernity, as embodied by the freeway, the shopping mall, and television, has created "an ontology of everyday distraction."[28] Although this argument, born in urbanized America, is seminal to the study of the formation of a transnational imagination, it needs to be problematized and destabilized to take into account the modern and premodern social-economic realities of everyday life in China, particularly in rural areas. When applied to television in a Chinese village, the question to ask, therefore, is not whether television contributes to this everyday ontology of distraction, but how television reworks an everyday ontology in spite of—perhaps even because of—the absence of other kinds of mobilities made possible by the ubiquitous freeways and shopping malls of the developed world.

In other words, I understand the strategy of displacement as methodologically enabling in terms of both destabilizing established concepts and arguments and regrounding these concepts and arguments in location-specific social spaces. For instance, the ways in which the Chinese state and the nation's history still carry enormous weight with Chinese people, both within and outside the PRC and despite the forces of globalization, seem to refute the scenario of the "diasporic public sphere," which, according to Appadurai, "confounds theories that depend on the continued salience of the nation-states."[29] For this reason, I want to point to the danger of understanding Chinese transnational modernities as generally being "flexible,"[30] deterritorialized, and thus, in Appadurai's terms, "at large."[31] In the case of PRC Chinese, including those who have left, modernity may well be an experience that is possible not in spite of the Chinese state, but precisely because of it.

THEORIES AND THEMES

In taking as my focal point the relationship between formations of transnational subjectivities and media production, representation, and consumption, I am confronted with the inevitable question of how, on the one hand, to engage critically with theorizations of place, mobility, home, body, and exile—themes central to postcolonial critiques—and how, on the other hand, to make such theorizations useful in explaining the politics of media and communications. Many studies that examine the role of the media in the formation of "imagined communities"[32] take as a given the delineation of space into homologous binaries—be it center versus periphery, global versus local, urban versus rural. Such stable configurations of space and place, however, become problematic when both people and images are mobile and displaced. This is because the "center" and "periphery" are reduplicated within both the world cities[33] and Third World cities.

Given that the media are principally held responsible for creating a "sense of place,"[34] and that the construction of identities through media production and consumption of place is also contingent upon the media being able to assume the intended audience to be in a space that is "enclosed' and 'bounded," the project of examining the formation of a (trans)national imaginary is made even more complicated by the process of displacement and, subsequently, "emplacement" within a new context. My analysis of the formation of a transnational imagination activates a number of levels at which space can be examined: symbolic and representational space, as in television, cinema, and cyber-texts; political and social space, such as rural to urban, premodern to modern, national to postnational; and psychic space—desire, fear, anxiety, and ambivalence. What most interests me in this project is how movement across, and engagement with, these spaces takes place, as well as the mutual imbrication that exists between them.

Studying the imagination of spaces and places in the specific context of migration—of both people and media images—makes the concept of travel central in both theoretical and methodological terms. I understand these theorizations to be relevant for a number of reasons. First, the communication medium in question—television, film, the Internet—needs to be looked at as a means of "transport" akin to traditional modes of travel, such as trains and planes. For instance, the staging of national media events in Tiananmen Square requires both domestic and diasporic audiences from disparate and remote regions within and beyond China to be "transported" there, in order for them to be witnesses to such events, hence giving rise to the need for diverse strategies for bringing them "there." The CCTV's euphoric coverage of Beijing's success in bidding for the 2008 Games suggests that nationalist media events are increasingly staged with both domestic and diasporic communities in mind. Similarly, state television also has a political motive in "transporting" live global media events into distant corners of the nation, packaged in the guise of familiar images and narratives. Finally, while the products of cyber-technology, including e-mail and the Web, provide powerful compensation to those who are "absent," "not at home," or "not there," they also raise questions about the relationship between the body, the home, the community, the city, the nation, and the global.

Broadcasting performs its "transportation" function by way of "mobile privatization," a mechanism that allows one to stay at home while "going places." Television, for instance, posits the audience in what Morse calls a "liminal space" between inside and outside, private and public, which in fact can also be seen as a "nonspace"—a "ground within which communication . . . between virtuality and actuality . . . can take place."[35] The capacity of television to afford virtualities is, according to Morse, akin to that of the modern shopping mall and highway. She also argues that it is through the displacement and dislocation enabled by the shared images of television that individuals in disparate locations and regions can become social subjects in a sovereign "nation." Increasingly, other visual media such as video, VCD, and DVD are jostling with television to occupy this nonspace. The broadcasting media's capacity for "mobile privatization" is further enhanced by its growing use of satellite technologies, which are seen by some as producing new definitions of space and time.[36] The satellite, designed to overcome the tyranny of distance, is particularly powerful for a nation-state such as China, which often perceives itself as having a "large territory and bountiful resources" (*di da wu bo*). Morley's caution is useful here: Although satellite technologies may well be reworking definitions of space and time, they are not necessarily replacing, but rather are overlaying, old configurations of distance and duration.[37]

At a material level, with the growing rate at which people and images traverse borders of various kinds—be they rural/urban, intraprovincial/interprovincial, or national/transnational—media and identity are no longer research topics that can be pursued within the boundaries of a conventional "place." Ong and Nonini's observation[38] that the locus of investigation of villagers may no longer be the village, but the movement itself of the villagers, is particularly relevant at a time when villagers increasingly leave home and are "on the road." At a geopolitical level, the displacement of the migrant body has the effect of destabilizing fixed categories such as "home" and "center"[39] and also of calling into question the dominant spatial configurations of places, as well as the unequal yet independent connection of places. Finally, at a more abstract level, travel can be a metaphor for displacement not only of the body, but also of the mind—one's way of imagining. Being neither "here" nor "there," being "absent" but still "present," being somewhat real but somewhat virtual, a patriotic cyber hacker inhabits a liminal space[40] and acquires what Bhabha describes as "online epistemology," "e-mail ontology,"[41] or a tendency to imagine places in a way that is more inscribed with a sense of "routes," instead of "roots," as the daily reality.[42] A series of cyber-wars between the Chinese hackers and their enemy counterparts—the most recent one being between Honker (red hackers) Union of China and the Poizon Box (an American hackers' organization) over the incident of the spy plane in Hainan in early 2001—testify to the curious interface between cyber-nation and national sovereignty.

I am, however, mindful of the risk of reading travel as a promise of total emancipation. After all, mobility is imbricated with power,[43] and travel is a social activity that is not only gendered,[44] but is also inscribed with a Western desire for exploration and colonization,[45] and is specific to socioeconomic power. Although the metaphor of travel may be useful in attempting to destabilize and rework global power relations, taking the activity of travel for granted may reinforce or even perpetuate the inequality between those who can travel and those who either do not, cannot, or have travel imposed upon them. I am equally alert to the risk of simplistically equating the media consumer with the imaginary traveler. Theorizations of "television as travel"[46] and recent theorizations of cyber-travel both point to the fact that imaginary travel is equally marked with unequal access and structural hierarchy.

Most important, I am interested in extending and developing the theory of travel in a way that may be useful in understanding the politics of "travel in time," as well as "travel in space." Migration—internal or diasporic; temporary or permanent—has created images and narratives of spaces and places that are inscribed by the "geography of power,"[47] but also the history and memory that are (in)formed by that geography of power. Displacement gives rise to the need to rework a sense of time. For the migrant who has left home, the past may be strategically useful in negotiations with present reality, and for this reason the quotidian activity of remembering or forgetting the past may become crucial in the formation of a new identity in the present. Through engaging with issues of collective memory, I want to explore the possibility of extending the use of the travel metaphor to include a temporal, as well as a spatial, dimension, in the study of the notions of "home," "homeland," and "exile."[48]

Furthermore, by linking cultural memory with displacement, I hope to suggest a useful reading position in understanding the imbricative relationship between place and time—that is, the spatialization of time and the temporalization of place. This may refer not so much to a postmodern condition described as the space-time compression[49] as to the interesting here/now versus then/there homology. Physical displacement, coupled with cultural memory, creates a curious situation whereby time is often signified in spatial terms and place in temporal terms.

PLAN OF THE BOOK

The book has eight chapters, with each two chapters dealing with one particular aspect or form of media production and consumption. The formation and transformation of the national imaginary since the start of economic reforms has often been discussed in the context of national cinema. While "fifth-generation" filmmakers have largely turned to nature, "peasants," and "the primitive" for answers to China's place in the world,[50] sixth-generation (as well as some fifth-generation) filmmakers are more responsive to the issues and phenomena of the reform era. Chapters 1 and 2 explore the ways in which mainland Chinese films have negotiated the tensions between various translocal practices, and how these films, as examples of a popular cultural form akin to television, have contributed to the formation of transnational subjectivities through an array of spatial representations of the "village," the "city," and "abroad."

I have chosen two Chinese villages as the locale of chapter 1. Zhou Xiaowen's film *Ermo* and Zhang Yimou's *Not One Less* are the focus of discussion in this chapter, and they have two things in common: Both films feature a village woman going to town, and both present television, in one form or another, as the object of these women's desires. Toward the end of each film, the women have returned to their respective villages. However, the films reach quite different conclusions about the relationship between mobility and the formation of a transnational imagination, as well as about the roles that villagers—women villagers in particular—are made to play in embodying the paradoxes and dilemmas of modernity. Through an analysis of a variety of cinematic representations, this chapter ruminates on the possibility of television as "virtual travel," but these cinematic representations of the village woman are also, where possible, juxtaposed with the experiences of some real women who have left their villages to work in the city, in order to add a material dimension to the discussion of mobility.

Since people experience different types of dilemma and paradox at different junctures of becoming modern, the definition of what is parochial and what is cosmopolitan is open to interrogation. While chapter 1 focuses on *jing cheng* (going to the city) in the (translocal) context of peasants leaving their villages, chapter 2 extends this theme of mobility into the realms of the transnational imagination. Its point of departure shifts to the city, where it deals with *chuguo* (going abroad)—a perennial locus of reverie among urban residents in China. My reading of the urban dilemma—to go or not to go abroad—underlying this preoccupation proceeds via an analysis of the spatial production in a number of films from sixth-generation filmmakers. It points to an increasing ambivalence and unresolved complexity in the way the national Chinese self is imagined in relation to "America," the ultimate signifier of "the West" or "the world outside China."

Chapters 3 and 4 look at a revealing disjuncture between the production and consumption of television dramas. Like the current decade, the 1980s and the first half of the 1990s were the decades of television in China. They were also the decades that saw an exodus of mainland Chinese intellectuals, scholars, and scientists—people who, voluntarily or involuntarily, forsook their homeland for the metropolitan cities of the West. Television drama was the most popular genre of this period, and of particular interest to both domestic audiences and exilic Chinese communities alike was a narrative form that may be described as the "Chinese in the New World" genre. These are stories of survival, in which the characters are usually mainland Chinese students who have gone to the West.

Chapter 3 extends the rural–urban trajectory outlined in section 1 and considers the production of a cluster of narratives about those Chinese who have left their home(land) and are now living in the "new world" of the global cities. It takes some stories of world cities as important cultural texts, through which Chinese identities are rewritten to negotiate the new intersections of space, place, and the self that have been brought about by migration in an era when global economic forces increasingly hold sway. It seeks to identify important moments in the last two decades, at which travel and displacement have been experienced at various junctures of becoming modern. It also argues that any attempt to study the formation of transnational subjectivities at the end of the twentieth century must look not only at how space and place are talked about, but also at how they are visualized. In particular, it must explore the tension, ambiguity, and ambivalence created by the technologized images of television.

Another significant dimension to the production and consumption of this cluster of television dramas is that the Chinese exiles whose lives form their "narrative fodder" are also avid viewers of these dramas. Following the movements of this group of emigrants, chapter 4 considers the various uses that these Chinese from the PRC who are now living overseas make of these cultural products from "home," in their attempts to articulate and reinforce a national imaginary specific to that group. The globalization of cultural products and the technology of home video, VCD, and DVD cooperate to give "the absent" access to "home-grown" products. That Chinese exiles are themselves watching the video versions of these television series about the experiences of Chinese exiles, produced in China for mainland audiences, is an interesting phenomenon—similar to someone catching a glimpse of him- or herself in someone else's mirror. I demonstrate that if the visuality of the world cities depicted in these dramas invites the voyeuristic gaze of Chinese domestic audiences, the pleasure of consumption of the same products by the exilic community is much more complex. Although living in a transnational space, these exilic individuals' imagination appears to operate largely within a template of national space and time.

For a collectivity to form a sense of identity, two things seem to be necessary: a shared memory of the specific events and things that have significance for the entire community and access to the cultural forms that enable these memories to be continuously refreshed and articulated. During the last few years, the Internet has increasingly made these two things possible. In chapters 5 and 6, which are still situated in the space between homeland and the place of exile, I have chosen two topics that, in very different ways, illuminate the relationship between new technologies, such as the Internet, and cultural memory, "time travel," storytelling, and the migrant's displaced body. The first is the memory of the most traumatic historical experience in living Chinese memory. Chapter 5 takes the case of websites dedicated to the Nanjing Massacre during the Japanese War and unravels an intriguing process through which cyber-identity, supposedly memoryless and deterritorialized, is grafted onto the Chinese government's version of China—a nation unified by a common past and defined by territorial borders. In this chapter, I point to the disjuncture between the geographically displaced, fractured lives of migrants and their ways of imagining "our" nation—ways that operate according to a spatial and temporal reality that takes precedence over their displacement and fracture. This case study points to the powerful mechanism of "stepping back in time" that has been enabled by cyber-technology—an increasingly regular activity among Chinese exiles all around the world, in their construction and maintenance of a collective fantasy of the "motherland."

The second topic of chapters 5 and 6 is food consumption—the most everyday activity of the individual. Still looking at the Internet, but shifting from a recent historical trauma to the contemporary life of the everyday, I argue in chapter 6 that in no other place are the two elements of collective identity—a shared memory and common cultural forms—more clearly embodied, both literally and figuratively, than in food and the memories associated with food. Eating is, moreover, an enduring topic on websites maintained by expatriate Chinese. What happens to the migrant's palate and memories of eating when she or he decides to leave home and live in a foreign land, where people not only eat different food, but also eat food differently? How do migrants talk about food not only in their "multicultural" host countries, but also in the cyber era of the disappearing body, in ways that allow them to articulate and negotiate a new sense of belonging, while at the same time resisting hegemonic representations of "ethnicity"? In this chapter, I pose some questions about the relationship between food as a mundane topic and eating food as a chronic topic on Chinese websites, with a view to examining its particular significance in the formation of a diasporic consciousness. In looking at the connection between "home(land)" and "homepage," I draw on expatriate Chinese writings taken from the Internet, as well as a series of interviews I conducted with a geographically dispersed group of diasporic Chinese who left the PRC to settle in places such as Australia, New Zealand, Canada, the United States, and Europe during the last decade or so. I argue that it is the constant remembering of somatic experiences associated with "home" that allows these displaced individuals to negotiate a coexistence between "homeland"—the national space of the past—and "homepage," the transnational space of the present.

Chapters 7 and 8 bring the narrative of mobility, media, and the Chinese transnational imagination to its full circle, by considering the scenario of the "global Chinese village" brought about by the arrival of satellite technology. I look at the importation of various media formats and practices into the Chinese media and consider the ways in which this inbound "travel" of an important media practice—the "media event"—affects the workings of the Chinese mediasphere and what its subsequent impact on the (trans)national imagination might be. In seeking to rework and develop existing theories of the phenomenon of the media event, my aim is twofold: first, to assess the relevance of media-event theory—which originated in Western media studies—in understanding the staging of media events in non-Western societies such as China; and second, to consider how global media events outside China are (re)produced for and (re)interpreted by local/national audiences within the PRC. Chapter 7 focuses on a series of media events on Chinese state television during the late 1990s and considers the relationship between the state, spectacles, and television. In taking this focus, I argue that in order to yield insight into the complexity and ambiguity of the Chinese mediasphere, media events need to be studied alongside what I refer to as "media stories"—a genre that performs different functions from media events in the construction of a sense of national time. I further demonstrate that while media events are about spectacles, official time, and grand history, media stories are mostly about everyday life, unofficial time, and individual memory. Finally, I argue that although media events and media stories perform different spatial and temporal duties and functions in the imagining of the nation, evidence from the Chinese media suggests as much convergence—both ideologically and symbolically—as divergence between the two genres.

For the same reason that I start the book with the Chinese village, I finish, in chapter 8, with the idea of a "global Chinese village." This chapter continues the focus on media events, but asks a different question: When a media event is staged outside China and transmitted globally, how is it reproduced for and reinterpreted by China's "national audiences"? I also consider a related question: What happens in the minds of diasporic audiences who are not "back there" to experience such a global media event along with the national audience at home? The television and Internet coverage of the recent Sydney Olympic Games gave rise to the most globally consumed sporting event in history; however, the imagery and symbolism deployed in the opening and closing ceremonies of the Games were quite place-specific. This chapter considers an array of strategies for constructing cultural citizenship in the context of watching the 27th Olympic Games, taking as a case study the viewing experiences of a number of Chinese spectators—both mainland Chinese viewing the Games "from home" and former PRC migrants now living overseas.

It is my hope that this journey, starting from the traditional Chinese village and finishing with the globalizing Chinese electronic village, will bring mobility, media, and transnationalism together, presenting a nuanced and multifaceted account of the relationship between media and the formation of transnational subjectivity, consciousness, and imagination at various junctures of becoming modern in contemporary China.

NOTES

1. "Chinese Students Rally at U.S. Embassy in Tokyo," *Asian Political News,* May 17, 1999, <www.findarticles.com> (accessed August 2001).

2. See "American Enterprises Online," <www.findarticles.com> (accessed August 2001).

3. "China Urges Japan to Release Feng Jinhua Who Threw Paint over Yasukuni Shrine," *Australian Chinese Times,* August 29, 2001, 20.

4. *Asian Economic News,* September 18, 2000, <www.findarticles.com> (accessed August 2001).

5. *Asian Economic News,* February 15, 1999, <www.findarticles.com> (accessed September 2001).

6. "Snakeheads Seen Linked to Truck Holding 58 Dead Immigrants," *Asian Economic News,* June 28, 2000, <www.findarticles.com> (accessed August 2001).

7. Zhang Youxue, *"Liuxue renyuan huiguo chuangye xianzhang fengxi"* ("An Analysis of the Chinese Students Who Have Returned from Overseas Study"), *Sheng Zhou Xue Ren (Chinese Scholars Abroad)* 134, no. 4 (2001), <www.chisa.edu.cn.> (accessed August 2001).

8. "Tokyo's New Overseas Chinese Community Thriving," *Asian Economic News,* March 22, 1999, <www.findarticles.com/cf_0/m0WDP> (accessed August 2001).

9. *"Dilin liuxue, chongshuo fenyun"* ("The Pros and Cons of Young Children Studying Abroad"), *Chinese Scholars Abroad Monthly* 136 (June 2001), <www.chisa.edu.cn> (accessed November 2001).

10. <www.cctvbase.net/data_center/data_content.asp?id=186> (accessed September 2001).

11. Arjun Appadurai, *Modernity at Large: Cultural Dimensions of Globalization* (Minneapolis: University of Minnesota Press, 1996), 4.

12. Appadurai, *Modernity at Large*, 4.

13. Homi Bhabha, "Arrivals and Departures," in *Home, Exile, Homeland: Film, Media, and the Politics of Place*, ed. Hamid Naficy (London and New York: Routledge, 1999), 1–16.

14. Wang Xiaomin, for instance, has written eloquently about the contingent and contiguous relationship between four social groups that have been born out of the economic reforms. They are the "new rich," white-collar workers, unemployed or wageless pensioners, and rural migrants. See Wang Xiaomin, "Preface," in *Zai Xin Yishixingtai De Longzhao Xia* (Under the Dominance of the New Ideology), ed. Wang Xiaomin (Nanjing: Jiangsu People's Press, 2000), 1–26.

15. See, for example, Aihwa Ong and Donald M. Nonini, eds., *Ungrounded Empires: The Cultural Politics of Modern Chinese Transnationalism* (New York and London: Routledge, 1997).

16. See Junhao Hong, *The Internationalization of Television in China: The Evolution of Ideology, Society, and Media since the Reform* (Westport, Conn.: Praeger, 1998).

17. See, for example, Sheldon Hsiao-peng Lu, ed., *Transnational Chinese Cinemas: Identity, Nationhood, Gender* (Honolulu: University of Hawaii Press, 1997); Stephen Teo, *Hong Kong Cinema: The Extra Dimensions* (London: BFI, 1997); and Mayfair Yang, ed., *Spaces of Their Own: Women's Public Sphere in Transnational China* (Minneapolis: University of Minnesota Press, 1999).

18. Anthony Smith, "Towards a Global Culture?" in *Global Culture: Nationalism, Globalisation and Modernity*, ed. Mike Featherstone (London: Sage, 1990).

19. Tu argues that cultural China can be examined in terms of a continuous interaction of three symbolic universes, consisting of mainland China, Taiwan, Hong Kong, and Singapore in the first universe, and the Chinese communities throughout the world as the second universe. Tu's third universe consists of individual international scholars and media people who construct images of China for the consumption of their own linguistic communities. See Tu Weiming, *The Living Tree: The Changing Meaning of Being Chinese Today*, ed. Tu Wei-ming (Stanford, Calif.: Stanford University Press, 1994).

20. Ong and Nonini, eds., *Ungrounded Empires*.

21. Stephan Chan, "What Is This Thing Called Chinese Diaspora?" *Contemporary Review* 1 (February 1999): 3.

22. Hamid Naficy talks about the difference between diaspora and exile in his earlier book, *The Making of Exile Cultures: Iranian Television in Los Angeles* (Minneapolis: University of Minnesota Press, 1993). He later defines the cultural exile in *Home, Exile, Homeland: Film, Media, and the Politics of Place* (London and New York: Routledge, 1999).

23. Aihwa Ong, "On the Edge of Empires: Flexible Citizenship among Chinese in Diaspora," *Positions* 1, no. 3 (1993): 745–77.

24. Appadurai, *Modernity at Large*, 22.

25. Michel de Certeau, *The Practice of Everyday Life* (Berkeley: University of California Press, 1984).

26. Here I have feminist writers such as bell hooks and Trinh Minh-Ha in mind. Both writers are cited in Edward Soja, *Thirdspace: Journeys to Los Angeles and Other Real-and-Imagined Places* (Oxford and Cambridge, Mass.: Blackwell, 1996).

27. Soja, *Thirdspace*.

28. Margaret Morse, *Virtualities: Television, Media Art, and Cyberculture* (Bloomington: Indiana University Press, 1998), 99.

29. Appadurai, *Modernity at Large*, 4.

30. Ong and Nonini, *Ungrounded Empires*; and Ong, "On the Edge of Empires."

31. Appadurai, *Modernity at Large*, 19.

32. Benedict Anderson, *Imagined Communities: Reflections on the Origins and Spread of Nationalism* (London: Verso, 1983).

33. See, for example, Paul Wollen, "The World City and the Global Village," *Emergences: Journal for the Study of Media and Composite Cultures* 9, no. 1 (1999): 69–78; and Ulf Hannerz, *Transnational Connections: Culture, People, Places* (London: Routledge, 1996).

34. Doreen Massey, "Imagining the World," in *Geographical Worlds*, ed. J. Allen and Doreen Massey (Oxford: Oxford University Press and Open University, 1995).

35. Morse, *Virtualities*, 102.

36. Shaun Moores, "Television, Geography and 'Mobile Privatization,'" *European Journal of Communication* 8 (1993): 365–79; Shaun Moores, *Satellite Television and Everyday Life: Articulating Technology* (Bedfordshire: University of Luton Press, 1996).

37. David Morley, "Bounded Realms: Household, Family, Community, and Nation," in Naficy, ed., *Home, Exile, Homeland*, 158–59.

38. Ong and Nonini, *Ungrounded Empires*.

39. James Clifford, "Traveling Cultures," in *Cultural Studies*, ed. Larry Grossberg, Carry Nelson, and Paula Treicher (New York: Routledge, 1992).

40. Naficy, *The Making of Exile Cultures*; and Naficy, ed., *Home, Exile, Homeland*.

41. Bhabha, "Arrivals and Departures."

42. Stuart Hall, "Cultural Identity and Diaspora," in *Undoing Place? A Geographical Reader*, ed. Linda McDowell (London: Arnold, 1995), 231–42.

43. Doreen Massey and Pat Jess, *A Place in the World?* (London: Open University Press and Oxford University Press, 1995).

44. Janet Wolff, *Feminine Sentences: Essays on Women and Culture* (Cambridge, U.K.: Polity Press, 1990); Elizabeth Wilson, *Sphinx in the City* (London: Virago, 1991); and Janet Wolff, "On the Road Again: Metaphors of Travel in Cultural Criticism," in *Undoing Place?* ed. Linda McDowell, 180–94.

45. John Durham Peters, "Exile, Nomadism, and the Diaspora: The Stakes of Mobility in the Western Canon," in *Home, Exile, Homeland*, ed. Naficy, 17–44.

46. See, for example, James Lull, *China Turned On: Television, Reform and Resistance* (London: Routledge, 1991); and Yosefa Loshitzky, "Travelling Culture/Travelling Television," *Screen* 37, no. 4 (1996): 334.

47. Massey, "Imagining the World."

48. Naficy, ed., *Home, Exile, Homeland*.

49. David Harvey, *The Condition of Postmodernity* (Oxford: Blackwell, 1989).

50. Rey Chow, *Primitive Passions: Visuality, Sexuality, Ethnography, and Contemporary Chinese Cinema* (New York: Columbia University Press, 1995).

1

✛

Going Home or Going Places: Television in the Village

Ermo, the main character in a film by the same name, is a peasant woman in a village in northern China. She earns a living by making and selling twisted noodles. Life is relatively calm and predictable for her, until one day her neighbor's television set becomes the object of her envy. As a result, Ermo decides that she wants to buy the biggest color television set in the shop in the nearby township—something even the mayor of the town cannot afford to do. To satisfy this desire, she leaves her village and gets a job in town. When Ermo has finally saved enough money and goes back to buy the television set she has had her eye on, she is indeed perplexed: The last time she was in the shop, some blonde characters on the screen were speaking "our language," but this time a Chinese person, on the English-language channel of China Central Television, is speaking a foreign language!

Comparing some of the "earlier forms of modernity" such as the railroad, the movies, and the boutique shop, Morse argues that television, shopping malls, and the freeway have resulted in the increasing rate of "mobile privatisation,"[1] a process by which new forms of communication, such as television, and transport, such as automobiles, are bringing individuals further and further into their interior world, a "phantasmagoria of the interior."[2] This is central to the experience of TV consumption, which, according to Shaun Moores, is about "simultaneously staying home and, imaginatively at least, going places."[3] Ermo's initial fascination with images of faraway exotic places suggests that the everyday departure from home and travel to virtual places, usually considered a truly postmodern phenomenon, has indeed taken place in the Chinese village. Writing about the arrival of cinema as a cultural industry, Hortense Powdermaker compares Hollywood to a "dream factory," but argues that fantasy is not necessarily a bad thing:

> One can escape into a world of imagination and come from it refreshed and with new understanding. One can expand limited experiences into broad ones. . . . Hollywood provides ready-made fantasies or day-dreams; the problem is whether these are productive or nonproductive, whether the audience is psychologically enriched or impoverished.[4]

Ermo's initial encounter with television, as described previously, can be seen as a moment when fantasy takes hold of the mind of a village woman. In spite of the very public setting in which it takes place, Ermo enters a world that is both public and profoundly private. She is seen to wander into a crowded television shop and stop in front of the counter where television sets are displayed. Indifferent to the bustling crowds around her, Ermo stands there, her eyes fixated on the television screen, which at that moment features a slim female swimming instructor in a pink swimsuit showing audiences how to exercise body muscles in the water in order to stay in good shape. Describing this moment, Stephanie Donald astutely points to the possibility of television as a portal that takes Ermo into a private, imaginary world:

> The moment encapsulates the intensity of Ermo's privacy. Despite "seeing" her relationships with her husband, son, neighbour, and lover in some detail, it becomes clear in the intimacy of the shot exchange with the television that Ermo is committed only to visions of something different from the present she inhabits.[5]

Ermo and her villagers' relationship to television is akin to that of Hollywood audiences to the cinema in its early phase. Ermo's fascination with television images signifies the birth of what Morse calls "the nonspace" in the life of villagers, a space of interface between the real and the imaginary created by television.[6] This is not to ignore the fact that Ermo's village is yet to achieve some of the earlier forms of modernity. For Ermo, going to the town means either walking for hours on a dirt road or getting an occasional lift, sitting on top of someone's fully loaded truck. The freeway and the shopping malls in the American society described by Morse have not arrived together with television in Ermo's village. We are reminded of the uneven and disjunctive nature of the modernization process and the possibility of travel it brings with it.[7] This difference points to the importance of paying attention to the simultaneous existence of, and the connection and the uneven relationship between, two kinds of "village" in the world: that of the "traditional, local and non-urban community"[8] and that of the interconnected global village famously depicted by Marshall McLuhan. It also points to the double-edged impact of television as potentially both emancipatory and disempowering. Given this, any perspective that privileges one at the expense of the other is both naïve and misleading.

Based on this premise, this chapter juxtaposes Zhou Xiaowen's *Ermo* with Zhang Yimou's *Not One Less*.[9] These films have two things in common: both feature a village woman going to town, and both have television as the object of these women's desires. Both films end with the protagonist going back to her village with a television set, but the question of what is to be done about the arrival of this modern object is left unresolved in both films. It is my contention that the two stories reach different conclusions about the connection among the modernization process, mobility, and the formation of a transnational imagination. They also seem to offer a different perspective on the place of television in such processes of formation. Through a construction of their respective relationships to television, the women in these films play pivotal roles in negotiating the uneven and disjunctive relationship between mobility, modernity, and transnational imagination.

I will demonstrate the logic of this argument by constructing, in juxtaposition, a reading of the two films. My reading is admittedly retrospective, interpreting what is within the film and drawing on the wisdom of hindsight by bringing extra-textual materials to bear on these texts. It is also reconstructive, both engaging with and diverging from critiques and discourses discernible within existing readings of these films, and is ultimately deconstructive, because, rather than reading the stories within the expected, or perhaps intended, narrative mode, I sometimes throw doubt on the very form of narration adopted and, when it suits me, opt to read them differently or even oppositionally. Central to my reading is a concern with the contradictory and disjunctive nature of the globalization and modernization process as it is experienced in a village. In this reading, I locate the village women in town as represented in the films alongside a number of real rural migrants from Anhui Province, who have during the last few years or so left their villages to work in Shanghai. What emerges from this contextualized description of the films' representation of television and modernity is an insight into the forces that are seen either to assist or to prohibit the formation of transnational subjectivities among Chinese peasants, who, to this day, make up the predominant proportion of the Chinese population.

ERMO AND TELEVISION: TAKING ISSUE WITH SOME READINGS

Ermo lives with her husband and ekes out a living by making and selling twisted noodles. Life is getting on just fine, except that her son causes her trouble by constantly going to visit their neighbor, who has a television set. Ermo forbids her son to do this, promising that she will buy him a bigger TV than the neighbors' once she saves enough money. One day Ermo gets a lift to the nearby town and, having sold her noodles, wanders into a shop that sells television sets. She sets her sights on the largest set in the shop and, as she stands in front of the object of desire, is mesmerized by the images on the screen. Dreamily, she says to herself, "It is really a big TV. You can see every blonde hair on the foreigners' skin!"

To save enough money to buy the television, Ermo leaves her village and gets a job in the city supervising the production of noodles. There, she lives and works like most rural women migrant workers, sleeping in a dormitory and working hard for her boss. She worries about the cost of eating a meal in a restaurant and tries to maintain an equilibrium between supporting her impotent husband, while sleeping with a virile and (relatively more) understanding man. In order to maintain her dignity and independence and at the same time boost her savings for the television, she sells blood to the hospital. The film's story ends with Ermo sitting in her village home, fast asleep in front of the television, with all her guests—everybody from the village she has invited to watch television—gone. The television announcer is nonchalantly reading the temperature and weather conditions of the major cities of the world: Tokyo, Vancouver, New York, Frankfurt, Paris, Sydney, and London. As the name of each of these global cities is read out, an icon of that city flashes onto the screen. The film finishes with the closing announcement from the television station and the camera zooming in on the flickering, snowy screen we all know so well from our own television-viewing experiences.

Director Zhou Xiaowen said that he had thought about three ways of ending the story of Ermo.[10] The first shows Ermo finally saving enough money to bring home the largest television, but she cannot watch it—she has become emaciated due to selling blood too often and finally loses her sight. The second option has Ermo's husband moving the television set from the house to the village theater, where he sells viewing tickets to the local villagers. Business is good. Every night, people flock to the village theater, except for Ermo, who continues to make noodles in her own courtyard. The third option, sketched in the previous paragraph, is what the audience eventually gets to see. The first scenario outlined by Zhou clearly is the darkest and most damning one, since Ermo's loss of blood in exchange for a television set symbolizes the irresistible, yet dangerous, seduction of modernity. However, this account of Zhou Xiaowen's three options interests me, not so much because the choice he finally made marks a shift in, or casts doubt on, prevailing attitudes toward modernity, as because all of these options point to an absolute lack of an alternative—or, dare I say, bright—future for Ermo.

Imagine, for a moment, that there may be a fourth option: Ermo buys the biggest television in town and as a result learns a lot about the world beyond her village. One day, she watches a documentary about a village woman who goes to the city alone and eventually becomes a successful entrepreneur. Ermo decides to follow suit. She packs up—as she did previously to go to the nearby town—and sets off on the road again. This is not an implausible scenario. Indeed, as we learn from the film, there is not much to hold Ermo back: She is tired of waiting on her impotent and misogynist husband; she feels betrayed by her secret lover, her neighbor Xiazi, yet has no moral platform from which to seek justice; she is suffocated by oppressive social values about "female virtues"; and her experience of working in town has proven to her that she is a capable worker. We also know that throughout the 1990s, and particularly since the mid-1990s, thousands of rural women, single or married, have left home to become *dagongmei* (working girls), working in rural township factories and in the city, in search of paid employment and an alternative lifestyle.[11]

That Zhou Xiaowen could not possibly envisage such a conclusion to Ermo's story is understandable. After all, for him, Ermo embodies the predicament and conundrum of rural China in the process of modernization, not the possibility and potential that modernity can bring to a village woman. Her dream of owning the biggest television in town is not driven by a desire for "going places," but for social mobility. For this reason, she must continue to live in suffocation, both sexually and morally. In addition, as an embodiment of the tension between the city and village, Ermo is not to be granted the option to choose between the village and the city. In fact, it is tempting to conclude that neither the city nor the village promises redemption for Ermo. Furthermore, Zhou's ironic use of television as both the metaphor and metonym of the downside of modernity rules out any possibility of television as a source of knowledge and as a facilitator in the formation and transformation of a spatial imagination that is no longer confined to the physical and psychic world known to Ermo.

The appearance of *Ermo* coincided with the beginning of a profound change that has swept China's rural spaces since the 1970s. Seen in this light, Zhou's choice of ending for the film does not seem that inevitable. Here I want to revisit *Ermo* with a view to rescuing the possibility of a reconciliation between the two different possible scenarios awaiting Ermo. This is because, while it is important to read any text, in part, by returning to its historical context (*Ermo* was made in the early 1990s), an alternative reading that benefits from the wisdom of hindsight would yield insight into a specific moment that marked the beginning of the coming together of modernity, television, and the formation of transnational subjectivities in reform-era China. This is also, of course, a more optimistic reading.

Ermo's resolve to buy the television set (so big that even the mayor cannot afford it) is driven by a desire for status—she wants to get even with her neighbor, who has both a television and a virile man. Her preoccupation, therefore, is with the immediate social implications of owning a television set, rather than with what television can deliver. For this reason she relates to the object of her desire with awe and incomprehension, but at the same time treats it as an expensive piece of furniture. She demands that the shop assistant turn off the set she intends to buy because it will "wear out" if it is used too often, and she tells people not to touch it in case they damage it.

Zhou Xiaowen's somewhat poignant and definitely ironic ending to the film suggests a disenchantment with modernity. The blonde foreigners flirting on Ermo's television—*Dynasty*, dubbed into Mandarin—appear as ludicrous as the detached weather report on the world's major cities that flashes across the television screen at the end of the film. According to Dai Jinhua, the story of Ermo embodies the director's profound doubts about modernity. For Zhou Xiaowen, Dai suggests,

> modernity does not provide a powerful and effective redemption; it is not a much-anticipated dream. It can only create a myriad of desires or some modes of meeting these desires. It can offer individuals no more than some choices in a choiceless world.[12]

While I concur with Dai on the point of Zhou's attitude to modernity, I depart from her reading of the role of television in the film. According to Dai, Ermo's obsession does not mean that television embodies her real desire and purpose; nor does it signify the inevitable arrival of television—an index of postindustrialism—into China's rural life. Although this may be true, I do not read Ermo's obsession with television as "fortuitous" to the narrative and as embodying a mere "fantasy" and a "cruel irony," as Dai suggests. This is because, while Ermo's decision to buy the biggest television is fortuitous—her neighbor happens to have a television set, which evokes her envy—her son's fascination with television is inevitable. Television, though as much an index of modernity as washing machines or vacuum cleaners, is different from other such commodities, in that it does not offer a quicker or more efficient way of doing housework. Rather, it promises to bring home, on a daily basis, a new and different way of knowing, thinking about, and imagining the world or, in Morse's phrase, an "ontology of everyday distraction." It is probably for this reason that Ermo's son keeps going next door to watch TV against his mother's instructions. It would be hard to imagine him being so keen to visit the neighbors, day after day, if, instead of a TV set, they had a new washing machine or vacuum cleaner.

Television, unlike other tokens of modernity, offers these village children glimpses of a world their own parents do not know and cannot deliver to them. In this sense, although Ermo's promise to buy her son a bigger television is seen to be a product of her vanity and neighborly rivalry, we may also speculate that it may be an indication of her realization—however inchoate—that television is destined to play an important role in the life of her son, and that buying a TV set would be a most effective exercise of her parental care and responsibility. Looked at in this way, Ermo's decision is also remarkably modern. We should note that Ermo's husband initially opposes the idea of buying a television, preferring to spend their hard-earned money on building a new house. In his typical "peasant" fashion, he proclaims that "television is only an egg, but a house is a hen."

Zhou Xiaowen has given us many clues to understand Ermo's motives for wanting a television, but leaves us wondering about Ermo's life after she gets it. What lies ahead for her? Zhou's ending is a deliberately ambiguous one. In fact, he does not leave us with much hope. With the flickering snowy screen fading out and the credits starting to roll, Ermo's singsong voice selling "twisted noodles" starts again, implying that Ermo's life goes back to where she began. It is in a similarly ambivalent, perhaps even more doubtful, vein that Dai offers her cheerless, or even chilly, prediction of Ermo's days to come. For Dai, the end of the film also marks the end of Ermo's quest; her future prospects appear bleak: "For Ermo, what lies ahead are the long and lonely nights of her village in the mountains, and those endless and monotonous days."[13] This kind of life, Dai predicts, will eventually turn Ermo into one of those wooden, expressionless old women sitting on the hill, staring numbly into the distance.

This is another point on which I want to diverge from Dai, who seems to underestimate the powerful pedagogic potential of television. It may be that Ermo has not had much to do with television before she decides to buy one; however, once she sets eyes on the biggest television set in town, she starts to develop an intellectual curiosity for and fascination with what she sees on the screen. Her first contact with television in the shop is deeply baffling to her. Seeing a dubbed foreign movie on the screen, she asks why blonde foreigners (*waiguoren*) speak "our" language. Xiazi, who owns a truck and comes to town often and seems more savvy than Ermo, explains to her that "TV stations can speak whatever language they like." When Ermo goes back to buy the TV set, she is even more intrigued: This time a Chinese person, on China Central Television's English channel, is speaking a foreign language (*waiguohua*)! Again, Xiazi reassures her, "They speak foreign languages only for a little while each day." Ermo's questions about television, which seem intended to demonstrate the parochial nature of a premodern consciousness, can in fact be read as astute questions about the workings of globalizing images on television.

Writing about Chinese television viewers in the early 1990s, Lull found that they considered television to have the ability to open their minds, providing them not only with new ideas, but also with a whole new way of thinking:

A key argument I will now make is that television has become the main reference point which Chinese people use to compare and evaluate their own national status, a development that has inspired viewers to dream of a better future while at the same time they have become frustrated and angered by the barriers that stand in the way.[14]

By now, we can see that Ermo's fascination with television has taken on an intellectual dimension, though it is expressed in an intuitive manner. Her naïve questions are a result of what Lull refers to as "selectively attentive viewing," which is driven by an intense curiosity about the "similarities and dissimilarities between . . . [her] country and the rest of the world."[15] Ermo's capacity to develop critical perspectives on the outside world is real. In addition, considering the reality of Ermo's life, being physically "stuck" in a village in the mountains, the singularity of television as a way out of this phobic space—a possible source of information and images of the world outside—is not to be underestimated. Here it may be useful to note that the time—late 1980s and early 1990s—when television entered Ermo's, and indeed many other rural people's, household coincided with the time of rapid expansion of imported programs on Chinese television. During the period of the 1970s and early 1980s, imported programs consisted of no more than 2 percent; by the early 1990s, however, the national average percentage of imported programming is estimated to have reached 25 percent. These foreign programs, accessible to the Chinese viewers, such as Ermo and her family and neighbors in the village, included, first, news programs—CCTV expanded its evening news bulletin from 15 minutes to 30 minutes, due to its regular importation of foreign news; second, education programs, including language education; third, entertainment programming, such as teleplays, miniseries, sitcoms, and soap operas, children's cartoons, variety shows, sports programs, and arts performances. These entertainment programs came from various countries; however, the great proportion of them originated in the United States.[16]

Although television connects the place of the "idyll" to other geographically distant, but communicationally present, places,[17] it serves a different purpose to people of different social contexts. While Margaret Morse's American urban modernity that features shopping malls, television, and freeway is congruent with the idea of *freedom to* pursue individualism and pleasure, the Chinese villagers' existence, which features television without freeways and shopping malls, is more about *freedom from* the stifling realities of village life. In her work on small-town American housewives who read romance genre novels, Janice Radway finds that reading romance functions as a "combative" and "compensatory" strategy.[18] Many women use reading to retreat to their own interior space, to be alone, which allows them to refuse the other-directed social role prescribed for them. Her work challenges a common assumption of a woman as a "docile audience" and argues that the reading of romance by these women is a creative activity that empowers them in their everyday lives. Similarly, we know from the story that Ermo's quest for television sets her on the road to self-realization of sexuality and independence. She is also seen to be a quick learner in consuming and participating in the modernity afforded by the city. That Zhou Xiaowen opts to end the story by "returning" Ermo to the village—showing her to be too tired and disillusioned to pay attention to foreign people or foreign places on television—says more about his disapproval of the globalization process than about the (im)possibility of Ermo continuing to be intrigued, inspired, and indeed educated by television.

Will television eventually lose its status-giving power and cease to be the exotic object of a commodity fetish? Will it ever become an ordinary item of household furniture, which, like any furniture, has a practical function in the house apart from looking good?[19] Will it eventually become a window onto the world beyond, taking Ermo and her family to unknown places to experience unknown things? Answers to these questions are mostly positive and lie, of course, outside the frame of the film. By the mid-1990s, there were 0.28 billion television sets in China, and the size of the Chinese television audience had swelled to 0.8 billion. Most of these viewers (0.6 billion) were of peasant origin[20]—the most disadvantaged and powerless majority of the Chinese population. Lull observes that although most Chinese viewers of the early 1990s had no opportunities to travel outside China, images of foreign places allowed them the pleasure of "vicarious travel."[21] Through their consumption of images of travel in everyday life, and their identification with characters in foreign places on television, Chinese villagers' spatial imagination has acquired a transnational dimension.[22] In other words, the incorporation of television as an everyday object into most rural households—it is not hard to imagine that many other houses in Ermo's village will soon acquire a television—marks the beginning of a new way of imagining the world, as well as one's place in it. Although, at the end of the film, Ermo and her family are dozing off and too tired to engage with the images of the world cities, it is by no means far-fetched to imagine that television will eventually become an everyday object for them. In fact, this is exactly what has happened in the Chinese countryside. Images of these faraway places may then take a firmer and more tangible hold on Ermo's and—perhaps more likely—her son's imagination. "Vancouver," "Paris," and "Frankfurt" may become more than exotic names to them.

ERMO AND THE CITY: AN ALTERNATIVE READING

For the reasons I have given so far, I believe that Ermo does not necessarily have to become, as Dai predicts, one of the numb, wooden old women dotting the contemporary rural landscape. This is because Ermo lives in an era that is characterized by both unprecedented physical mobility and an expanding horizon of imaginary space brought about by television. Thanks to this piece of furniture called television, Ermo and her fellow villagers' horizon of imagination has suddenly expanded. Now they can watch American soap-operas—it was *Dynasty*, dubbed into Mandarin, that Ermo and her fellow villagers were watching, lifestyle variety shows promoting modern cosmopolitan living. Note the gaze of Ermo on the scantily dressed female swimming instructor floating in the pool and, of course, the incessant lure of the world outside—seen in the images of Sydney, Tokyo, Paris, and New York. Unlike these other old women, Ermo is a traveler in both the literal and the epistemic sense. Her decision to go to town is motivated by money, but her desire to *consume* modernity, thereby gaining status, is overtaken by the sheer speed at which she participates in modernity. In the city, she is away from her impotent and oppressive husband, free from village gossip and social conventions, and able to act independently in making decisions about sexual pleasure, money, and work.

Ermo gets what she wants—the biggest television in town—much to the pride of her husband. However, she seems to realize that she may have paid too high a price for it: She suffers a blackout from selling too much blood, and Xiazi's empty promise to marry her, while attempting to "keep" her by secretly topping up her wages through her boss, leaves a sour taste in her mouth. When the television set finally arrives—via the window, as it is too big to fit through the door—it has to sit on the bed, as there is no other place in the house for it. Ermo leans against it, looking emaciated and forlorn. All she can muster enough strength to say is, "My strainer is now being used as the antenna. What can I use to make my noodles with?"

This is where Zhou Xiaowen's, and indeed Dai's, thinking on modernity becomes inconsistent. On the one hand, as Dai points out,[23] the film shows that Ermo's story is but one episode from the rural Chinese life, which has already been infiltrated by modernity: The neighbor has a truck and a television set, and Ermo's income comes from selling goods rather than working in the field. On the other hand, Ermo's surrender to the sheer weight of village ways of life seems to point to the absolute incommensurability between this life and modernity. This contradiction can only be explained in terms of the prevalent sense of being stuck. Stephanie Donald notes that the cinematic space inhabited by Ermo is "claustrophobic," invoking a sense of both desperation and inevitability.[24] It is perhaps this sense of inevitability that also accounts for the fact that Zhou and his critics—such as Dai—are reluctant to consider the possibility of Ermo's sojourn in the city as having a transformative effect on her subjectivity. After all, in Zhou's view, neither the village nor the city offers any possibility of a way out for her.

However, Ermo's experience in the city points to the possibility of alternative readings. It is apparent that Ermo neither loathes nor adores the city; it is just a place where she can make quick money so that she can buy the television set much sooner. Nevertheless, unshackled by the village constraints and scrutiny, she wears a bra to look like city girls, has a clandestine affair with her friendly neighbor Xiazi, and even learns to order a meal in a restaurant like city folks do. Ermo's encounter with urban life involves an obscure

town that lies close to the county where her village is located, and so her experience of going to the city (*jin cheng*) is unremarkable, in the general
scheme of nationwide rural–urban migration. Indeed, tens of millions of rural residents have traveled far in search of work in the city. However, this
town, though not even a provincial capital, presents the possibility of epistemological transition in Ermo's inadvertent journey of becoming modern.
Her identity in town is that of a contract worker (*da gong*), not a peasant, and
as a worker, she no longer works alone but as part of an assembly line with
other workers. She even gets over her initial shock at the harshness of industrial work when one of her fellow workers has a hand mangled in the
noodle-making machine. As a worker, Ermo no longer generates income
from subsistence, but earns a wage from her employer. Not knowing how
the wage system works, she nevertheless learns new ways of making money
in the city, such as selling her blood to the hospital.

Ermo operates within a clear spatial/temporal nexus composed of economic reforms, marketization, rural migration, urbanization, and the increasing mobility of the 1990s. However, the film deemphasizes these social
and national specificities, thus making the story of Ermo an antimodernity allegory. Such an allegory requires the exclusion of an alternative narrative possibility, one that allows space for Ermo's subjectivity to be transformed by her
experiences—which is a likely consequence for a rural migrant whose subjectivity has obviously acquired a number of modern dimensions.

Zhou's Ermo is a typical "peasant" woman. She is "inarticulate" and un-
burdened by gracious conversational skills and refined manners. Indeed, she
seeks to extract justice from her neighbor through nonverbal means, such as
fistfights and foul play (she poisons their pig). In the film, Ermo is often seen
wandering in a somewhat trance-like fashion from one place to another in
town, riveted by almost everything she sees. The city often presents itself in
the shape of a question mark. Most of what Ermo has to say in town is in the
form of asking naïve questions. "What's this? It looks like blood," she says,
when offered a red cordial in the restaurant. "What is stock-taking?" she in-
quires, when she learns that the shop is stock-taking (*pan dian*). "What good
does it do?" she wonders, when her lover gives her a gift of some antiwrinkle
cream. "What does it mean 'to be paid each according to one's ability' [*an lao
qu chou*]?" she asks, when she receives her first pay from her boss. Ermo's lack
of sophistication about how the city works is in stark contrast to the conventional figure of a detective-anthropologist, often identified in modernist urban films. In James Donald's work on the cinema and the city, he points to
the notable cinematic tradition of using the character of a detective or an anthropologist as a way of understanding the city.[25] The detective or the anthropologist is necessary to the narrative of the city, because, as he argues, unlike "us," who are too much a part of the urban landscape, the detective and
the anthropologist are able to maintain both a distance and an intimate

knowledge of the city. Like the detective or the anthropologist, Ermo is not as involved in the city as "we" are. Her questioning is a constant source of amusement, which endears her to the urban spectators who are curious and voyeuristic about, yet almost always contemptuous of, peasant mentalities. However, Ermo's "peasant-like" questions are not easy to answer. For instance, "Stock-taking means that the shop is closed" is the answer she is given to one of her questions. Here, rather than casting Ermo as an ignorant peasant, I choose to read these questions as her intuitive interrogation of the widely assumed inevitability of modernization. Ermo's first contact with the city gives her the vantage point of a detached observer of life. Her questions about the workings of the city are those of a naïve anthropologist or even a cultural "agent provocateur," and they turn our own common assumptions about modernity on their head. In other words, Ermo in the city follows the tradition of using the point of view of the "villager," whereby, as Frederic Jameson observes, it is useful to use the "peasant as witness" seeing the metropolis for the first time.[26] In this sense, Zhou uses Ermo as a mouthpiece for his own interrogation of modernity, while at the time refusing to attribute the possibility of her own agency. What Zhou—and indeed Dai—fails to acknowledge is that Ermo's subjectivity may be subject to transformation not only because of her experience of living and working in the city, but also because of her imagination or her capacity to imagine traveling beyond the physical spaces she inhabits.

The final scene of the film emphasizes the incongruence of the towering presence of a brand-new television set in a shabby old house, hence implying that television has no place in the rural villagers' lives. Zhou thereby signifies his refusal to consider the various uses that can be made of television in such a context. However, Hartley forcefully argues, television is "transmodern," capable of performing social functions that are both premodern and modern.[27] Ermo's husband's invitation to the entire village to watch TV in his house— despite his initial opposition to buying a TV set—reasserts his power and masculinity as the former village chief and is clearly socially motivated. However, television also has an important pedagogic role, informing citizens about their community, their nation, and the world. Although "education" in the form of everyday media consumption is entertainment-oriented and can be seen as deeply banal, it is crucial in facilitating the construction of cultural citizenship.[28] The pedagogic role of television is clearly visible in the ways in which these Chinese villagers watch television. Consider the following fragment of dialogue between village spectators of a rugby match on Ermo's television:

A: Look! Foreigners are fighting. It must be a gang fight.
B: No, it's a ball game.
A: What ball game is that?
B: It's softball.

This snippet could be seen as a mockery of the villagers' lack of cross-cultural literacy. Indeed, this is the reading offered by Ciecko and Lu.[29] While I concur with their reading of Ermo and her fellow villagers' relationship to television as embodying "ironies and paradoxes" of globalization, and while I also accept their claim that *Ermo*, like some other fifth-generation films, partakes of the self-orientalization of the Chinese villages in order to engage the gaze of the transnational film market, I nevertheless do not agree with their view of these village viewers as totally disinterested, inarticulate, and unable to return the gaze of the urban and international audiences.[30] In fact, Ermo's remarks about the workings of television, as well as the dialogue quoted previously, may be read as a sign of their incipient cross-cultural curiosity. In the same way that Ermo's insistent, albeit intuitive, questions about the workings of modernity in the city are self-ethnographic, the comments of these village spectators of foreign images also betray curious minds at work, pointing to the possible beginnings of a more informed understanding of the world outside. Again, Lull's argument on the impact of television on Chinese viewers in the 1990s is worth considering:

> Television has irreversibly altered the consciousness of the Chinese public. It has introduced, reinforced, and popularized ideas and images that have fuelled the imagination of the people in ways that far exceed what government planners had in mind when they first promoted the medium's widespread adoption.[31]

Writing about modernity and the Chinese cinema, Stephanie Donald observes that modernity does not arrive everywhere at the same time, nor does it arrive in the same sequences of forms.[32] That aside, I argue, modernity may also arrive again and again, layer upon layer, and as a result we must deal with it each time it manifests itself in different shape and color and, accordingly, consider its implications. The consumption of television in everyday life is now crucial to the formation of subjectivity, community, and transnational imagination in every corner of the world to which it has spread. Although Zhou is entitled to articulate his doubts about or even aversion to modernity—just as Dai is entitled to her prediction of Ermo's bleak future—his argument is nevertheless premised on an unwarranted conflation of television with other signifiers of modernity. An important point I have tried to make, via the example of Ermo and her fellow viewers in the village, is that although television as an object can be an icon of modernity, the arrival of television as an everyday consumption item in rural Chinese homes marks the beginning of the formation and transformation of a transnational imagination in such communities. In other words, the incipient "nonspace" in the village life created by the arrival of television may give rise to conditions for the formation of transnational subjectivities, which may manifest themselves in various ways ranging from, on the one hand, a growing capacity to understand or identify with the people living in different national and cultural spaces and, on the other hand, an acquisition of a reworked, "modern," or even postmodern outlook on the selfhood, place, time, and social relationships. It would be hard to conceive that the daily exposure to things both new and different and routine identification with imaginary characters in faraway places will leave the villagers' horizon of imagination unaltered.

This claim, however, should be qualified by the sobering fact that vicarious travel through television consumption does not necessarily go hand-in-hand with village women's actual physical mobility. My extensive interviews with a group of domestic maids and corporate cleaners from villages of Anhui Province indicate that media consumption of rural migrants has diminished, rather than increased, since their arrival in the city.[33] While television used to be a daily reality back in the village, these village women now working in the city either do not have a television in their dormitories or are too tired after a long day's work to watch television. Some tell me that they can only afford to read newspapers that are thrown out by people whose offices they clean, since newspapers cost money. Recruited to contribute to the project of modernity and globalization, these women who clean urban spaces remain invisible figures in the transnational space. Through conversations about space and place with young women who clean the public spaces of Shanghai International Airport,[34] I realize that not everyone who traverses that international space equates airports with the freedom to travel. My request to each of them to give me a wish-list of the places they would really like to go repeatedly drew blank looks and subsequent giggles. After much prompting, Huang, age twenty, from a village in Anhui Province, says: "I dare not imagine" (*wo bugan xiang*). Ge, her colleague from the same county, says that she is prepared to go to any place in the world as long as there is money to be made. Their transnational imagining seems short-circuited, rather than facilitated, by their decision to leave the village. Juxtaposing their experience with that of Ermo, whose relationship with television starts and ends in her village, we see the contradiction of mobility. With the former, the everyday experience of virtual travel—of being transported to places imaginatively by television— may need to stop due to the need for the body to remain mobile and "in circulation" in the domain of transnational capital, whereas with the latter, the body has to remain immobile so that the mind can travel. In both cases, what is described as "mobile privatization" seems a remote possibility.

ZHANG YIMOU AND TELEVISION:
THE POLITICS OF COMPASSION

Like *Ermo*, *Not One Less* tells the story of a young village woman for whom television assumes a central importance. Wei Minzhi is a thirteen-year-old village girl, and, like Ermo, she is obstinate, inarticulate, and bereft of refined manners and cultivated social skills. Although she has not had proper schooling, she has been enticed to take a job as a substitute teacher for the reward of 50 yuan, plus a 10 yuan bonus. Wei is not a good teacher, and her salary is contingent upon her making sure that no one goes missing from the class. However, it so happens that a poverty-stricken boy does disappear from her class, which sets Minzhi off on a wild goose chase. She goes to the city to look for the lost boy and meets with nothing but cold indifference and apathy from city folks. Alone and helpless, she decides that she might find her student if she can manage to get herself seen on television. Driven by this naïve faith, Wei begs and pesters—with a peasant's graceless stubbornness—the television station's security guards for permission to enter the station. Her efforts finally pay off when the station manager, by pure chance, stumbles across this persistent girl, who has by now become a fixture at the entrance to the building. As it happens, the manager is a compassionate man, and from then on, Wei's fortunes take a turn for the better. She appears on television and makes a tearful plea for her wandering student to come home. The film ends with Wei and her pupil happily going back to the village, with boxes of school stationery, two television sets, and a big bundle of cash donated by urban television viewers.

Although the story of Ermo unfolds as an allegory, the social issues in *Not One Less*—poverty and the lack of educational opportunities for rural children—are represented in a much more realistic manner. In fact, it was Zhang's declared intention to make the film as close to a "subdocumentary" as possible.[35] This supposed desire for the effect of proximity to real life has been the cause of both controversy and recognition in international film festival communities and domestic circles alike.[36] However, does Zhang succeed in being as faithful to the rural life as he claims to be?

Here we may do well to consult the novel on which the film is based.[37] In the original story, a peasant school girl, Xiaofang, leaves her village and finds a job in the city, to escape the imminent fate of being married off to a rich man by her parents, who are in debt. Her teacher, Zhang, follows her to the city and tries everything, including appealing to Xiaofang on television, to go back to school. While Xiaofang's teachers, classmates, and the village chief put their resources together to pay off her parents' debt, Xiaofang herself is nowhere to be found, and in the meantime, the rich man who has "bought" Xiaofang, acting in complicity with the powerful prefecture chief, is threatening to decimate the already struggling school by ordering the transfer of the school's principal, Mr. Wang.

In comparison with the original story, Zhang Yimou's adaptation has a less cluttered plotline and a happier ending. But what are some of the narrative strategies that enable Zhang to transform a messy story—no more messy than real life, though—with a plausible, though "unsatisfying," ending into a "feel-good" story? Here, I want to point out that in representing poverty and the woeful state of rural education in the ways that he does, Zhang mirrors the behavior of his own characters in the film: Like the television journalists he portrays, Zhang is guilty of perpetuating a romanticized discourse of compassion. In other words, the fictitious world in which Wei, the peasant girl, forms a relationship to television as the pitiable, recognizable Other for urban television viewers is poignantly similar to the urban space inhabited by rural migrants who have become the objects of both sympathy and derision to city folks. What is ultimately ironic is that in attempting to do a good deed for the future of rural children by making a film about poverty and rural education, while at the same time telling a good story, *Not One Less* resorts to reproducing the familiar images and tropes one associates conventionally with poverty, women, and rural life on television. Hence, the film becomes metonymic of the politics of representing these issues in the media in general.

Some elaboration on these claims is in order. Like perennial news stories on television, *Not One Less* operates on the logic of compromise. The complexity of human relationships and the dynamics of the power structures represented in the original story have been both reduced and flattened out in order to maximize the story's appeal. In lieu of abusive individuals with power and wealth, and in the absence of any questioning of a social structure that conditions and legitimates systematic inequalities, *poverty*, an abstract and rarefied concept, becomes the public enemy. By offering compassion as the effective solution to the social problem, *Not One Less* inadvertently draws attention to the political nature—and limitations—of such a discourse.

Moreover, like news stories on television, which adhere relentlessly to the logic of sound bites, visual imperatives, and time constraints, and for which narrative economy consists of offering only "narrative sketches"[38] to be recognized and activated by implied audiences, Zhang Yimou also resorts to the deployment of "narrative sketches." One tactic for eliciting predictable spectatorial responses is the deployment of a familiar homology, which, in the case of Zhang's film about Wei, operates on the default association between poverty, women, children, and rural life. It is exactly the seduction of this homology that may account for the ways in which Zhang tinkers with the original story. Explaining the appeal of *Not One Less* to urban audiences, Liu Jianzi makes a telling point about the film that is equally true of the ways in which stories of rural poverty are read by television audiences:

> It must be pointed out that films cannot have the intended effect without the complicity of the spectator. In other words, the fact that audiences are moved by the film's realistic touch in its portrayal of rural China is not a result of the film's painstaking efforts to record life as it is, but rather a result of the concepts and images that are already easily associated with women, poverty and rural life in the popular consciousness.[39]

RURAL WOMEN AND TELEVISION: ON HOW TO GET ON TV

Television is crucial to the narrative resolution in the film. Wei Minzhi manages to get herself on television, appealing, with tears streaming down her face, for her student to return. This appearance changes the lives of everyone, including the children in her village, who are desperate for a proper school. Here we are encouraged to think that television offers an all-too-easy solution to social problems and that the media publicity is remarkably "effective" in generating city folks' sympathy and charitable support. Important though these issues may be, I am nevertheless more interested in asking a different question. A considerable time in *Not One Less* is spent on Wei's supposedly laughably naïve and excruciatingly ineffectual attempts to get herself on television. And, admittedly, her discovery by the station manager is purely serendipitous. So what do poor rural women like Wei—and, indeed, Ermo—need to do in order to get themselves on television?

Wei's dogged determination to appear on television is indeed thought-provoking. One may even be tempted to think that although she has no understanding of the politics of television, her desire indicates a powerful moment at which millions of Chinese television viewers like her—female, poor, rural, uneducated—are beginning to have a taste of what it is like to participate actively in modernity. Indeed, it is not too far-fetched to detect in her action some kind of inchoate and intuitive expression of what Hartley calls a "citizen of media"[40]—however unsophisticated that expression may be. Are we, the audience, to blame if we want to regard Wei as an example of "little people" who have discovered the possibility of participating in the construction of citizenship, albeit in a mediated way?

Here I want to point to some important dimensions to the politics of representing female peasants. First, in order to turn an ordinary peasant girl like Wei Minzhi into one with maximum cinematic appeal, she must remain inarticulate, clumsy, and, in short, unmodern. Helpless and clueless, Wei appeals to the "metropolitan gaze"[41] of urban television viewers within the film—as well as of the film audience itself—not in spite of, but precisely because of, her gracelessness and clumsiness. For this reason, her pursuit of modernity via television must be held in check. Her television appearance objectifies, rather than emancipates, her. To ensure her status as the recipient of urban sympathy and support, Wei must not only appear incapable of becoming modern, but she must also be content never to want to become the speaking subject. When her wish to appear on television finally materializes, she does not know what to say; all she can do is cry into the camera. Unable to speak for herself, she becomes an object to be constructed and produced, and it is television, the epitome of the technology of control, that assumes this role.

This is a second dimension to the politics of representing the rural poor in China. On the one hand, the production of modernity, consonant with the state agenda and newly configured class interests, requires that people like Minzhi be incorporated within its scope. On the other hand, the status quo depends upon people like her to continue to be inarticulate and unquestioning. At the turn of the new century, in spite of commercialization, television is still state-owned and controlled, and managed by people with middle-class urban sensibilities. Wei Minzhi's future—and, indeed, the future of all those like her—lies in playing the role she has been cast in: subordinate, marginal, and voiceless. In other words, television functions for Wei as a two-edged sword: She is allowed to participate in modernity, as long as she accepts modernity's conditions and consequences.

BETWEEN THE VILLAGE AND THE CITY: DEPARTURES AND ARRIVALS

Both films feature a departure from the village, an arrival in the city, and a final return to the village. Both Ermo's and Minzhi's lives are seen to be transformed by this departure and return. However, it is the television, not the women's experience in the city, that is seen to be the agent of change. In the case of Ermo, the television she brings back is seen to decimate the traditional way of the village life, whereas in the case of Minzhi, the television she returns with is seen to "save" her village. In both cases, the experience of the women in the city is represented as aberrant, and the narrative closure can only be realized with their return.

Here I argue that there are at least two reasons why mobilities are gendered fictions. First, the narrative of the final return of the two women back to the village becomes meaningful when juxtaposed with that of the final departure of men from the village. I have in mind examples such as *The Road Home—My Father and My Mother* (*Wode fuqin, wode muqin*) and *Shower* (*Xizao*).[42] The gender-specific narrative of departure and return is consistent with the unevenness in the process of mobility and increasing stratification, along the lines of gender, geography, and educational level. Second, and I believe more seriously, returning women to the village as a narrative solution is incongruent with the palpable reality of more and more women departing from, rather than returning to, the village in the nationwide mobility and hence risks further reducing the social visibility of these rural women who have left home and are trying to survive in the niche of transnational space.

Although Zhou situates Ermo and her fellow village viewers in front of the box—that is, as the spectators of television—Zhang's character, Wei Minzhi, wants to appear on television and, in part, ends up being "constructed" by television. For this reason, while *Ermo* gives me a launching pad from which to open up a discussion on modernity, media consumption in rural China, and the possibility of transnational imagination, *Not One Less* provides me with an angle to consider both the possibility of and difficulties with such imagination. For the same reason that Zhou's antimodern allegory does not leave me disillusioned, the happy end of Zhang's *Not One Less* does not leave me feeling uplifted, morally or emotionally. I depart from both Zhou's intention in, and Dai's reading of, *Ermo* and opt for a more empowering view of the television audience depicted in the film and the role ascribed to television in Chinese rural life. However, I also want to diverge from the intention of *Not One Less* by casting doubt on the power of television to transform the fate of the poor, rural girls and women who are the objects of the compassionate story told on television within the film.

In their critique of *Ermo*, Ciecko and Lu rightly observe that films such as *Ermo* embody a tendency of self-orientalization, in that the Chinese village life is again displayed for the gaze of transnational spectators.[43] Here I want to add that it is not just transnationals who participate in the gazing; it is also the Chinese urban. In other words, since cinematic spectatorship is largely an urban experience—unlike televisual spectatorship, which has also become a common rural experience—the poignancy of the fantasy of social mobility and economic success in the plot of a peasant woman's quest either to own a television or to appear on it is intended to resonate mostly with urban spectators. As the object, rather than the subject, of the gaze, Ermo and Minzhi may have the right and capacity for fantasy, but are seen to have no access to determining how that fantasy is represented, let alone access to opportunities to act it out.

Although television is put to different uses in the two films, I argue that in both works, it is to be read as both metonymic of the modernizing process and metaphoric of the paradoxes and contradictions that puncture this process. Television is seen to be at once empowering and disempowering, liberating and restricting. And it is the experiences of these rustic, "uncivilized" women that not only give these metaphors potency but also render them theoretically useful. A gender-reversed scenario—say, Ermo's husband or Wei Minzhi's brother going to the city and coming back with a television set— would be not only less appealing to urban filmgoers, but also less workable as a plot. This is because modernity is invariably a gendered phenomenon, and women such as Ermo and Wei Minzhi are perceived to be likely transgressors in both spatial and moral terms—urban versus rural, traditional versus modern—in the process of modernization. The body of the female peasant in an urban space functions discursively to make class interests invisible by erecting the familiar tropes of "city versus country," "tradition versus modernity." Moreover, unlike the equivalent process in many other places, modernization in China—a nationwide project ushered in by the Party-state—bears the imprint of the state at every juncture. For this reason, although women are potentially the agents of modernization, the modernity they "perform"[44] is scripted in such a way that they become available for subjugation, co-optation, and regulation by the state. The idea of rural women, unshackled by traditions and roaming freely in urban transnational spaces, has already proved to be disquieting for both the urban genteel and the state.[45] That cinema reflects this intense curiosity in, and anxiety about, this group of people is both natural and understandable. I hence argue that the question of what constitutes the "transnational" must necessarily start with the question of what constitutes the "national," which in turn is made up by unequal, yet interdependent, relations between the rural and the city. Hence to trace the impact of mobility on the contour and texture of transnational imagination, there is no better place to start than the politics of leaving the village.

NOTES

1. The concept "mobile privatization," first used by Raymond Williams, is defined by later television academics as a mechanism that combines mobility with privacy. It refers to the dramatic retreat of social life into privatized settings, on the one hand, and opportunities for viewers to be transported to destinations well beyond the confines of home, on the other. See Raymond Williams, *Television: Technology and Cultural Form* (London: Fontana, 1974); and Shaun Moores, "Television, Geography and 'Mobile Privatization,'" *European Journal of Communication* 8 (1993): 365.

2. Margaret Morse, *Virtualities: Television, Media Art, and Cyberculture* (Bloomington: Indiana University Press, 1998), 100.

3. Moores, "Television, Geography," 365.

4. Hortense Powdermaker, *Hollywood the Dream Factory: An Anthropologist Looks at Movie Makers* (London: Secker & Warburg, 1950), 12–13.

5. Stephanie Donald, *Public Secrets, Public Spaces: Cinema and Civility in China* (Lanham, Md.: Rowman & Littlefield, 2000), 122.

6. Morse, *Virtualities*, 102.

7. This disjunctive and uneven nature of the globalization process is also noted in Anne Ciecko and Sheldon Hsiao-peng Lu's reading of *Ermo* in their article "Televisuality, Capital and the Global Village," *Jump Cut* 42 (1999): 77–83.

8. Paul Wollen, "The World City and the Global Village," *Emergence: Journal for the Study of Media and Composite Cultures* 9, no. 1 (1999): 70.

9. *Ermo*, 1994, and *Yige Ye Buneng Shao*, 1998.

10. These three options were outlined by Zhou Xiaowen in his interview with Dai Jinhua (2000). See Dai Jinhua, *Wu Zhong Feng Jing* (Sceneries in the Fog: Chinese Cinema 1978–1998) (Beijing: Beijing University Press, 2000).

11. For information about internal migration in China, including female rural migration, see Dorothy Solinger, *Contesting Citizenship in Urban China: Peasant Migration, the State, and the Logic of the Market* (Berkeley: University of California Press, 1999); Delia Davin, *Internal Migration in Contemporary China* (London: Macmillan, 1999); and Tamara Jacka, "My Life as a Migrant Worker," *Intersections* 4

(September 2000), <wwwsshe.murdoch.edu.au/intersections/issue4/> (accessed November 2001).

12. Dai, *Sceneries in the Fog*, 369.

13. Dai, *Sceneries in the Fog*, 370.

14. James Lull, *China Turned On: Television, Reform and Resistance* (London: Routledge, 1991), 170.

15. Lull, *China Turned On*, 174.

16. For a thorough account of the internationalization of television programs on Chinese television, including its policies and economics, see Hong Junhao, *The Internationalization of Television in China: The Evolution of Ideology, Society, and Media since the Reform* (Westport, Conn.: Praeger, 1998).

17. David Morley, "Bounded Realms: Household, Family, Community, and Nation," in *Home, Exile, Homeland: Film, Media and the Politics of Place*, ed. Hamid Naficy (New York: Routledge, 1999), 153–54.

18. Janice Radway, "Reading the Romance," in *The Communication Theory Reader*, ed. Paul Cobley (London: Routledge, 1996), 462.

19. It may be relevant to mention here that village viewers in the film talk about "watching the television set" (*kan dian shi ji*), rather than "watching television" (*kan dian shi*). Although this may be just a difference of expression, we can also read it as a linguistic index of people's initial fascination with the form, rather than the content, of television.

20. He Chunhui, "*Kan jiao dian fang tan*" ("Looking at the Focal Point"), in *Ju jiao jian dian fang tan* (Focusing on the Focal Point), ed. Yuan Zhengmin and Liang Jianzhen (Beijing: China Encyclopaedia Press, 1999).

21. Lull, *China Turned On*.

22. Liu Xin, "Space, Mobility, and Flexibility: Chinese Villagers and Scholars Negotiate Power at Home and Abroad," in *Ungrounded Empires: The Cultural Politics of Modern Chinese Transnationalism*, ed. Aihwa Ong and Donald M. Nonini (New York: Routledge, 1997).

23. Dai, *Sceneries in the Fog*.

24. Stephanie Donald, *Public Secrets*, 122.

25. James Donald, *Imagining the Modern City* (London: Athlone, 1999).

26. Frederic Jameson, "Remapping Taipei," in *New Chinese Cinemas: Forms, Identities, Politics*, ed. Nick Browne, Paul G. Pickowicz, Vivian Sobshack, and Esther Yau (New York: Cambridge University Press, 1994), 148.

27. John Hartley, *Uses of Television* (London: Routledge, 1999).

28. John Hartley, *Popular Reality: Journalism, Modernity, Popular Culture* (London: Arnold, 1996); Hartley, *Uses of Television*; and David Rowe, *Sport, Culture and the Media* (Buckingham: Open University Press, 1999).

29. Ciecko and Lu, "Televisuality."

30. Ciecko and Lu, "Televisuality," 82.

31. Lull, *China Turned On*, 170.

32. Stephanie Donald, *Public Secrets*.

33. Wuwei is a county in Anhui Province that has a tradition of exporting domestic servants to middle-class families in Shanghai, Beijing, and other big Chinese cities. I have conducted some in-depth interviews with domestic workers from Wuwei and contract cleaners from Mengcheng County Anhui, all of whom are presently working

in Shanghai. See Wanning Sun, "Anhui Working Girls in Shanghai: Gender, Class and a Sense of Place" (paper presented to the workshop on Space and Place: Popular Culture in China, Hangzhou, China, June 18–21, 2001b).

34. These interviews took place in April 2001. Again, the interviews were conducted in Chinese and translations are mine.

35. Liu Jianzi, *"Tao guan tian guan de qi shi"* ("Inspirations from Clay Pots and Iron Pots"), *Dushu* (Readings) 258, no. 9 (2000): 72–80.

36. Zhang withdrew the film from the Cannes festival in 1999 to protest against claims that the film was functioning as propaganda for the state. In China, *Not One Less* won Zhang considerable political mileage, and the film has been described as a tribute to the state-sponsored Hope Project, a nationwide scheme to boost education in poor, remote country areas. See Dai, *Sceneries in the Fog.*

37. The original story is called *There Is a Sun in the Sky (Tian shang you ge tan yang).* For bibliographic details and a brief account, see Liu Jianzi, "Inspirations from Clay Pots."

38. Tony Wilson, *Watching Television: Hermeneutics, Reception and Popular Culture* (Cambridge: Polity, 1993).

39. Liu, "Inspirations from Clay Pots," 74–75.

40. Hartley, *Popular Reality.*

41. Vera Mackie, "The Metropolitan Gaze: Travelers, Bodies, Spaces," *Intersections* 4 (September 2000), <wwwsshe.murdoch.edu.au/intersections/issue4/> (accessed October 2000).

42. *The Road Home—My Father and My Mother (Wode fuqin, wode muqin)* (1999) and *Shower (Xizao* 2000). For a critical analysis of these two films, see Stephanie Donald and Wanning Sun, "Going Home: History, Nation, and the Mournful Landscapes of Home," *Metro* 129–30 (September 2001): 140–51.

43. Ciecko and Lu, "Televisuality."

44. Louisa Schein, "Performing Modernity," *Cultural Anthropology* 14, no. 3 (1999): 361–95.

45. Michael Dutton, *Streetlife China* (Melbourne: Cambridge University Press, 1998).

2

✦

Going Abroad or Staying Home: Cinema, Fantasy, and the World City

The two enduring tropes of mobility in contemporary Chinese urban folklore are "going to the city" (*jincheng*) and "going abroad" (*chuguo*). While the former features villagers like Ermo and Minzhi on the road to the urban spaces in China, the latter centers upon city folks on their way to becoming transnationals. Although these are parallel processes, they also stand for the metaphor for one another. In addition, they are not only parallel processes, but are also in many instances sequential and linked, although many millions take the first step, whereas only smaller numbers take the second. The dream of leaving one's home(land) for the global cities is akin to that of leaving one's home village for the "internal global cities" in China, in that the traveler in each case has to negotiate a spatial relationship marked with a peripheral versus center inequality. In my interviews with some Shanghai residents who employ maids and domestic part-time cleaners from rural areas of other provinces,[1] Shanghai was over and over again described—implicitly—as the center of China. Ms. Zhang, a retired senior journalist who employs a maid from a village in Jiangsu Province, says that Shanghai is the best place to be if *chuguo* is not an option. Mr. Mi, a young businessman dealing in computing equipment who employs a domestic cleaner from Anhui—an adjacent poor and largely rural province—describes Anhui as the "Philippines of China." His comparison of Anhui to the Philippines is interesting. By equating a "poor" hinterland rural province in China with a poor Asian country, Mi subscribes to the language of a global power, but appropriates the power associated with that speaking position in defining his relation to Anhui. In identifying against Anhui within a global geopolitical framework, he brings to light the discursive complicity between global centers and national ones. In other words, by mobilizing a global configuration of space and place to define and describe Anhui—a place he has never been to, but that nevertheless produces a servant class for his consumption—Mi points to the increasing possibility of replicating global power relations within a national space. Indeed, as Ulf Hannerz correctly points out, there is a third world in every first world and a first world in every third world.[2]

In addition, the traveler in both tropes of mobility, rural–urban, national–transnational, is confronted with the—sometimes frightening, sometimes exciting—prospect of departing from the familiar and familial spaces and arriving at the unknown and unchartered territories. Furthermore, the traveler is constantly compelled to negotiate the desire and anguish of being simultaneously "here" and "there," and the sense of loss brought about by the displacement. Nowhere are the intensity and potency of such desires and anguishes captured more effectively than on the cinema screen. The state of trance and reverie that marks Ermo's initial fixation upon the images on the television screen is a testimony to the power of the camera to convey the subjective world of a desiring spectator. Equally, the intensity and anguish are effectively captured in the helpless and pleading eyes of Minzhi, fixated on the camera. Compared with television, cinema, due to the intimate yet collective viewing in the darkness, provides so powerful a means of acting out the fantasy and desires that it is often described as the "dream factory."[3] Writing on the relationship between social mobility and the fantastic in German silent cinema, Elsaesser observes that the possibility of improving one's fortunes is a subject that appeals to a wide spectrum of viewers.[4] Cinema, in representing economic success and social mobility, often resorts to fantasy.[5] Given this, Elsaesser argues that film analyses need to ask the question as to how the motif of social mobility is encoded in fantastic forms. As an imaginative space whereby dreams, fantasies, and desires are acted out, as well as ambivalences, dilemmas, and fears, the cinematic representations feed *off* and *into* whatever crazes happen to infect the collective imagination. What enables this dual process to occur is the intimate, yet public, nature of viewing. To put it another way, the impact of cinematic spectatorship on the formation of transnational imagination lies in both the personal and the public nature of filmic experience. This point is most cogently argued in Stephanie Donald's work on cinema and civility in China. She states:

> [B]efore we settle on terms such as "national" or even "transnational" cinema, we need to acknowledge the publicness of cinema. Cinema's contribution to, say, the concepts of national and transnational, lies in the wide-ranging possibilities of cinematic cultural space. Cinema is both discursive and creative. Films not only explore individual and social fantasies, they also produce the space in which those fantasies become available in public.[6]

In the same way that Ermo fantasizes about having the biggest television in town, one of the objects of desire for city folks is a passport to go overseas, in spite of the fact that many more can travel overseas today than two decades ago. Both fantasies are equally powerful. As I mention in the introduction and chapter 1, the formation of transnational imagination can take place in a number of ways: first, through one's engagement with the imagination of people in other places, especially in other national spaces; second, through producing and consuming a reworked sense of place brought about by transnational movements of people, capital, and images; and third, via the impact of globalization of media formats and practices in the construction of a national identity. Extending the theme of cinema, mobility, and transnational subjectivity within these parameters, this chapter shifts the focus from the village to the city and concentrates on the fears and desires of city folks who are enmeshed in their own dreams. In doing so, I hope to further the argument on the relationship between spectatorship, cinematic space, and transnational imagination. As shown in chapter 1, while the arrival of television in the village may make it possible for villagers to imagine transnationally, the possibility of virtual travel may be curtailed or circumscribed by the actual village-to-city migration, which is motivated by a desire to escape the village. Following where the previous chapter leaves off, this chapter continues to lay bare the politics, as well as the variegated nature of transnational imagination, from the perspective of those who are willing to and capable of participating in the social and physical mobility and those who are resistant, reluctant, or unable to do so.

TO GO OR NOT TO GO:
A "STORYBOARD" OF COLLECTIVE FANTASY

Story #1 (1990)

Ah Hong, a woman in a small town in southern China, has applied for a visa to go to America many times and finally is granted one. She heads for New York, leaving Nansheng, her husband, and son behind. She writes home frequently, expressing the desire to return home, as life is too hard in New York. Nansheng tells her to stick it out, for the future of their son. Eventually, he receives a letter from Ah Hong, demanding a divorce. Distraught, Nansheng arrives in New York via Mexico, as an illegal immigrant, penniless, with no English, and hell-bent to find his wife. New York is as cruel to him as it was to Ah Hong. Just as Nansheng has given up looking, he stumbles on his wife. However, Ah Hong has transformed into a swindler—scheming, seductive, and, above all, a total stranger who has no memory of who Nansheng is. In his desperate attempt to talk sense to her, he grabs Ah Hong, only to be stabbed by her, and he falls to the ground in a pool of his own blood. This is the story of *Farewell China* (*Ai Zai Tai Xiang De Ji Jie*), a film directed by Clara Law and starring Maggie Chung as the chameleon-like An Hong.

Story #2 (1995)

Ma Lixin lives in Beijing, where he breeds and sells goldfish. He loses his first girlfriend, a beautiful ballet dancer, because he cannot make up his mind about whether to go to America or not. New girlfriend Haiying gets him as far as the Beijing airport before he chickens out of flying to San Francisco. Trouble is, they have already said farewell to their family and friends and would lose face if they went back. So the couple goes into hiding in a rented farmhouse outside Beijing, pretending to be abroad. Ma misses his mother and rings her from a phone booth near her flat so as to catch a glimpse of her. He tells his mother that he is doing well in America, but wants to come home. His mother tells him not to return until he has finally "made it" over there. Ma and his girlfriend have no choice but to go on hiding. This is the story of *Goldfish* (*Huangjin Yu*),[7] a film produced by Wu Di, an independent filmmaker in China.

Story #3 (1999)

Liu Yuan, a young man from mainland China, has lived in Los Angeles for more than ten years. He meets Li Qin, who has just arrived in America and is uncertain of her future there. Liu tells Li that America is not what she thinks and that it is "not for fun" (*bu hao wai*) . Following his advice, Li decides to go back to China, only to change her mind before boarding. She sells her plane ticket, finds a job, and "bumps into"—literally—Liu again on the street a year later. The two fall in love, but, since the course of love never runs smooth, the couple is never too far away from police, crime, and pure bad luck. Life, however, smiles on them after all, and the story ends with the happy couple flying together to Beijing to be with Liu's ailing mother. This side-splittingly funny story, *Be There or Be Square* (1999), owes much to the deadpan humor of Ge You and is one of many Happy New Year releases— new films marking the Chinese New Year. It was produced by the most prolific and successful—in box office terms—director Feng Xiaogang, who also directed the popular television drama series *A Beijing Native in New York* several years ago.

The previous is a deliberately chronologically arranged "storyboard" of change and continuity in the ways in which the theme of "going to America" was represented in popular cultural forms throughout the 1990s. Since the start of economic reform and the national "open-door" policy, China has seen millions of people, including many of the best educated, leave the country to make their home in large metropolitan cities in the West. The "storyboard" outlines a broad spectrum of the ways in which America is imagined by the people of the PRC. Such a spectrum ranges from those who want to go to America, but cannot; those who can go to America, but do not want to go; those who have been to America, "made it" there, and decided to come back; those who think they want to go to America, but who change their minds just before departure; those who do not want to go, but are pressured by social expectations to go; those who have gone to America, but want to come back; those who can never go to America, but nevertheless never stop fantasizing about going; and those whose loved ones (children, spouses) have gone to America and who tell their loved ones not to come back until they have achieved their American dream.

These films all deal with migration and can be considered akin to, in a particular sense, the "border cinema,"[8] although the genre usually refers to the large number of films made in the United States about Mexico border crossers.[9] This is because the characters invariably have some kind of relationship to the border separating China—a place they want to leave—and America, a place they want to be. Moreover, the storyline of "going to America"—applying for visas, having applications rejected or approved, leaving and arriving at the airport—is essential to the narrative. Where they differ from American border films is that while the Mexican border-crossers, both prospective and potential, are represented from the speaking position of the "center" (the U.S. film industry), the Chinese films are represented from the perspective of the "periphery," the "self," the Third World film industry. Although the border is not literal—as in the case of Mexicans wanting to go to the United States—but symbolic, as Fregoso argues, it figures as a trope of "absolute alterity."[10] Like the border in its physical form, the imaginary border in these films—embodied in the lines of people outside U.S. consulates in metropolitan cities of China, waiting for visa approval; in the departure lounges of international airports in both American and Chinese cities; or in the "par avion" envelopes bearing American stamps—exerts a fascination on spectators that is no less intense and powerful than the real one. In addition, the border can even be literal, as in the case of Nansheng, the husband in *Farewell China*, who is smuggled into America via Mexico as an illegal immigrant in search of his estranged wife. Furthermore, in these films, as well as in the American border films, "America" is seen to be the ultimate object of collective fantasy, and the borders separating the United States and Mexico/China are symptomatic of a pathological desire for the "freedom," "wealth," and "power" that "America" promises.

With the exception of Clara Law's *Farewell China*, which is set partly in China and partly in America, the other films mentioned here are seldom perceived to belong to the transnational genre, in terms of production, marketing, spectatorship, or subject matter. They are stories about urban Chinese going about living their lives, making decisions about what to do and where to go. In *Goldfish*, Ma Linxin's journey to America abruptly halts at Beijing airport, and Liu Yuan, in *Ripped Off Once*, never even makes it to the U.S. embassy in Beijing. However, although "America" is absent in terms of cinematic space, the lives of these people are seen to have been irreversibly changed because of their decision to go to America.

Writing about spatial configuration in transnational cinema, Naficy argues that there is a reciprocal relationship between genre formation and society, and that each epoch creates its own genres and narratives.[11] If this is true, questions arise as to what we can say about this fascination with the "border" and the persistent topic of going to America in the Chinese cinema and how these films correlate with the process of transnational imaginings in China in the era of reforms.

Stories of going to America have been the perennial stories in popular representations in China—in cinematic, televisual terms, as well as in literature—and have duly generated ongoing interest among writers concerned with cultural production and national imaginary.[12] Little critical attention, however, has been given to narratives of *not* going to America. This omission is both understandable—narrative is tied to the concept of a journey, the going from one place to another, and for this reason mobility provides better narrative fodder than immobility—and surprising, since those Chinese who enjoy transnational mobility are a minuscule part of the Chinese population. For the overwhelming majority of Chinese, "America" remains a symbolic space. This omission also represents a theoretical blind-spot in understanding the ways in which popular imaginations of space and place impact the formation of citizenship and transnational imagination in reform-era China. My analysis here is an attempt to address this omission by taking into consideration some narratives about not going to America. In doing so, I am concerned with one particular dimension of Chinese transnational cinema: the representation and consumption of images and narratives of Chinese and un-Chinese places and spaces.[13]

Writing about Turkish and Iranian transnational films, Naficy finds that transnational films are inscribed with phobic spaces, spatial configurations that are marked with paranoia, panic, and eruption of memory:

> A sense of claustrophobia pervades the worldview, mise-en-scene, shot composition, and plot development of many transnational films. These are films of liminal panic, of retrenchment in the face of what is perceived to be a foreign, often hostile, host culture and media representation.[14]

A sense of claustrophobia permeating the spatial configuration, narratives, and aesthetics, according to Naficy, is more the consequence of the "conditions of exile" of the filmmakers than of the subject matter or place of production. This argument on the production of phobic spaces in transnational films has for me a significant relevance: In our attempt to understand films and the formation of the transnational subjectivity, it is as important to pay as much attention to the conditions of making films—economic, political, and social factors in production and consumption—as it is to the style and content of the films per se.

PHOBIA, PANIC, AND CLARA LAW'S *FAREWELL CHINA*

Farewell China clearly bears the imprimature of Clara Law. Together with *Farewell China*, Law has made two other films on migration: *Autumn Moon*, about a Hong Kong–based girl about to migrate to Canada; and *Floating Life*, about a Hong Kong family that migrates to Australia. Law is a Hong Kong-Australian filmmaker; her work, in terms of both production mode and aesthetics, can be described as "interstitial" and "transnational." It may be noteworthy that these films were made during the years prior to Hong Kong's return to China, when Hong Kongers' desire to leave Hong Kong was paralleled by the Chinese nationals' desire to leave China.[15] *Farewell China* is partly set in China (Guangzhou and Shanghai), but stars Maggie Chung, a mega star based in Hong Kong. Funded by money from Hong Kong, the production team spans Hong Kong, the PRC, and the United States. For this reason, although the film is set in the PRC and tells the story of PRC citizens going to America, the viewers or audience—at least, during the initial phase of distribution—were also interstitial and outside the national audience of the PRC.

Law's work bears the mark of exilic and diasporic filmmakers. Diasporic filmmakers often make films that are "distressing and dystopian" and marked with "incredible tension and agony."[16] This sense of agony, clearly present in Law's other two migration films, is communicated with a spatial configuration marked with paranoia and panic.[17] In *Floating Life*, Bing, a migrant from Hong Kong who lives in a Sydney suburb, shuts herself up in a fortress-like house. She is rigid, uptight, and at times hysterical. She constantly talks about the dangers of being robbed, being bitten by poisonous spiders, and being burned by the sun. The sense of her claustrophobia is also realized through the use of overexposed and washed-out light in the shots of the Australian suburbs and streets. They are seen to be open, bare, and disorienting.

The spaces in *Farewell China* are even more phobic. The outside spaces of New York that are traversed by Ah Hong and her husband are seen to be overpowering and disorientating. Arriving in New York—in fact, literally belched into the street from a coach, as one of the two survivors from the PRC smuggled to the United States via Mexico—Nansheng staggers in the middle of the street, with cars and pedestrians rushing past, indifferent. Nansheng looks up and sees buildings and bridges towering over him, imposing and menacing. He looks for shelter in dark enclosed spaces, yet finds himself besieged by homeless people, drunkards, drug-dealers, prostitutes, and gangsters. Stumbling and scrambling along, Nansheng has nowhere to go and nowhere to hide. The phobic space—fearing both going in and getting out—is also powerfully realized through the use of a number of signifiers in Nansheng's search for his vanished wife in Brooklyn, Harlem, and Long Island. He looks up to see the spiraling staircase inside the building where a friend lives, the grilled security door of the Chinese take-out, and the stuffy crowded space of the Chinese laundry. On one occasion, feverish, delirious, and exhausted, Nansheng faints and collapses on the street. This sense of distress and spatial phobia becomes particularly pronounced after Nansheng finally manages to call his parents in southern China from a public phone booth. He says that he wants to go back home because life is too hard. His parents tell him not to come back until he succeeds in what he wants to do, unless he has reached the point of having no food to eat or being seriously ill—exactly what he has told his wife at the beginning of the film.

Another important feature of diasporic films that is clearly present in Law's work is the blurring of memories. Law herself describes *Farewell China*, which is set in a Chinese town in the first half and in New York in the second half, as part naturalistic and part fantasy.[18] The past and present are (con)fused, and so is the space of (home)land and host land. In *Farewell China*, this disjuncture is found in the ambiguous narrative of the chameleon-like Ah Hong, who is seen to have amnesia (or split personality) and thus is unable to recognize her own husband. Has Ah Hong forgotten her past, or has Nansheng lost his grip on reality? Talking about cinema and the city, James Donald observes that if cinema is a "dream factory," then it is possible to talk about its capacity to reproduce "nightmares." Pushing this relationship further, he argues that the city is often represented as a dream space, a "delirious world of psychic projection."[19] By telling the story in two locations—a nostalgia-inducing Chinese rural setting and a dystopian New York—*Farewell China* presents the dream, as well as the subsequent nightmarish consequences of acting out this dream. A temporal-spatial disjuncture is also further enhanced by the use of music throughout the film. The emotional and psychic tensions experienced by Nansheng and Ah Hong in New York are many times brought out through the repetitive use of a song called "A Big River" (*yitiao dahe*), a well-known sentimental song about "my motherland" and "revolutionary fighters" from a film set in China's socialist era.[20]

At the beginning of the film, audiences are told that Ah Hong has applied for a visa to go to America many times, but was refused. She is told that as she has no children and is too pretty, she is considered a potential immigrant. Ah Hong applies, again, and since she has had a son, is eventually allowed to go. To pay her airfare, Ah Hong and her husband borrow a lot of money.

Throughout the film, however, Ah Hong's reasons for wanting to go to America are never spelled out. To a Chinese spectator in the early 1990s, going to America seems the most desirable thing to do, and such desire is absolute, unquestionable, and pre-suppositional. Produced in 1990 and at the cusp of political change in China following the June 4th Tiananmen Incident, the film records the pathological yearning for "America," the global city, the Other. It was also a moment when the Chinese state was keen to discredit that foreign vision and the people who shared it, taking pains to demonstrate the dystopian aspects of the United States and the Western world in general. The dystopian vision of the global city experienced by the Third World migrants poignantly speaks to the specificity of the Third World in the trajectory of travel in the era of globalization. While travel may destabilize the divide between center and periphery, it may also reinforce or perpetuate the already unequal global power relations.[21]

TO GO OR NOT TO GO:
THE STORY OF THE ABSENT AMERICA

Ma Linxin, in *Goldfish*, is an ordinary young man in Beijing, trying to make up his mind about what he wants from life. Migrating to the United States is an option, since he has families and relatives who are prepared to sponsor him. For this reason, he is the object of envy to many friends and acquaintances, who are not endowed with such good opportunities. Going abroad (*chuguo*), after all, is the game in town, and "America" is the place to go. Besides, life in Beijing is not perfect: Ma envies the freedom—and perhaps even the purposelessness—of the goldfish he breeds and sells.

Ma cannot help but feel, however, that the decision to go to America has been somewhat made by someone else on his behalf, not by himself. Social pressure is one factor. Going abroad is undoubtedly the most enviable, trendy, and desirable thing to do. To be able to go, to be in the process of going, or even to appear to talk knowledgeably about how to go about taking steps toward going bring one some kind of clout. Conversely, not to go when one can is a sign of weakness, stupidity, and even failure. In the 1990s, going abroad fired the imagination of the urban Chinese and made the entire nation feverish with American dreams. Ma does not live in a social vacuum and does not want to appear a loser. In addition, he has the expectations of families and the girlfriend to think about. Going overseas, making money, buying a house and car, and becoming successful give one's parents pride and joy and increase their status, and a man who succeeds in his application to migrate to America has maximum sex appeal. Ma has already lost his first girlfriend due to his indecision, and his current girlfriend is putting pressure on him to go, too.

It is not until Ma and his new girlfriend finish saying farewell to their ad-
miring friends and arrive in the Beijing airport, ready to board the plane to
San Francisco, that he realizes that he has no good reason to go to America.
America does not need him, nor does he need America. Yet not to go would
be incomprehensible to families and friends. Ma's decision to hide in a farmhouse on the outskirts of Beijing, pretending to be in America, seems a most
absurd, yet at the same time perfectly logical, solution. It points to the
predicament of individuals who succumb to the sheer force of a frantic, feverish pursuit of an American dream, yet lack the courage to defy it. By hiding,
Ma and his girlfriend find a refuge from, first, the maelstrom of going abroad
that is taking the imagination of the entire town by storm; second, the fear of
the prospect of not being able to realize that dream when he goes to America; and third, the reality of having to choose between the two. By hiding, Ma
becomes a fugitive, an exile, and invariably an excommunicate. He has for-
saken not only the opportunity to fulfill his American dream, but also the natural right to be at home in one's own environs. A chaser of freedom, Ma ends
up being chased. This somewhat absurdist feature of dark humor was made
by Wu Di,[22] one of the so-called sixth-generation independent filmmakers in
China,[23] who made a number of "underground" films outside of the state film
industry.

Goldfish, in this sense, makes an astute comment on the fear and desire that
mark the transnational imagination of urban Chinese in the 1990s. More important, it articulates the dilemmas of individuals who are swept into the maelstrom of the reform era, but do not share the aspirations and fervor of the urban Chinese. "America," in the popular consciousness of the late 1980s and
early 1990s, embodied the promise of everything that China wanted but
lacked—wealth, modernity, freedom, adventure, and, above all, exotica—and
was so imagined by both those who had access to mobility and those who did
not. When such perceptions took a concrete form in the context of social relations in reform-era China, they manifested themselves in the accumulation
of social power and cultural capital by those who are seen to either have the
means to migrate to America or have some kind of connection with American
people and things. Being an unemployed and peripheral loafer, bereft of political or social ambitions, Ma is by no means an exemplary citizen in the eyes
of official ideology and, in fact, has no political clout to speak of. His perceived
privilege does not derive from political, cultural, or economic power, but from
his prospect of mobility. What Ma possesses is a passport to "America," a place
that occupies the highest rung in the hierarchy of the social meaning of space
in the imagination of the Chinese population in the 1990s.

Ma's situation of being stuck, of being immobilized by the social expectations of mobility, reveals a discontinuity between the spatial imagination of
the general public and the spatial practice of individuals. While a public
imagination of "going to America" in the Chinese consciousness operates on

the level of fantasy, desiring the unattainable and impossible at a safe distance, the individuals who are leaving for America nevertheless have to face the fear of the real, unknown, and uncertain. The tension between fear and desire in the private selves of those who are going to America is played out on the cusp of "imagining" and "experiencing" America.[24] This is exactly the moment Ma is at. In opting not to go, Ma lets his fear of America ultimately get the better of his desire for it. And in deciding to hide, he lets us know that his fear, though real and strong enough to himself, cannot compete with the desire of the general public. While he is seen to have little confidence in interrogating the public desire by simply making a statement such as "I don't want to go" or asking what would appear to be the most justifiable question, "Why should I go to America?" he is inevitably confronted with the dilemma of whether to go with the flow and act out a collective fantasy or be truthful to his own ambivalence. Ma is hiding in both the spatial sense—he is hiding from urban Beijing, as well as from America—and the temporal sense: he is hiding from the past, as well as the future.

What constitutes narrative tension in Ma's case is his freedom to travel— the most desirable asset in social terms—and his own desire for the freedom to make up his own mind about mobility. The story in the film is one of not wanting to go to America; however, Ma's reluctance to leave the "motherland" cannot be simply explained away by some kind of allegiance to the state ideology of patriotism. The force of a primordial nativist sentiment also seems strained as a possible reason to account for his lack of enthusiasm for America. It may well be that Ma simply wants to be himself and to feel at home in his environment. What he is reacting against, therefore, is the difficulty, if not the impossibility, of having the freedom to work out his own ambivalence and to escape from being implicated in the sheer force of that social desire, which he is not part of.

One of the most powerful moments in the film is the scene in the phone booth. Ma, who has been hiding from his family and friends, misses his mother so much that he finds a phone booth outside her house, where he can see her when she answers the phone. Ma, pretending to be calling from San Francisco, tells his mother that he wants to come home. This brings us back to Nansheng in the New York City phone booth in *Farewell China*, whose parents tell him exactly the same thing. These are powerfully poignant moments, and it is hardly a surprise or a coincidence that the scenario appears in two films produced in entirely different contexts. Both Nansheng and Ma have "boxed" themselves into a phobic transnational space. "America" does not want them, and their families do not want them to come back. Between the brutal realities of surviving on the margin in the global cities and the sheer forces of social expectations back home, these liminars are exiles in both a physical and a psychic sense. In both films, this collective desire is presented as an unchallenged and unchallengeable force.

How do we read the texture of social imagination of these films, which take *chuguo* as their subject matter but center around individuals who nevertheless decide not to go? How are these narratives likely to rework the Chinese audience's imagination of space and place? One can only start to answer this question by returning to the larger query of the relationship between cinema and national culture. Here, Rey Chow's argument is useful, regarding the power of technologized images to affect the ways in which the nation is imagined in modern and postmodern culture. In discussing the relationship between electronic media and the formation of modern subjectivities, Chow points to the "immediacy and efficacy" of the electronic media, which threaten to "usurp and supplant" the role traditionally enjoyed by literature and writing. She argues that images delivered by electronic media are powerful because, compared with writing, they are "clear, direct and seemingly transparent," hence allowing "entire histories, nations and peoples to be exposed, revealed, captured on the screen, made visible as images."[25]

Although place, in the cinema of the socialist era, is represented to promote a sense of space and history within the ideological parameters of the CCP, new Chinese cinema—notably, the films of the so-called fifth-generation directors in the 1980s—presented space and place as allegories of China in the juncture of tradition and modernity. In many fifth-generation films, images of children, women, animals, and the countryside are used in the ethnographic self-writing of the Chinese history.[26] And for this reason, images of yellow earth, the Yellow River—the nature/history trope—are played out according to an aesthetic of timeless landscape and a discourse of the triumph of space over time.[27] As Stephanie Donald points out succinctly, Chinese "landscape provides not just a backdrop for the drama of history, but becomes part of a process of rewriting, or reinscribing, history."[28]

In contrast to fifth-generations films such as the *Yellow Earth, Red Sorghum, Ju Dou,* and *Old Well,* many films in the 1990s turn to urban spaces to tell ordinary stories about ordinary people. These films are therefore, in Dai's words, "antiallegorical" *(fan yu yan).*[29] This does not mean, however, that space is no longer allegorical and hence spatial representation no longer has anything to do with the nation as an imagined community. Here I argue that besides an "either allegorical or antiallegorical" framework of analysis lies an alternative way of theorizing the relationship between cinematic space and the national imaginary. Central to this point is the notion of place as fantasy, a nonplace, which, though occupying no real space, nevertheless permeates the film. "America" in *Goldfish* is a place of fantasy and has a similar function to Yan'an, in that they are both symbolic spaces[30] to yearn for, but not to arrive at. In *Yellow Earth,* Cui Qiao is unable to go to Yan'an, the land of freedom, as Gu Qin, her communist savior, promises. However, her yearning for it and her final failure to arrive there are enabling motifs that propel the narrative forward.

I also want to add that although the place of destination is never "arrived at" and thus never represented, it has a direct correlation to, and an impact on, the way in which the inhabited space of the character is presented. The sense of predicament that Ma lives in is figuratively realized through both a claustrophobic and an agoraphobic sense of space. Ma's fear of the unknown, America, and the known—the urban milieu in Beijing—forces him to retreat to a closed rural space. Ma also appears to have a fear of open spaces: He hides in a farmhouse on the outskirts of Beijing and in a public phone booth near his mother's house. While these closed spaces function as a temporary sanctuary for not making a decision about life, they are represented to the audience as dark, enclosing, and oppressive. It is this double-edged use of urban space that marks Ma's—and, indeed, many urban Chinese'—predicament about what he wants from life and how much "America," overseas, or the outside world should feature in his imagination. It also operates, on both metaphoric and metonymic levels, to signify the profound ambivalence in the imagining of the national self/otherness on a collective level, as well as the dilemmas of individuals who are faced with the imminent challenge of transgressing the space.

By juxtaposing *Goldfish*, which operates on the trope of an "absent America," with *Farewell China*, in which the space of "America" figures prominently, I argue that the construction of transnational subjectivity exists in an unpredictable place and manifests itself in unexpected time. The space of urban Beijing, writ with transnational longings and anxieties, may turn out to be as phobic and disorientating as that of New York.[31] It can be found not only in the "liminal" "slip-zone"[32] of transnational cinema, but also in "national" places that are usually considered to be outside of transnational cinema. Transnational subjectivity is formed in the imagining of those whose subjectivity has taken on a transnational dimension, even though their bodies are still confined to, or hiding within, the national space. In other words, transnational subjectivity may be formed in the liminal space between homeland and host land, as Naficy demonstrates, but also in the absence of the host land: In these narratives "America" as a destination is never "reached" or represented; however, as a fantasy space of transnational imagination, its enigma is enhanced not in spite of, but precisely because of, its absence.

More important, the remarkable commonality between *Farewell China*, a certifiable work about transnational liminality, and *Goldfish*, a film produced within the national space, in terms of spatial configuration, themes, and aesthetics, signals the need to problematize the conception of what is "liminal." I argue that just as it is risky to exclude the category of the "national" in transnational imaginaries, it is important to recognize that transnational liminality does not necessarily start only when national borders are crossed. It may start, as in the case of Ma in *Goldfish* and the filmmaker who made it, within the national space. In other words, in our understanding of the formation of transnational subjectivity, deterritorialization warrants consideration as both a physical and a psychic phenomenon.

Such juxtaposition has another important benefit. It brings to light that there is another level on which the paradoxical use of space in the *Goldfish* can be interpreted. Though much less well-known than its contemporaries, Wu Di's film bears the trademark of Chinese underground independent filmmakers of the 1990s, being "gritty" and "realistic."[33] The film is virtually unknown to mainland, as well as Western, mainstream audiences, but is, however, screened to limited transnational spectators during international film festivals.[34] For this reason, I concur with Donald's argument that the independent films made in China during the 1990s should be understood "in tandem with the idea of transnational imaginaries."[35] The liminal space of Ma in the film is metaphoric of both claustrophobic and agoraphobic space in the cultural production sector in the 1990s for filmmakers such as Wu Di,[36] who operate outside both the state film industry and the commercial mainstream. Wedged between the two, independent filmmakers want to resist the hegemonic ideology of the mainstream, which may include both that of the state and commercial production, on the one hand, and that of imperialistic readings of Chinese films by transnational audiences looking for spectacles of the Orient, on the other.[37] In other words, the fugitive status that Ma gets himself into, due to his inability to choose between two sorts of freedom—the "freedom to do something" and the "freedom from doing something"—is also the everyday reality of "underground" filmmakers.

Writing about the autobiographical tendency of independent filmmakers, Dai says:

> Sixth-generation filmmakers and the characters in their films tend to be iconoclastic, wedged between rejection and loss, search and trauma. . . . They wander among the derelict lanes of metropolitan cities, surviving in the liminal space between the legitimate and illegitimate, between searching and drifting, and between fragile sensitivity to cruel apathy. . . . They are telling their own stories and presenting their own lives.[38]

In this sense, Wu Di's *Goldfish*—and, indeed, some other independent films of the genre—are evocative of what Naficy refers to as the "phobic spaces and liminal panics" of the independent transnational films that cut across previously defined geographic, cultural, national, and cinematic boundaries.[39] In this light, the story of Ma, who cannot bring himself to get on the America-bound plane and at the same time cannot face going back home, can be read as a narrative of transition, of liminality, and, above all, of resistance. Refusing to go to America—hence, rejecting the ideology of the everyday urban life, but at the same time hiding from its social expectations—Ma's is the autobiographical story of the filmmakers, whose work deals with hybrid identities in transition and formation. As such, they are indeed doomed to the status of "squatters" in the cultural production of China, inhabiting a shadowy space, being unable to claim a significant role in the construction of national imaginary and the formation of transnational imagination. In this context, the story of Ma having "cold feet" about America becomes doubly significant in unraveling the relationship between cinema and national imaginary. It is telling not only in terms of the private anxieties of individuals who live through the times of mobility and transnationalism, but also in terms of the voices of dissonance in an increasingly globalized environment of cultural production.

In contrast to the angst-ridden contemplation of Ma in Wu Di's film on the question of emigration, He Qun's *Ripped Off Once* is a sunny and lighthearted narrative in which Liu Yuan, a young man in Beijing, resists the social pressure to go to America. Liu is less neurotic than Ma and seems at ease with his environment. Liu does not share the soul-searching of Ma in *Goldfish;* he simply keeps telling people that he may go sometime later. Liu's strategy of managing a public ambivalence—here embodied by "America"—mirrors that of his creators, commercial filmmakers in China who must master acrobatic skills in balancing the need to please both the state and the market.[40] Unlike the story of the *Goldfish*, where the international airport marks the border between the self and the other, the city he lives in is already a transnational space. The restaurant called "Ripped Off Once" that he frequents is located in the vicinity of Beijing's foreign embassies and diplomatic organizations and holds a special power in the spatial imagination of the city's residents. Going to the restaurant is a transnational experience, as the restaurant itself is a microscope of transnational capitalism. Mrs. Xu, the proprietor with an entrepreneurial instinct, is running a vibrant business that caters to both Chinese and foreign customers. She herself has been overseas in the *chuguo* rush, but has come back to make her mark where she belongs. People come here to meet and exchange woeful or successful stories of emigration. They talk about the pros and cons of *chuguo*, while being waited on efficiently and subserviently by Russian waiters. Here the audience learns that the queues waiting to go to America outside the American embassy are long and patient, but "America" is not a destination for everybody. In the restaurant with *chuguo* as the daily subject matter, personal anxieties are revealed, collective desires are reinforced or interrogated, and spectators are invited to identify with the anxieties or happiness of those caught in the waves of emigration, therefore participating, publicly and vicariously, in the transnational imagination of spaces and places.

Beijing, while providing an urban setting for both *Goldfish* and *Ripped Off Once*, is represented very differently in the two films. I argue that this difference underscores the importance of the notion of publicness or civic space in the formation of citizenship and transnational imagination. Publicness is absent in *Goldfish*. Ma has the choice of either flying out of a *national* space or hiding in his *individual* world. Truthful exchange with the public, including his mother, friends, and relatives, is impossible. This difficulty of rendering his personal ambivalence public accounts for Ma's sense of alienation. Audiences are hence forced into a closed situation of either having to identify with or having to reject his decision. In contrast, the restaurant that Liu frequents in *Ripped Off Once* is a civic space in which private ambivalence is daily played out and made public through the participation of the spectators. It is for this reason a much more open and accessible space, in the sense that it accommodates social and individual fantasies of mobility; that it opens up "psychic space"[41] for spectators by visualizing the transnationalization of national space, hence pointing to the possibility of mobility in both spatial and intellectual terms.

Goldfish and *Ripped Off Once*, two films produced in the 1990s, are indeed obscure, both as examples of their respective trademarks—independent films and commercial films—and as examples of Chinese films made in the 1990s. By rescuing them from obscurity, I bring to light the trope of "absent America" in cultural production of the reform era, as well as the danger of omission in analyzing the ways in which "moments" in the circuit of culture—production and consumption, representation—work in the spatial imagination of the Chinese in 1990s. Throughout the analysis, I lay bare the tension between private ambivalences and collective desires, thereby reinforcing that cinema provides a powerful space to articulate and negotiate this tension.

BE THERE OR BE SQUARE:
SUNNY AND FUNNY LOS ANGELES

Liu Yuan, the insouciant man in *Ripped Off Once*, is played by Ge You,[42] the comedian known to Chinese audiences for his deadpan humor and antihero characterizations. Unlike Jiang Wen, who plays the heroic Wang Qiming in Feng Xiaogang's earlier work, *A Beijing Native in New York*, Ge You signals to the audiences a different mode of storytelling and a style known for "pleasure seeking and foul play," qualities that are described as "Wang Shuoesque."[43] Ge has appeared in Feng Xiaogang's comedies many times before, but for the first time he plays a Chinese living in America in *Be There or Be Square*. Loafing around in Los Angeles, driving a beaten-up van and living in a bus in a park, Liu Shan seems to be in his element. He does everything to make a buck, including selling insurance and burial ground and being a tourist guide for visitors from mainland China. The Los Angeles experienced by Liu Yuan is suburban and remarkably different from the New York Wang Qiming experiences—modern, sublime, yet inaccessible (as is apparent in the next chapter)—and the New York experienced by Nansheng, which is phobic, disorientating, and menacing. To be sure, crimes abound. The film starts with a burglary, followed by an armed robbery in the Chinese restaurant and a raid by Immigration officers; however, they seem to be merely plot devices to facilitate a love story. Los Angeles is full of thugs, criminals, and small-time crooks, but Liu Yuan and his girlfriend seem to take these events in stride and are capable of dealing with them as they come. The sense of paranoia, panic, and anxiety permeating the urban spaces of America in *Farewell China* is conspicuously absent, nor is Los Angeles represented as exotic, alluring, and modern. It is mundane and familiar. When Li Qin, Liu Yuan's lover, comments that she feels as if she has migrated to Guangzhou—referring to the Chinese laundries, newspapers, and television in Los Angeles, Liu Yuan replies facetiously, "Guangzhou? No way! More like the rural township outside Guangzhou."

A number of factors may account for these differences in the spatial configuration, as well as the representation of the characters' relationship to space. Between the time Wang Qiming lands in New York in *A Beijing Native in New York* in the early 1990s and the time Li Qing lands in Los Angeles in *Be There* at the end of the 1990s, a decade has passed during which China has become easier to leave and return to. Popular imagination of "America" has changed from one marked with an intensive collective fetish to one marked with ambivalence and growing—albeit partly mediated—familiarity. "New York," "San Francisco," and "Los Angeles" have changed from utopian spaces that PRC citizens wanted to go to at any cost, as refugees, illegal immigrants, and poverty-stricken students, to an array of transnational spaces—a background against which a newly configured Chinese national imaginary is played out. While the former scenario calls for narratives of "arrival"—legal or illegal—in "America" and a journey of no return, the latter scenario features constant traversing between host land and homeland.

In addition, the decade also sees the trajectory by which PRC filmmakers adjust and readjust their positions in relation to both the state and the market. If the films of so-called underground independent filmmakers in the mid-1990s can be seen as a refusal to succumb to both the state and market forces, the commercially successful films dominating the national cinema toward the end of the century have found a way of pleasing both, although at the expense of what Feng Xiaofang calls "creativity." In other words, while the spatial metaphor in the former scenario is that of being stuck, trapped, and thus "phobic," that in the latter is one of becoming unstuck, dynamic, and expansive. Unlike the first two films analyzed in this chapter, *Be There* features both arrivals in the United States and departures from it. Like so many comedies made in this mode, *Be There* is playful in the use of language, self-referential—characters in the film refer to television dramas such as *A Beijing Native in New York*—and hilarious. Above all, the film pleased both officialdom and the market. Though the story of a Chinese migrant teaching

LA police Chinese through Chairman Mao's quotations provides a good laugh, and hence is not meant to be taken at face value, it pleases the audience as well as the Party. Indeed, many comedies made in the late 1990s are products of the successful marriage between market-derived imperatives for entertainment value and state ideological indoctrination. Feng Xiaogang is the master of such a balancing act. "To be politically correct and economically successful is not really that difficult," says Feng, as long as "you can find a point that accommodates the three olds."[44] This perhaps accounts for Feng's phenomenal success in securing funding. In contrast to independent filmmakers who please neither the state nor potential investors, Feng thrives in the shared space between the state and market. Steering a middle way between the two, Feng's films package official values and positions in wisecracks, sarcastic remarks, and funny observations, leaving it to the audience to decide whether or not to take them seriously. Liu Yuan, in *Be There or Be Square*, is as disparaging of "America" as Wang Qiming is in *A Beijing Native in New York*: "America is no fun [*mei guo bu hao wan*]," he says on one occasion, and on another occasion, he tells new arrivals from the PRC, "If you want to live a comfortable life, America is not for you. Here you have to rough it [*chi ku*]." On the one hand, Feng's stories promote nationalism, a basic ideological tenet of the Party, in a tongue-in-cheek fashion, but on the other hand, they embrace with open arms the advent of transnational capitalism.

DEPARTURE LOUNGE AND ARRIVAL HALL: GAPS IN TRANSNATIONAL IMAGINATION

I have looked at a number of ways in which the city, both American and Chinese, is imagined and represented in spatial terms, as well as the ways in which "Third World" migrants experience these spaces. Focusing on a number of films about borders and migration, we see that the tapestry of the Chinese transnational imaginary is woven with input from an array of speaking positions, including those outside the national semiosis,[45] those inside but existing on the margin of national culture, and those thriving within the mainstream national culture. There is also a diversity of modes of production, including diasporic and exilic films, which exist between national spaces; independent/underground films, which exist within national spaces; and commercially successful films. It is apparent that no one has a monopoly over the field. An "interstitial" mode exists inside, as well as outside, of the national space—as in the case of *Goldfish*. By the same token, liminality is not necessarily the default trademark of transnational narrative—as in the case of *Be There*. Moreover, these modes of production sometimes overlap and sometimes contradict each other in the construction of the space of "us" and "them."

I said at the beginning of this chapter that cinema provides a powerful space to reenact the urban residents' transnational dreams and fantasies. Indeed, the fears and desires articulated in these cinematic spaces are predominantly urban. So, is there a connection between the imaginings of the villagers—as discussed in the previous chapter—and those of the urbanites? Alternatively, what have rural migrants got to do with city folks' American dreams? Here I argue that the answer to this question lies in the contingent and contiguous relationship between an urban mobility and a rural one. What delineates these two forms of mobility is that while the latter may be denied the possibility of acting out fantasies and dreams created by global images, the former is more free to act them out. In addition, while mobility and media consumption facilitate the emergence of a transnational imagination among both those who travel and those who do not, the construction of a transnational, hence (post)modern, subjectivity produces various forms of "internal orientalism,"[46] in the sense that those who fail to assimilate the transnational ethos become the new Other, regardless of gender, geography, wealth, and other such social attributes. This process therefore mobilizes a homology between the modern, male, urban, and wealthy and the backward, female, rural, and poor. As a result of this homology, Wei Minzhi in *Not One Less*, for instance, is useful not only discursively, but also politically, in the formation of a transnational imagination. My interviews with a number of domestic servants from Wuwei country, Anhui Province, and now working in Shanghai, as well as their employers, again testify to this. For instance, "Anhui *baomu*"(maids) are considered inferior to local maids in Shanghai because the latter are more capable of running modern household electrical appliances. Like Minzhi, Anhui maids are perceived as clumsy and unrefined. "Anhui maids command a less competitive price also because they come from somewhere else and have no fixed address, and thus are less trustworthy," said one of the employers I talked to.[47] It is clear that the maid, although homologous with an apartment, a passport, or a car in signifying a modern lifestyle and affluent status, also embodies both the contradictory and unequal process of becoming modern. She is a perennial reminder of the fact that claims to modernity and transnational space may be either a consequence of another group having to remain premodern or are contingent upon the privilege of one group being able to define what is "modern" on behalf of another group.

The cluster of films dwelling on the theme of *chuguo* invariably invokes the transitional and transnational space of the international airport and its departure lounge and arrival halls. Because they are repetitively represented as the gateway to an(other) world, such spaces are to be read both literally, where mobility takes place, and symbolically—people who traverse that space are inscribed with privilege and status. Again and again, the fear and desire in the city folks' imagination of "America," "the West," or "overseas" (*wai guo*) are played out in, and inscribed onto, these spaces. This does not mean, however, that these spaces are experienced and perceived in such a way by all. We will do well here to remind ourselves of the Anhui girls in the previous chapters whose job it is to clean the Shanghai International Airport. Spatial configurations, after all, are shaped by one's place in society. This is also evidenced in the answers to my question—"Where would they most like to go if they had unlimited access and mobility?"—from a number of domestic maids from villages of Anhui and now working in Shanghai. Chen, a middle-aged woman, answered, "I would like my son to become either a car mechanic or a driver," while another Chen answered, "I would most like to work in a factory, where I can clock in and clock out punctually." These *dagongmei*'s conflation of a geographic space with a social one is worth considering: The ways in which a place is imagined are contingent upon how a place is experienced. For this reason, those who assume the place of the center—"citadel"—of the city are bound to imagine the city differently from those at the margin, the "ghetto," of the city.[48]

A number of points can be made about the role of cinema in the formation of transnational imagination. First, in reading the formations of a transnational imagination, we must pay attention not only to the main melodies, but also to the jarring and splintering in the imagining process. More important, in reading the texture of transnational imagining, we should look for alliances and convergences at unpredictable places and times. Last, but not least, it is crucial to understand transnational cinema as not only films that are produced, distributed, and viewed in what is conventionally perceived to be the "transnational space," but also films outside of this defined space, but that nevertheless share the subject matter, aesthetics, narrative strategies, and cinematic language with transnational cinema.

NOTES

1. These interviews took place in April 2001. All interviews were conducted in Chinese and the translations are mine.

2. Ulf Hannerz, *Transnational Connections: Culture, People, Places* (London: Routledge, 1996).

3. Hortense Powdermaker, *Hollywood the Dream Factory: An Anthropologist Looks at the Movie Makers* (London: Secker & Warburg, 1950).

4. Thomas Elsaesser, "Social Mobility and the Fantastic: German Silent Cinema," in *Fantasy and Cinema*, ed. James Donald (London: BFI, 1989).

5. This is obviously not the place to go into a detailed discussion of the notion of fantasy. However, for a good work that exemplifies the relationship, see James Donald, ed., *Fantasy and Cinema*.

6. Stephanie Donald, *Public Secrets, Public Spaces: Cinema and Civility in China* (Lanham, Md.: Rowman & Littlefield, 2000), vii.

7. I am thankful to Justine Lloyd for tracking down the filmographic detail of this film from the Vancouver International Film Festival.

8. For an explanation of "border cinema" see Rosa Linda Fregoso, "Recycling Colonialist Fantasies on the Texas Borderlands," in *Home, Exile, Homeland: Film, Media, and the Politics of Place*, ed. Hamid Naficy (New York: Routledge, 1999).

9. Rosa Linda Fregoso, "Colonialist Fantasies."

10. Rosa Linda Fregoso, "Colonialist Fantasies," 178.

11. Hamid Naficy, "Phobic Spaces and Liminal Panics: Independent Transnational Film Genre," *East/West Film Journal* 8, no. 2 (1994): 4.

12. The best-known work of this kind is *A Beijing Native in New York*, which, due to its popularity both at home and abroad, has provided textual fodder for a number of works on Chinese culture and representation, including Geremie Barmé, "To Screw Foreigners Is Patriotic: China's Avant-Garde Nationalists," *The China Journal* 34 (1995): 209–34; Mayfair Yang, "Mass Media and Transnational Subjectivity in Shanghai: Notes on (Re)Cosmopolitanism in a Chinese Metropolis," in *Ungrounded Empire: The Cultural Politics of Modern Chinese Transnationalism*, ed. Aihwa Ong and Donald M. Nonini (London: Routledge, 1997); Michael Keane, "Ethics and Pragmatics: China's Television Products Confront the Cultural Market," *Media International Australia* 89 (1998): 75–86; Stephanie Donald, *Public Secrets*; Lydia Liu, "Beijing Sojourners in New York: Postsocialism and the Question of Ideology in Global Media Culture," *Positions: East Asia Culture Critique* 7, no. 3 (1999): 763–96; and Wanning Sun, "A Chinese in the New World: Television Dramas, Global Cities, and Travels to Modernity," *Inter-Asia Cultural Studies* 2, no. 1 (2001a): 81–94.

13. Sheldon Hsiao-peng Lu outlines several levels at which transnationalism in Chinese cinemas can be studied. These include the plurality of Chinese cinemas; the globalization of production, marketing, and consumption of Chinese film; and the representation of national, cultural, political, ethnic, and gender identities. See Sheldon Hsiao-peng Lu, ed., *Transnational Chinese Cinemas: Identity, Nationhood, Gender* (Honolulu: University of Hawaii Press, 1997).

14. Hamid Naficy, "Phobic Spaces," 14.

15. For a brief discussion of *Farewell China* and Law's work as an example of Hong Kong filmmakers' "China Syndrome," see Stephen Teo, *Hong Kong Cinema: The Extra Dimensions* (London: BFI, 1997).

16. Hamid Naficy, "Between Rocks and Hard Places" in *Home, Exile, Homeland*, ed. Naficy, 142.

17. For a detailed reading of *Floating Life*, see Tony Mitchell, "Boxing the Roo: Clara Law's Floating Life and Transnational Hong Kong-Australian Identities," *UTS Review* 6, no. 2 (2000): 103–14; and for an analysis of *Autumn Moon*, see Audrey Yue, "Migration-as-Transition: Clara Law's Autumn Moon," *Intersections* 4 (September 2000), <wwwsshe.murdoch.edu.au/intersections/issue4/yue.html> (accessed October 2000).

18. Interview with Clara Law by Julia Rigg on Radio National, Australia, April 28th, 2001.

19. James Donald, *Imagining the Modern City* (London: Athlone, 1999), 86.

20. The song, sung by Guo Lanyin, the famous female singer in the PRC from the 1950s, goes something like this: "This is my heroic motherland. It's the place where I

was born and brought up. In the vast and glorious land, there is sunshine and spring everywhere."

21. Yosefa Loshitzky, "Travelling Culture/Travelling Television." *Screen* 37, no. 4 (1996): 323–35.

22. Wu Di is also the cinematographer for *The Days* (Ri Zi) and *Postman* (You Chai).

23. For an account of the sixth-generation filmmakers, see Stephanie Donald, *Public Secrets;* and for independent filmmaking, see Dai Jinhua, *Wu Zhong Feng Jing* (Sceneries in the Fog: Chinese Cinema 1978–1998) (Beijing: Beijing University Press, 2000).

24. I borrow these terms from Henri Lefebrve's work on different ways of spatial production. See Henri Lefebrve, *The Production of Space* (Oxford: Blackwell, 1991).

25. Rey Chow, *Primitive Passions* (New York: Columbia University Press, 1995), 10.

26. Rey Chow, *Primitive Passions.*

27. Dai Jinhua, *Sceneries in the Fog.*

28. Stephanie Donald, *Public Secrets,* 68.

29. Dai Jinhua, *Sceneries in the Fog,* 370.

30. I am indebted here to Stephanie Donald's discussion of Apter and Saich's account of the symbolic importance of Yan'an in revolutionary discourses in early Chinese revolutionary films. See Stephanie Donald, *Public Secrets.*

31. Tang Xiaobing's study of the cinematic representation of Beijing as a modern space in a number of films, including Xie Fei's *Black Snow* (1989), seems to reinforce this. See Tang Xiaobing, "Configuring the Modern Space: Cinematic Representation of Beijing and its Politics," *East-West Film Journal* 8, no. 2 (1994): 47–69.

32. Hamid Naficy, "Phobic Spaces."

33. Tony Ryans, "'Goldfish,' Dragons and Tigers: The Cinema of East Asia," Vancouver Asian Film Festival Film Catalogue, 1995, n.p.

34. *Goldfish,* for instance, was screened as part of the Asian Film Festival in Vancouver in 1995.

35. Stephanie Donald, *Public Secrets,* 106.

36. For an account of the independent filmmakers in the 1990s, see Dai, *Sceneries in the Fog.*

37. See Dai, *Sceneries in the Fog.*

38. Dai, *Sceneries in the Fog,* 412. The quote is in Chinese and the translation is my own.

39. See Naficy, "Phobic Spaces," 1.

40. For an account of how filmmakers in the 1990s manage to do this, see Keane and Tao's interview with Feng Xiaogang, the most successful filmmaker of this kind, Michael Keane and Tao Dongfeng, "Interview with Feng Xiaogang," *Positions* 7, no. 1 (1999): 193–99.

41. The concept of psychic space is essential to Stephanie Donald's work, and she argues that it is necessary for a shared imaginary.

42. Ge You is China's most popular comedian, best known for his deadpan humor, mockeries, and sarcastic remarks. He starred in many of Feng Xiaogang's works, including *Be There or Be Square, Party A and Party B, The Story of Editorial Office,* etc.

43. For a detailed account of the so-called Wang Shuo phenomenon, see Jing Wang, *High Culture Fever: Politics, Aesthetics and Ideology in Deng's Era* (Berkeley: University of California Press, 1996), 262.

44. Keane and Tao, "Interview with Feng Xiaogang," 193–99. The "Three Olds" are *laoganbu,* old cadres; *laoban,* boss; and *laobaixing,* ordinary people. This is a clever way of summarizing the various forces filmmakers have to reckon with—i.e., the state, the funding bodies, and the audience.

45. The notion of "national semiosis" is put forward and elaborated in John Hartley's *Uses of Television* (London: Routledge, 1999), where he argues that *semiosis* refers to the general practice of sense-making, and *national semiosis* refers to the ways in which meaning is made and understood across the nation.

46. Louisa Schein, "Gender and Internal Orientalism in China," *Modern China* 23, no. 1 (1997): 69–98.

47. I have also interviewed a number of employers who hire either Anhui maids or Shanghai maids. The impressions quoted here come from Ms. Xu, a young scientist working in a transnational pharmaceutical company in Shanghai, which requires her to travel to France at least a couple of times a year. Ms. Xu also lived in Paris for ten years prior to returning to Shanghai.

48. For a good discussion of the metaphor of "citadel" versus that of the "ghetto" in the global city, see Hamid Naficy, *The Making of Exile Culture: Iranian TV in Los Angeles* (Minneapolis: University of Minnesota Press, 1993); and Edward Soja, *Thirdspace: Journeys to Los Angeles and Other Real-and-Imagined Places* (Oxford and Cambridge, Mass.: Blackwell, 1996). My interviews reveal that the village women now working in Shanghai mostly experience the city as an inaccessible place. Huang went to Puxi (west of the Huang River) a year ago, with some friends. The other two have never been to downtown Shanghai. They do their shopping—for clothes and groceries—in the local district and literally have no relationship with Shanghai. With little money and no local dialect, getting around the metropolitan areas of Shanghai is not only a daunting logistical task, but also forbiddingly expensive. For these women, whose spatial practices are circumscribed by a lack of economic, cultural, and social capital, Shanghai remains another world, a "forbidden city," marked with invisible yet real boundaries.

3

+

Arriving at the Global City: Television Dramas and Spatial Imagination

In Pursuit of Melbourne (*Zuei Zhu Mo Er Ben*) is a multiple-episode television drama produced jointly by China Central Television (CCTV) and Xiamen Television in southern coastal China. When it was shown nationally early in 1999, it was watched with intense interest by my parents, my brother, and my sister-in-law living in Anhui Province. Anticipating my visit from Australia later that year, they had taped the show in case I was interested. On arriving home, I was initially reluctant to embark on a viewing marathon, considering I had only one week in China. However, once I started, I could not stop. I spent most of that week sitting in front of the television set with my family, obsessively watching a local production about the lives of a group of Chinese now living in Australia.

In Pursuit of Melbourne is about Chinese students who go to Melbourne to study and who find themselves living in a group house. Zhao Yulin, the main character, is a scholar-turned-businessman who, after many trials and tribulations, finally "makes it" in Australia. His success wins the recognition of both the Australian business world and older-generation Chinese migrant communities in Australia. His commitment to work forces him to put his personal life "on the backburner," but the talented and beautiful heiress to a Taiwan business tycoon, who also becomes a strong business partner with him, is present throughout the show. Zhao's friends include Li Suang, who has lived and worked illegally during most of his time in Australia because his visa has expired. He is eventually sent back to China by Australian immigration authorities, but the show ends with his triumphant return as the Chinese representative in an Australia–China joint business venture.

The show is not very different from many other television dramas of the same genre. During the past decade, Chinese television audiences, including my family, have seen *A Shanghainese Native in Tokyo* (*Shanghai Ren Zai Dongjing*), *The New World* (*Xin Da Lu*), *Broadway No. 100* (*Bei Lao Hui Yi Bai Hao*), *Chinese Tenants in an American House* (*Liumei Fangke*), *The Green Card Class* (*Luka Zu*), *Entering Europe* (*Zouru Ouzhou*), *Dignity* (*Zun Yan*), and *The Blue Danube and the Yellow Sun* (*Duo Nao He Huang Taiyang*). Most of these dramas consist of between eight and thirty episodes, with each episode lasting from thirty minutes to an hour. However, the earliest, most popular, and most widely watched production of this kind of narrative is *A Beijing Native in New York* (*Beijing Ren Zai Niuyue*).[1] Produced by Feng Xiaogang for CCTV in late 1993, the twenty-one-episode series centers around the life of Wang Qiming, a cellist from Beijing who goes to New York with his wife, Quo Yan, to start a new life. Wang starts as a waiter in a Chinese restaurant; loses his wife to David, his American business rival; becomes enamored of Ah Chun, a Westernized Chinese woman; and becomes a rich philanthropist. This genre shows no sign of decline.[2] Since the new millennium, Chinese television audiences have seen *Our Lives as Overseas Students* (*Wo Men De Liu Xue Sheng Huo*), a ten-episode documentary about Chinese students in Japan, and *My Beloved Homeland* (*Wo Qin Ai De Zu Guo*), a forty-episode drama about the lives of Chinese students and scholars who went overseas to study during the few decades prior to the founding of the People's Republic of China in 1949 and decided to come back to China to participate in building Chinese socialism.

Apart from wanting to spend time with me, my family had another agenda in watching *In Pursuit of Melbourne* again. They wanted to know what I thought of the show—whether I thought the storyline was realistic and plausible. Between many waiting moments while another tape was inserted, ejected, or rewound, and when tears were wiped and noses blown, questions were put to me: Is Melbourne—and Australia—really like that? Is that what life is like for Chinese students living there?

Economic reforms and the open door policy at the end of the 1970s saw the beginning of the first wave of mainland Chinese students going overseas, mostly to the United States, Canada, Australia, New Zealand, and Japan to study, work, and live. The trend has continued unabated. Having voluntarily or involuntarily left their country, many members of this group of people have been slow, reluctant, or unable to assimilate into their host society or have found it difficult to do so. While they may have decided to "cut the umbilical cord" by seeking foreign citizenship, their primary cultural ties may still be to the "motherland," although a return in an emotional or intellectual sense is already out of the question.

While this group of people was desperately, if not futilely, attempting to forge a sense of home in the "New World," a most important change was beginning to take place in the minds of many Chinese still living in China in the

1980s and 1990s—a change in their perception of the West and in their ways of imagining the nation in relation to the Other. The "West" of the Chinese imagination in the early 1980s was predominantly an ideal world: materially affluent, culturally sophisticated, and morally superior. An expression that was frequently heard throughout the 1980s was: "Things like this would never happen in the West;" or "Only the Chinese are capable of such behavior." This self-loathing was often reinforced by the impressions of a handful of Chinese who had, since the late 1970s, had a chance to go abroad briefly and had become instantly enamored of everything they saw there. Writings containing such anecdotal impressions of the West often compared what the travelers had briefly seen in the West with life in China. Their vision of the West tended to be a projection of the writers' own sentiments, very often flowing more from the desires and frustrations of "the self" than from the realities of "the Other."

The exodus of mainland Chinese students to the West in the 1980s and the beginning of the 1990s signaled a start to the dismantling of such a one-sided view of the West. Not incidentally, "the West" in the Chinese imagination had been almost synonymous with the United States. These people left China to start "from scratch" in their respective new countries, and many of them had to borrow huge sums of money to pay for their trips. The experiences of individuals varied tremendously, ranging from those fortunate ones who quickly settled down and found a place for themselves in their new home, to those who had a hard time trying to fit in and survive. Although their experiences are hard to generalize, one thing is certain: The experience of translocation has produced a myriad of narratives—stories of success and failure, separation and reunion, alienation and displacement—which have become an important part of the urban legends of contemporary China.[3] Some of these narratives are mundane, while others are stories of how larger political and historical transformations impact individuals in one way or another. Qian Ning's nonfiction work "Student Lives in the USA" (*Liu Xue Mei Guo*), for instance, a realistic account of a variety of these experiences, strikes a chord of recognition and resonance among many of the Chinese students who left their country at this time.[4]

This does not necessarily mean that these students' new lives abroad had quickly demystified a utopian view of the "West." In fact, ironically, some accounts of the West provided by these very students may continue to contribute to such a utopian view. A frequent remark among them is that "unless they [folks at home] have experienced it, they will never realize how hard it is." This perceived difficulty of representing the "true," "authentic" experience of displacement was compounded by the students' reluctance to share their experiences—especially the painful ones—with their families in China, for fear of worrying them. A common practice, therefore, was to report selectively on their lives, focusing on the successful and happy side, since they believed that people back home could not understand no matter how much they might have wanted to. Another factor that contributed to the difficulty of giving an honest account of their life overseas was the students' desire to "save face": They feared looking like losers if the truth were told that their much-envied and celebrated departure from China had not quickly turned to success and prosperity in the New World.

For these reasons, although these people constitute only a tiny percentage of the Chinese population, their lives and experiences have been and remain the focus of intense curiosity. While those who have no prospects of traveling overseas, such as Ermo, Minzhi, and their fellow villagers, may travel vicariously by fantasizing about or identifying with the Chinese characters in foreign locations, those who do have prospects—like Ma Lixin in *Goldfish*, who gets cold feet about going to America—may watch these shows with more than mere curiosity or fascination. The difficulty, if not the impossibility, of knowing the "firsthand truth" about the lives of Chinese overseas is precisely why these narratives are so popular as a subgenre of television drama. This desire for the "authentic" experience of the Chinese now living overseas points to the limitation of virtual travel brought about by Margaret Morse's television, shopping malls, and freeway. In spite of the growing presence of McDonalds, Kentucky Fried Chicken, and Starbucks in China's urban spaces, and in spite of the global televisual images beaming into most people's livingrooms, vicarious travel to a new place is not that feasible. To most Chinese, who have never been overseas and will probably not be able to go in their lifetime, watching television representations of the countries to which their family members, friends, or fellow countrymen have migrated satisfies two curiosities: What exactly is the West—be it America or Australia—like, and more important, what is it like for a Chinese to be living there?

This is significant, considering that the Chinese audiences' perceptions of the West, until a decade or so ago, had come largely from American movies and other imported images of "exotic places" that have saturated Chinese television. However, since these images were not produced for the consumption of Chinese audiences, most people found it hard to relate to them. For this reason, for Chinese who have never left China, seeing images of "world cities" produced by domestic television is their closest approximation to traveling in exotic places. In other words, in these narratives, Chinese now living in the global cities perform the role of a de facto ethnographer/tour guide, taking the voyeuristic Chinese viewers into the hitherto unknown labyrinth of the foreign city. In lieu of real travel, viewing representations of these places at once fulfills and stimulates—to some extent—the wanderlust of homebound audiences. Moreover, watching and identifying with characters living in faraway foreign places provides, to some extent, a mediated experience of desired cosmopolitanism, hence performing a crucial function in the formation of (post)modern subjectivities.

For this reason, these television stories are important cultural texts, in which Chinese subjectivities are written to negotiate the new intersections of place, space, and self brought about by worldwide migrations. These texts may hold answers to questions about how a Chinese ambivalence toward modernity, which is identifiable in the cultural texts of the 1980s, continues to be negotiated and managed in a cluster of technologized images of world cities in the 1990s in these television dramas. Visualizations of mobility create new social meanings of place and space for both those who are "on the move" and those who are not, but who nevertheless actively consume images of movement. They constitute an important dimension in the unpredictable relationships between "motion and mediation"[5]—that is, between mass migrations and the irregular circulation of images as a result of these movements. Understanding the ways in which images of foreign places are constructed in these representations is a crucial starting point to unraveling the ways in which the (sometimes) conflicting images of places and mobility contribute to the formation of Chinese transnational subjectivities.

While cinema commands intense and collective engagement by enabling people to act out fantasies in the darkened yet intimate public space, television is about the "regular imagining"[6] of individuals in mundane, everyday, and domestic space. Since television is much more accessible to the Chinese population than cinema is—television, not cinema, comes to Ermo and Minzhi's village—its capacity to assist and facilitate transnational imagining is not to be underestimated. It should be clear from the last two chapters that although the entire nation of China seems to be on the move, mobility has taken different forms and followed different routes and itineraries. It is also clear that depending on the specificity of point of departures and arrivals, a sense of place is constantly reworked to articulate a new understanding of spatial hierarchy. Given this, how does a cluster of television dramas produced throughout the 1990s about the experiences of individuals who have left China for the global cities figure in the process of "imagining as an everyday social project"?[7] Or to put it more specifically, as a form of national fiction that evokes a technologized visuality, how do these televisual shows negotiate the tension between the visual and the verbal? How do these shows resolve the conflict between the desire to seduce audiences with images of world cities, on the one hand, and to promote patriotic or nationalist messages of the state, on the other? In addition, how is the city spatially represented to convey a sense of the "global" so as to accommodate a collective fantasy of the modern and Western and at the same time portray the not-so-alluring realities of Third World migrants who have moved to these places? Furthermore, if, as Naficy's study of Iranian television in Los Angeles suggests, there is a reciprocal relationship between forms of representation and society/community, and each epoch creates its own narratives,[8] how is the "Chinese in the New World" narrative similar to or different from other narratives of mobility that were created prior to, after, and parallel to it? How do these differences and similarities speak to the changing formations of Chinese social imagination in an era when everything—people, images, and capital—seems to be in constant and global circulation?

THE VISUAL VERSUS THE VERBAL

One could not understand the relationship between these television series and the formation of Chinese audiences' imagination of place without first considering the importance of visuality in the technology of television. By the early 1990s, many Chinese households, including rural households, had a color television, whereas the number of Chinese who had been overseas was still very small, considering the total population of China. This meant that television programs about foreign countries held a fascination for Chinese audiences, not only for their entertainment value but, more important, also for the visual information they contained. People simply wanted to *see*—literally—what foreign countries *looked* like. China had closed its door to the world for several decades, and few Chinese had seen (images of) other countries with their own eyes. Visual images of foreign places began to increase in the 1970s and exploded in the 1980s, with Deng Xiaoping's trip to the United States being the landmark. In such transitional times, the visuality of television acquired paramount importance for image-hungry Chinese audiences. Lull's study of Chinese television audiences at the beginning of the 1990s found that, contrary to the commonly held view that television is about glancing, while the cinema is about gazing,[9] Chinese audiences had a "collective curiosity" that resulted in "selectively attentive viewing styles."[10] This curiosity, according to Lull, would sometimes drive viewers to pay more attention to the details of domestic settings and street scenes from foreign countries than to the content of reporting that accompanied these pictures.[11] When a British-produced English-teaching program, *Follow Me*, was screened in China in the 1980s, for instance, Kathy Flower, the hostess of the show from the U.K., virtually became China's first foreign television star. It was found that a large number of viewers of the show were not English learners. They regularly watched it simply because the program was one of the few at the time that provided them with visual images of Western lifestyles.[12]

The visual representations of world cities in the "New World" dramas were the earliest technologized images of the West made available to mass audiences in China by Chinese television producers, and it is important that any analysis of them be considered in this context. The implication of this is important: Images and pictures of foreign places should not only be considered in conjunction with storylines, but more important, they should be seen as competing with the verbal messages associated with them. In this sense, television promises to "democratize," as it can assist viewers in their resistance to the preferred readings of state indoctrination. However, it is more than the televisual spectacle that accounts for the success of these shows. Rather, it is a combination of visual exotica and narrative familiarity. If the first spectatorial desire of Chinese audiences that is satisfied by these shows— to "see" exotic Western places—is a voyeuristic one, then the second, wanting to know what it is like for a Chinese to live and survive in foreign lands, is a desire to consume familiar stories and storytelling. The "New World" genre touches on many perennial themes: adventure, success, separation, reunion, human vicissitude and transformation, struggle and survival, fate and luck, romance, and, of course, exotica. Audiences may privilege certain genres, tropes, and themes over others, but, necessarily, their viewing pleasure comes from the familiarity and comfort of narrative convention, as well as from the experience of "vicarious traveling" delivered by visual images of unfamiliar and exotic places. The tension between the visual and verbal creates a pair of opposing homologies—between familiarity, similarity, and continuity, on the one hand, and exotica, difference, and discontinuity, on the other. I would suggest that in the negotiation of these tensions, the social imagination of space and place—a process crucial to the formation of the modern subject—is constantly reworked.

Writers on cultural representations in Chinese contexts hold differing views on the relationship between the verbal and visual. Reflecting on the power of technologized images to affect the ways in which the nation is imagined in modern and postmodern culture, Rey Chow[13] points to the "immediacy and efficacy" of the electronic media, which threaten to "usurp and supplant" the role traditionally enjoyed by literature and writing. She argues that images delivered by electronic media are powerful because, compared with writing, they are "clear, direct and seemingly transparent," hence allowing "entire histories, nation and peoples to be exposed, revealed, captured on the screen, made visible as images."[14]

In comparison with Chow's, Wang Jing's understanding of the relationship between verbal and visual impact is a more nuanced one.[15] Rather than "usurping" and "supplanting" the verbal, the visual, Wang argues, has the capacity to complement words to achieve polysemy and ambiguity. Writing on the visuality in Su Xiaokang's four-part documentary *Heshang* (River Elegy), the most important and influential critique of Chinese culture in the 1980s, Wang reminds us that *Heshang* is not just a verbal construct; it also speaks to the audience through the camera and, as a visual representation, is able to "transcend" the ideological closure determined by the written text. She also points out that the conflict between the visual and verbal results in "ambiguity," rather than exclusiveness:

The ending of *Heshang* thus tells us two different stories: one the conquest of the river by the ocean, the other, the miracle of a spatial breakthrough of the imprisoned. Because visual imagery has a life of its own and is less susceptible than verbal imagery to ideological constraints, the spectacle of the merger invites conflicting interpretations. In so much as the conclusion is seen rather than derived from a logical statement, the last few minutes of the documentary embody the tour de force of a conceptual ambiguity beyond the grasp of verbal logic.[16]

The tension between a visual effect and verbal construct identified in *Heshang* is also evident in many "Chinese in the New World" dramas. This tension manifests itself in the seductive and desirable images of the world cities, delivered visually by television, and the often anti-Western, nativist sentiments embodied in the narratives. Television delivers a visual "other" world that consists of alluring images of modernity. What is interesting about the "New World" narratives is their tendency to represent world cities in ways that are not dissimilar to the ways "the Orient" was constructed in Western representations of the previous century—an ironic reversal of visual orientalism. While oriental otherness is homologous to the premodern, the feminine, and the rural, and hence is different and exotic to the West, the exoticism of the world cities derives its meaning from its being (post)modern. New York, Chicago, Los Angeles, Tokyo, and even Budapest offer a life that is both exciting and enticing. For this purpose, identifiable signs usually associated with postcard images—such at the Danube River, the "Hollywood" sign on the hill of Los Angeles, and the Mt. Rushmore sculptured heads of American presidents—serve as signs of both authenticity and exotica.

The world cities on the television screen look exotic because they look "different." "Difference," when constructed by the camera, can be enticing. It suggests alternative lifestyles, possibilities of freedom, and dreams of success. It brings home a faraway foreign land, full of novel scenes and people. These images conjure up a city that, during the day, functions seamlessly, with no traffic congestion, no pollution, and no urban squalor. In the evening, the city is equally enticing, taking on a softer, more feminine touch. Well-lit streets, soft neon lights, and well-dressed city-slickers walking in and out of department stores and cafés all form part of the mise-en-scène. Such images disclose a world of sophistication and affluence to Chinese audiences, whose desire for a cosmopolitan lifestyle—their wanderlust—is temporarily displaced through what Mulvey calls a "scopophilic" gaze.[17] In this sense, Rey Chow is right in pointing out that "the East" can also be a gazer and a spectator. Such essentialist representations of the sublime of the modern city are to be contrasted with a more suburban look in later filmic representations of "America," as is discussed in the analysis of *Be There* in chapter 2.

The visual effect consistently delivered in these representations of world cities sits uncomfortably with the state's xenophobia and its reluctance to participate in the construction of a fantasy of the West. For example, in contrast to what the visual images suggest, *A Beijing Native in New York* embodies a strong nationalism and a high degree of ambivalence toward the West. Wang Qiming, a cellist in Beijing, comes to New York with his wife, Guo Yan, to start a new life. Wang becomes estranged from his wife, who later marries Wang's American business rival, David. Like Ermo and Minzhi, the two village women in the city we meet in chapter 1, the new arrivals in the global cities are often represented as the self-appointed anthropologists of the city. Throughout the story, there is a persistent desire to define and describe New York. Halfway through the series, the audience learns that New York is neither heaven nor hell. It is what Ah Chun, Wang's lover and business partner, a character who is given credibility to speak about America, calls a "battlefield," where only the strongest survive. According to Guo Yan, New York is alienating. "If I ever had a home, it would be in Beijing. It could never be in New York." Even Ah Chun, who is ostensibly the most Westernized woman in the story, says to Wang, "We [Chinese] had long been human beings when they [Americans] were still apes. Haven't you noticed the hair on their bodies?"

Similarly, the twenty-episode drama series *Broadway No. 100* tells the story of a Chinese group house in Los Angeles, whose inhabitants include a painter who refuses to compromise his artistic integrity for the sake of money and is hence living in poverty, a doctoral student who is too busy making a living to love his wife, and a postdoctoral researcher who becomes pregnant by the painter, while her husband in Shanghai is planning a visit. The doctoral student's wife, who has to work as a live-in maid for a rich and mean American woman, gets beaten up by her employer's son, a banker-cum-politician running for the Senate. When the Chinese woman decides to seek justice in the American courts, everyone in the house offers moral and financial support. The story ends with her winning the legal case against her American employer, who symbolizes the power, wealth, and racism of American society. On hearing the verdict, she demands a face-to-face apology in court from the defendant.

This narrative is supposedly based on real life. It is also a very powerful story since it resonates with the experiences of many Chinese students abroad in matters relating to race, gender, class, power, money, pride, dignity, and humiliation. Most probably for this reason, the plot was "recycled" in an eight-episode drama produced by Liaoning TV in 1998. Appropriately titled *Dignity*, the story focuses on the court case of a Chinese student, Lin Xue, against a rich and powerful American banker-politician, Mr. Edward, whose mother was Lin's employer. When the verdict against Edward is read out, Lin makes an emotional speech that can be read as a scathing comment on the United States in the new global order. Her story assumes a national dimension: "I am demanding an apology because what I want is not money, but dignity. America prides itself on its respect for human rights, equality, and the individual, but my experience tells me that this is a society governed by money. But money isn't the most important thing.

It would be wrong to assume that a nation can get away with murder simply because it is rich and powerful."

THE AERIAL VERSUS THE PEDESTRIAN:
SPATIAL CONFIGURATION OF THE CITY

In these television dramas, the city or the metropolis assumes a central place. Since these narratives describe the lives of some Chinese, such as Beijing natives or Shanghai natives, in the global cities—New York, Tokyo, or Melbourne—viewers are treated to a story with Chinese characters and a foreign location. What are the styles of imagining these cities, and, indeed, how is a sense of the city constructed on television, the most accessible and everyday means of going places without leaving home? Here, I want to argue, echoing the discussion of Ermo and television in chapter 1, that television has taken the place of cinema in facilitating and assisting the spatial imagination of space and place. I also want to demonstrate that the ways in which "the world city" in these Chinese television dramas in the 1990s and the beginning of the twenty-first century are imagined are akin to those in the classic cinema in the early part of the twentieth century. Furthermore, understanding how the city is spatially configured is crucial to unraveling the complexity and ambiguity that mark the urban Chinese imagination of the "modern" West in the era of globalization and mobility.

Writing about the cinema and the city, James Donald observes that the style of imagining the modern city consists of a bifurcated spatial configuration.[18] In his discussion of the Bernard Rose horror movie *Candyman*, he identifies an "aerial" view of Chicago, including its townscapes, traffic on freeways, and monumental buildings. This, according to Donald, presents a "God's eye view" of the city, which presents a "dehumanized geometry."[19] This is an abstract view in which individual human beings are either invisible or insignificant. This aerial view, Donald observes, is juxtaposed with a view from below, whereby, on the streets, individuals from different genders, races, and classes make sense of the city's irrationality in their respective ways. For this reason, this "juxtaposition between panorama and myth," Donald argues, bespeaks the "doubly textured" nature of the urban space, which has become the dominant cinematic style of imagining the city.

This argument of the "panorama-myth couplet" resonates with de Certeau's view of the city as consisting of a contrast between a "concept" city, which is associated with power, and a "pedestrian" view of the city, which is densely textured and fraught with the rich experiences of the individuals occupying and traversing that space.[20] In Donald's view of the cinematic city and de Certeau's configuration of the city of the everyday, a mismatch and a contradiction between an abstract city and the concrete city are identified.

And in explaining and understanding this mismatch lies the key to under-standing the power relations in the city, as well as the ways they are metaphorized in spatial terms.

This bifurcated style of representing the city is clearly replicated in the vi-sualization of the global cities of New York, Los Angeles, or Tokyo and of their metropolitan areas in the televisual dramas I am concerned with here. As mentioned earlier in this chapter, modernity, as a sign of difference, be-comes available for consumption by Chinese television audiences. It is a con-vention of many of these drama serials to start each episode with aerial shots of the city, usually consisting of the freeways, landmark bridges, and sky-scrapers. What is worth noting is that although aerial shots conjure the im-age of the "modern" in these television dramas, as they do in the classic ur-ban cinema, the "modernity" that these images conjure up is connotated differently. In Donald's cinema, the city is alienating and dehumanizing be-cause of its modernity, whereas in the television dramas that concern me here, the city is seductive and exotic not in spite of, but precisely because of, its modernity. This is evidenced in the fact that the space of the global cities is configured with fetishistic uses of clichéd icons of speed, such as cars gliding noiselessly (and seemingly pollution-free) along the surface of highways; power-imposing bottom-up shots of city skylines; and energy, suggested by sweeping shots of multilevel highways. A common observation of new ar-rivals from China is that Australia does not look as "modern" as they had imagined. In fact, it reminds them of the Chinese countryside, being mostly free from tall buildings, vertical highways, and the posh, expensive-looking shops that they associated with the modern city. The lack of expected signs of modernity can sometimes be as disappointing to Chinese arrivals in the "New World" as the experience of some Western tourists who arrive in some "Third World" places and fail to see signs of "tradition"—that is, "authentic-ity."

What is most ironic about these romanticized visualizations of the space of world cities is the apparent disjuncture between what these images suggest in terms of power and the structural inability of the Chinese characters living there to access this power. These cities, as signs of modernity, merely provide a setting and a background for an essentially Chinese story; and although the signs themselves are available for spectatorial consumption, the power asso-ciated with them is not similarly distributed and shared. This is most poignantly demonstrated in the scene of the fabled arrival of Wang Qiming and his wife at the New York airport and their subsequent taxi ride to what was to be their first home in the new country. Coming out of the airport, he and his wife look out of the moving taxi, and the architecture, streets, and people gliding past them form part of the mise-en-scène. To the music of Dvorak's "The New World," an elated and ecstatic Wang gesticulates in the taxi with a maestro's flourish and exclaims to the world: "America, here I come" (*meiguo, wo lai le*)! Wang seems to be on top of the world. His excitement about the new city is indeed infectious.

In my conversations with Chinese viewers about the show, many single out this beginning scene as an example of "America" as an exciting and stimulating place. Wang Qiming's initial ecstasy at his glimpses of modernity and affluence through the taxi window on the balmy night of his arrival in New York is quickly dashed when the taxi finally takes him to a tunnel-like, graffiti-covered basement, which his relatives have arranged for his and his wife's first home in America. While Wang cautiously enters the dark basement to "check it out," his wife, waiting on the pavement, mistakes a friendly black pedestrian who offers help for a potential robber. We are here momentarily brought back to the sense of phobia and panic experienced by the Chinese in American cities that I described in chapter 2.

The basement scene, I argue, can be read as a powerful spatial metaphor of the peripheral position of the "Third World" migrants in the global cities. If the space of global cities can be conceptualized into the sharp contrast between the "citadel" and the "ghetto,"[21] the basement signifies the marginality of socially invisible people struggling in the city. The symbolic use of the basement as a signifier of a pedestrian view of the city that is fraught with anxiety and the struggle of the little people surviving at the margin is evidenced in the final episode, when Wang, having finally "made it," moves to a mansion on Long Island. The show ends with Wang going to the airport to meet a friend from Beijing and taking him straight to the basement to start his new life. Here it becomes clear that although these dramas resort to romanticization and exoticization of the global city, the power that is associated with the global city is not easily accessible to those who arrive to inhabit this space.

This contradiction between the city of power and the powerlessness of many inhabitants of the city is also seen in the self-depiction of overseas students' lives in *Our Lives as Overseas Students*, an account of some Chinese students in their twenties, trying to survive in Tokyo in the period from 1996 to 1999. Like New York, the "Tokyo" recorded by the cameras of these students-documentarists also takes on a bifurcated visuality. While panoramic and sweeping shots linger on its affluence, its cosmopolitan exteriority, and its fast pace, an internal view of the living conditions of the Chinese tenants suggests the opposite. Most students who agree to be filmed live in an unfurnished dingy room of about six square meters (with no kitchen or bathroom). These spaces take on a much more claustrophobic dimension because some of the inhabitants have become illegal immigrants—having overstayed their visas and gone "black" (*hei*). This sense of phobia and marginalization, which marks the migrants' relation to the world city, is replicated in a cluster of domestically produced television dramas in recent years about the experience of rural migrants in Chinese cities. *Roughing It in Shanghai* (*Chuang Shanghai*), for instance, starts with four Henan rural migrants getting off a crowded train at Shanghai Central Railway Station. Frightened and dizzy from the speed at which the city moves, the group stumbles into a nearby construction site, where the migrants spend their first night in Shanghai stuck in an elevator in a yet-to-be-completed building site.

Both James Donald's cinematic city and the televisual city I am concerned with embody a contradiction between the knowable and transparent city and a mysterious, irrational city, or what Donald calls the "split between the will to visibility and the irredeemable opacity of the social."[22] Concurring with this reading, I want to add, however, that the opacity comes not only from the fact that margins are invested with the meaning, memory, and desire of the little people, but, more relevant to my analysis, it comes from these meanings, memories, and desires belonging to those whose subjectivities are informed by different temporal and spatial configurations. Sometimes, there is a deliberate mismatch between the two. In other words, in contrast to the highly essentialized and flat visual representations of the global city in spatial terms, there is, in these dramas, a strong sense of temporal depth.

For instance, a common way of bonding between the characters of these stories is the parodic, yet somewhat emotional, recycling of a political language that comes from a previous era. The setting for one poignant scene in *A Beijing Native in New York* is a Chinese party, where members of a crowd, moved by their own nostalgia and melancholy, sing a revolutionary song about Beijing: "Beijing, you are the heart of my motherland and symbol of our nation." Here, the revolutionary flavor of the song is deliberately ignored; sung in a foreign place and in an ahistorical time, it articulates a specific kind of yearning borne out of displacement—a function irrelevant to the original text. *The New World* provides another example, when a group of Chinese students celebrates a friend's marriage in a Chinese restaurant in downtown Chicago by singing a propaganda song denouncing the exploitative landlords of the pre-Communist era. These appropriative uses of revolutionary texts become a common strategy for expressing a particular kind of Chineseness that is united by a common experience and a collective memory of the nation's past.

These examples also highlight the centrality of nostalgia in the affective landscape of this paradiasporic community. In spite of the foreignness of the locations in which these stories are set, their sense of time is intensely Chinese. The historical time of China is collapsed into the space of world cities, or alternatively, a place in China is fused into the time of the global cities. "Beijing" is thereby a space that has acquired a temporal dimension. Time is spatialized: "The past" is equated with China, while "the present" is equated with places of migration; the past becomes *there*, and now becomes *here*. As Naficy's work suggests, the exile looks forward by looking back.[23]

PLACE, TIME, AND NEW SUBJECTIVITIES

Chinese students going to the West to start a new life are often compared to the "intellectual youth" (*zhi qing*) of the 1960s and 1970s, who were "sent down" to the countryside for resettlement and hence had to endure rural hardships.[24] In fact, many of those who went to the West were ex-"sent-down youth" (*xia fang zhi qing*), who, a decade and a half later, having previously found their way back to the city, found themselves again "enduring foreign hardships" (*yang cha dui*)—this time as a result of voluntary displacement. To these educated urban youths, both the poverty-stricken rural China of the 1970s and the prosperous Western world of the 1990s posed a challenge to their sense of worth and their ability to survive; and although hardships in the countryside were both material and psychological, while those in the West were mainly emotional, the ethos was similar in both cases. Loneliness, alienation, and displacement led to their inevitable redefinition or rediscovery of selfhood.

In *Sacrificed Youth* (*Qin Chun Ji*), a film about a young Han Chinese woman sent to live with ethnic Dai people in the far south during the Cultural Revolution, the landscape is psychologized to suggest a world of alienation. In Chen Kaige's *King of the Children* (*Hai Zi Wang*), a Shanghai youth is sent to teach school children in a poor and remote mountainous region. In the last decade, television audiences had also viewed numerous television drama series, including *Nie Zai* (Wages of Sin) and *Nian Lun* (Cycles of Life), that focused on the experiences of these former sent-down youths. In this sense, then, the "Chinese in the New World" genre is a continuation of the "sent-down youth" narrative, in which life presents itself as consisting of various kinds of challenges—be they the unbearable harshness of the country, the whims of Mao, the tyranny of China's political regime, or, in this case, the challenges posed by foreign cultures.

In this specific sense, I argue that in spite of their foreign locations, the "New World" narratives can be seen as a continuation of the ethos of the "educated youth literature" (*zhi qing wen xue*), in which the self goes through a process of dislocation, displacement, and subsequent transformation. Like the countryside to the educated youth, the world cities are, to these willing exiles from mainland China, places where ontological transformation takes place. New arrivals are told, very often by those Chinese who arrived before them, that "this is America; you must see, think, and act differently." "America," "Japan," or the "world cities" are often represented as agents for social reconfiguration in class, race, and gender terms. For example, the idea of couples growing apart, getting a divorce, and "shacking up" with someone else—often, a *gueilo*—is a common plot ingredient in the "New World" stories. The Chinese male in these narratives—like the urban male in the "educated youth literature" who fails to protect his female comrades from seduction by the powerful village leader—likewise frequently finds himself unable to defend his masculinity. "Every day," laments Cai, the philosopher-turned-kitchen-hand in *The New World*, "I see one of our beautiful women walking out of this door with a white man." In this and other stories, "New York," "Los Angeles," or "Chicago" becomes a powerful discursive space in which the self is constantly rewritten to negotiate the new intersections of class, race, and gender brought about by displacement.

In both the "educated-youth literature" and the "Chinese in the New World" narratives, characters are compelled to forsake their old selves in order to position themselves in relation to their newly constituted otherness. The treachery of country/abusive village chiefs/physical hardships/power in the former genre is comparable to that of city/foreigners/racism/money in the latter. In visualizing an "other" world, images of rural China become homologous with those of global cities.

There is another level on which we can perceive a similarity between these two genres. In her analysis of the "educated youth literature," Dai Jinhua astutely observes that despite the suffering and loss experienced by educated youth, what characterizes this body of literature is heroism.[25] I argue here that this heroism—the ability to survive in adversity—is also central to the "Chinese in the New World" narratives. "If you love him, send him to New York, for it is heaven; if you hate him, send him to New York, for it is hell." These words appear onscreen at the start of each episode of *A Beijing Native in New York* and introduce the audience to an unfamiliar space that seems to hold perpetual fascination, not in spite of, but precisely because of, the treacheries associated with it. The narrative of putting oneself in difficult and alienating circumstances and emerging from them stronger and transformed is common to Chinese students like Wang Qiming in *A Beijing Native in New York*, who went to America in their thirties and forties in the late 1980s and early 1990s, but also to the Chinese students in their early twenties who left China in the late 1990s. The pride of being able to *chiku* (eat bitterness)—endure hardship—is a theme that is brought up over and over again by the group of Chinese students in Tokyo in *Our Lives as Overseas Students*.

If the "sent-down youth" is a predecessor to the "Chinese in the New World" as a narrative of displacement and alienation, and of surviving in the liminal space between past and present, home and host, then the emergence of a literature on peasant and labor migrants within China in the 1990s and the beginning of the new millennium is a continuation of the theme of travel, mobility, and becoming modern. Starting in the early 1990s, an increasing number of Chinese peasants and labor migrants left home to seek work in China's prosperous rural areas and cities. As the new century has dawned, it seems that this trend of mobility remains unabated: villagers going to the city (*jing cheng*); domestic maids or sex workers going south (*nan xia*); inlanders journeying to the coast—all of them seeking work and income. Popular media, both television and print, contribute to the production of "migrant worker" stories, adding another narrative layer to the theme of mobility and travel. General interest in the experiences and adventures of peasants and other nonlocal workers has seen the production of numerous television and film representations, including the 1983 film *The Girl from the Yellow Mountain* (*Huang Shan Lai De Gu Niang*), the 1988 television drama *Erzi* (*Er Zi*), and the 1991 television series *Girls from Out of Town* (*Wai Lai Mei*). A number of newspapers and magazines, such as *Working Girls* (*Da Gong Mei*) and *Workers from Outside* (*Wai Lai Gong*), make the narratives of migrants their main focus. At the turn of the century, television dramas about the experiences of rural migrants in the city have proliferated, presenting a parallel narrative of mobility and migration to that about the diasporic group. Like *Shenzhen Working Girls* (*Shenzhen Dagongmei*) and *Sisters' Ventures in Beijing* (*Jiejie Meimei Chuang Beijing*), *Roughing It in Shanghai* (*Chuang Shanghai*), for instance, is the story of a group of rural migrants from Henan Province trying to—some are successful and some are not—become "Shanghairen" (Shanghai residents). He Wenchang, a rural schoolteacher in Henan, eventually becomes a "white collar" (a cleaning agent salesman) in Shanghai, but is told that in spite of his successes, he will never become a "Shanghairen" because of his accent and looks. The girl he is in love with, who comes to Shanghai with him on the same train, initially finds a job working as a maid, but ends up in a bar as a *xiaojie* (a euphemism for prostitute). These rural migrants, like Wang Qiming and his friends, exist in the shadowland of their host "countries" and tend to occupy the heaviest, dirtiest, and most dangerous niches of the labor market. Just as the functioning of world cities is contingent on the presence of various Third World populations,[26] so, too, do Chinese cities—especially large provincial capitals and cities in the south and on the coast—come to rely on the presence of migrant workers from the country, inland, and the north. Displacement and deterritorialization have reworked the ethnoscapes—the shifting populations of tourists, immigrants, refugees, guest workers, and other moving groups—of both world cities and southern, coastal, and capital cities of China. People of disparate social classes and places of origin make up each other's habitat and have an impact on each other's subjectivity.

In spite of, or because of, the codependent spatial relationship between urban people and rural migrants, the latter are treated with discrimination, derision, distrust, and disdain. The stereotypes of country people in the urban consciousness, government management and policing strategies, and popular media representations conspire to cast rural migrant workers into the shadowland of "foreigners," "subalterns," and "vagrants."[27] They are subjected to a similar process of ghettoization and peripheralization as Third World migrants are in the world cities. That both Chinese migrants overseas and rural migrants within the country are often perceived as threatening and unruly is evidenced in the similar metaphors evoked to describe their movements. While Western cities are flooded with "yellow tides" from Asia, internal migrants are often described in official documents and the media as *mangliu* (a blind, purposeless flow) or *dagongchao* (floods of laborers), in spite of the fact these rural migrants' work in the city has considerably revitalized the urban market and provided the much-needed income and capital for rural villages back at home.

When increasing numbers of Chinese are literally on the move, crossing borders, provinces, and socioeconomic boundaries, narratives of their travel and mobility also contribute to the reworking of the social meanings of place and space. Spatial imagination was relatively simple in Mao's era. Beijing was the political center of the nation, and the world was divided into "three worlds," with the Third World "our friends" and the First World "our superpower enemies." Economic reform, an open-door policy, massive outward migration of mainland Chinese, and, in the last decade, the internal movements of labor migrants have dramatically reorganized the hierarchy of place and space in people's imaginations.[28]

Those Chinese who have traversed these social spaces—even educated professionals like Wang Qiming and his wife, in *A Beijing Native in New York*—went to the world cities as Third World migrant laborers, working as kitchen hands in restaurants or sewing in clothing sweatshops. By the same token, Hong Kong, Shenzhen, Guangdong, Shanghai, Beijing—signifiers of urban, modern, and "enlightened" China—are what I call "internal world cities." In order to function effectively, these cities rely on migrant labor from the "internal Third World"—northern, rural, and inland provinces and regions such as Sichuan, Anhui, Guizhou, and Xinjiang. Urban media portray these places and their people as being in need of modernization and enlightenment, and in the popular mind they have been readily associated with poverty, backwardness, and primitiveness. The adventures and experiences of the *dagongmei* (working girls) and *wailaigong* (migrant laborers) have become an integral part of contemporary urban folklore. Characters in these narratives are spatially transformed by "going south" and "entering the city" and are confronted by the unpredictability and uncertainty of city life. And just as the "Chinese in the New World" cannot avoid the fate of being "ethnicized" by the (multi)cultural representations of their host societies, so, too, are internal peasant migrants constantly reminded by urban media and residents of the differences that set them apart from city folk.

A most interesting example of the parallel power dynamics of core–periphery inequality and interdependence between those two social groups can be found in the narrative of the maid. The experience of the Chinese student working as a live-in maid in a rich American household, mentioned earlier in this chapter, is remarkably resonant with those of hundreds and thousands of village women who have left home to become domestic servants, nannies, and cleaners in the city folks' houses in Beijing, Shanghai, Shenzhen, and other "internal global cities." Maids, as well as nannies and cleaners, are what McClintock calls "threshold figures," transgressing the public/private, waged/unwaged, inside family/outside family boundaries and a potential threat to the moral and sexual norm of the family.[29] The perennial fascination and anxiety about the maid, due to her threshold status, gives rise to the proliferation of popular narratives of the maid. In addition, compared with local maids, maids from rural provinces are doubly marginalized in the city, due to their perceived "foreignness." In both transnational and national spaces the rural migrant working as a maid is deemed a less competitive "product" than local maids because of her (dis)location. My ethnographic work with some maids from Anhui province—a Chinese province well known for maids—suggests that "Anhui maid" is seen as a metaphor for the gendered, unequal, and uneven relationship between Anhui and developed places such as Shanghai and Beijing.[30] Mobile, plentiful, and available any time, she also embodies the enduring potency of such a metaphor. The Anhui maid is a brand name, a product, whose cachet, authenticity, and desirability are made possible not in spite of, but precisely because of, the uniqueness of Anhui as a poor place. In this sense, the association of Anhui with poverty operates on a metaphoric level—Anhui is like a maid—and metonymic level: The maid stands for Anhui. While village women see going to the city as *baomu* (nannies) as an opportunity to raise their status, Chinese migrants in the world cities deliberately accept a lower status in order to earn income. In addition, what makes the maid in the transnational space different from her "sisters" in the national space is that while the former takes on a racial dimension and is therefore a useful figure in a nationalist discourse, the domestic (pun intended) maid embodies an urban and an increasingly middle-class anxiety and disquiet about the rural and social Other.[31] The maid, when caught in the class-based, rather than race-based, conflict, is more often than not interrogated and found wanting. This is most acutely evidenced in a popular twenty-two-episode television drama serial on Chinese television *The Twenty-Eight Maids in Professor Tian's House* (*Tian jiaoshou jiade ershiba ge baomu*). In the story, Professor Tian has a bedridden mother who is in need of constant attention. Professor Tian has at different stages employed twenty-eight maids because each of these maids in her own way fails to perform satisfactorily. Throughout the show, Professor Tian and his family try to live—uneasily—with the fact that they need, but cannot trust, their maid. They also struggle, each in his or her own way, to negotiate a class-based relationship with the maid. Professor Tian, for instance, feels guilty about exploiting the maid, while his wife, a factory cadre, insists on scrutinizing the maid to make sure that she works hard and does not steal or gossip.

Both of these constellations of mobility—transnational and national—are crucial cultural texts in considering the formation of what Mayfair Yang refers to as the "spatial mobility of subjectivity."[32] The identification of the immobile audience with mobile characters in these representations—be it those who travel to world cities such as New York and Sydney, or those who travel to Beijing and Shenzhen—makes it possible to talk about the cognitive mobility of audiences brought about by their vicarious travel. For this reason, Liu, in writing about the affinity between these two groups of travelers, argues that narratives such as *A Beijing Native in New York* and *A Shanghainese Native in Tokyo* are cultural interpretations of the formation of transnational identities.[33] Indeed, as Yang's survey of Shanghai viewers of *A Beijing Native in New York* demonstrates, the identification of mainland audiences with those who go abroad provides clues to the formation of a transnational Chinese imaginary.

METAPHOR, TRANSNATIONALISM, AND GLOBAL CAPITALISM

In their attempt to satisfy the two spectatorial desires discussed previously, the "Chinese in the New World" narratives betray a profound ambivalence toward the global and ambiguity in their view of the global modern. However, this ambivalence makes the representation of a particular group of "not-so-patriotic Chinese" on state television not only possible, but also strategically useful for the Party's nation-building agenda. And if, as Dai claims, the Chinese state is simultaneously saying "yes" and "no" to transnational capitalism,[34] then these stories textually embody such an ambiguous position.

In the same way that Su Xiaokang's visual image of the Yellow River in *Heshang* reveals his ambivalence toward the Chinese past, the images of modernity in these television dramas reveal Feng Xiaogang and his colleagues' unresolved emotional responses to "the West." If *Heshang* ends with a call for the "yellow civilization" to open up and embrace "the blue civilization," then the appearance of the "New World" narratives suggests that this call has been answered. "The West" is no longer symbolized by an azure ocean, as in *Heshang*. Rather, it is now a place where many Chinese are trying to build a new home—some successfully and others less successfully—and where many transnational Chinese subjectivities are (trans)formed. The habitat and experience of Chinese in these stories should be read as both a metaphor and a metonym for the dynamics of global capitalism and of China's place in it. The success or failure of these "Chinese in the New World" can thus be read as a symbol of what China needs to do, can do, and will do in the new global economic order. What Wang Qiming and other business "heroes" have lost in transition can be seen as the price China has to pay in order to become a global power. Seen in this light, the link between the production of these Chinese stories of global capitalism and China's eventual entry into the World Trade Organization is not as tenuous as it may appear.

If capital, or economic power, subordinates one group of people to another, then these narratives suggest that global capitalism creates a power dynamic characterized by shifting intersections of race, gender, and class. Many mainland Chinese students are portrayed in these dramas as having left their professional jobs at home to work for low pay—and often illegally—in the West. Such work is sometimes provided by another kind of Chinese, whose wealth and green cards allow them to exploit cheap labor from China. This portrayal of the downward social-economic mobility of most characters may also explain the Chinese state's willingness to make representational space for the experience of a group of "not-so-patriotic Chinese." These migrants' nostalgia for the "lost" homeland, together with the overtly anti-imperialistic sentiments resulting from their downward mobility, is in tune with the state's periodically unveiled anti-imperialistic agenda. Like the urban "educated youth" who were told that they needed to cleanse themselves of bourgeois values in order to become wholesome socialist beings, these estranged Chinese have always been liminal figures in the self/other configuration of the state. For this reason, giving voice to an exilic longing for a romanticized and imaginary "homeland" and presenting it to a domestic audience driven by a longing for faraway places is like parents telling those children still living at home that "it's a tough world out there" and "there's no place like home."

Political expediency, however, is not the only factor that determines what is created in cultural representations in contemporary China. State-supervised and -sponsored cultural production had already become more consumer-friendly and entertainment-oriented, both to attract revenue and to better win popular favor. Its need to diversify funding sources also meant that unless programs appealed to the widest spectrum of audiences, they would not be financially viable. For this reason, satisfying audiences' desires and titillating their fantasies became at least as important as meeting the political goals of the state—if not more so. And it is in the context of this structural tension between the state and market that some of the contradictions in the "New World" narratives can best be understood.

As a metaphor for China's position in the twenty-first century, the world cities where the Chinese have built their habitats point to the complex, ambiguous, and sometimes contradictory discourses in the transnational imaginary. On one hand, these narratives display a nativist, Sino-centric view of Chineseness; but on the other hand, they also betray a fetish for the "modern" icon of the "West." This ambivalence is heightened by the technology of the visual. In this sense, any attempt to study the constructions of the spatial imaginary at the beginning of the new century must look not only at how place is narrated, but also at how it is visualized —not to mention the tension, ambiguity, and ambivalence created by the marriage of spoken words with visualized images. This is particularly important because with the arrival of new communication and technologies such as VCR, DVD, HDTV, VCD, MTV, and computer games, national fiction is increasingly packaged and delivered in a mode that mixes the verbal with the visual. In addition, it is increasingly produced and consumed in spaces that are not strictly "national."

Given this, any analysis of national self-narrativization must continue to pay attention to the tension between anti-imperialistic, anti-Western discourses and the desire to critique an essentialist vision of China. The focus of such critical attention must go beyond representations set within the boundaries of national space and include stories set outside that space. And in an era when more and more Chinese traverse and inhabit the global spaces of transnational capitalism, this tension is bound to be continuously and creatively managed and negotiated in the narratives of, and by, those Chinese no longer living inside China. In addition, the movements of internal peasant and labor migrants and those of the Chinese in the New World need to be looked at as both parallel and intersecting processes, and representations of these groups of travelers should be considered articulations at specific junctures of the process of becoming "modern." Key to this process is the cognitive mobility of immobile, vicarious travelers in response to the images of places brought to them in stories of "genuine" travelers, and, in particular, the ways in which these audiences relate to and identify with characters in such tales of travel and mobility.

Finally, the experience of movement from, and shuttling back to, the home(land) makes "travel" a legitimate metaphor for the formation of migrant subjectivity, which is often marked by ambivalence, contradiction, and ambiguity. Connoting process, translation, transformation, and becoming, travel is both physical, allowing the migrant to go to the city from his or her village, hence leaving the old habitat for a new one, and epistemological—along with the change of habitat come fundamental, often uncertain, changes in the migrant's ways of being. It is for this reason that Nonini and Ong rightly argue that in studying various forms of Chinese modernity, the focus of ethnography should be on "travel" per se, rather than on "spatially delimited, fixed and local" places.[35]

NOTES

1. See note 12 in chapter 2 for a list of works on this television drama series.

2. Cao Guilin, whose novel *A Beijing Native in New York* was adapted into the television drama, has recently cashed in on the success of the book and produced a sequel, *The Green Card: A Beijing Girl in New York* (*Luka: Beijing Guniang Zai Nuyue*). Details of the publication are unavailable at this stage, but chapters of the novel can be read online, <www.shuku.net/dblx/html.01/4-2-1.html> (accessed November 2001).

3. A quick browse on the shelves in most Chinese bookstores would reveal numerous publications of this genre.

4. Qian Ning, *Liuxue Meiguo* (Studying in the U.S.) (Nanjing: Jiangsu Wenyi Chubanshe, 1996).

5. The relationship between electronic mediation and mass migration, according to Appadurai, is highly irregular and unpredictable because both viewers and images are likely to be in circulation. See Arjun Appadurai, *Modernity at Large: Cultural Dimensions of Globalization* (Minneapolis: University of Minnesota Press, 1996).

6. Colin Mercer discusses the role of the newspapers in the formation of a sense of collective identity. He argues that unlike novels, the quotidian nature of newspaper consumption contributes to the process of "regular imagining." See Colin Mercer, "Regular Imagining: The Newspaper and the Nation," in *Celebrating the Nation: A Study of Australia's Bicentenary*, ed. Tony Bennett, Pat Buckeridge, David Carter, and Colin Mercer (Sydney: Allen & Unwin, 1992).

7. Appadurai, *Modernity at Large*, 4.

8. Hamid Naficy, *The Making of Exile Cultures: Iranian Television in Los Angeles* (Minneapolis: University of Minnesota Press, 1993).

9. John Hartley, *Tele-Ology: Studies in Television* (London: Routledge, 1992).

10. James Lull, *China Turned On: Television, Reform and Resistance* (London: Routledge, 1991), 172.

11. Huang, a member of the Chinese diasporic audiences I interviewed, told me an anecdote about her parents in Sichuan who came to visit her in Australia and who wanted to bring some presents for her house. Not knowing what style of bedspreads and tablecloths—things they had decided to give as presents—would be suitable, they carefully watched for relevant details in some foreign shows and managed to find tablecloths and bedspreads of a similar style.

12. Hong Junhao, *The Internationalization of Television in China: The Evolution of Ideology, Society, and Media since the Reform* (Westport, Conn.: Praeger, 1998).

13. Rey Chow relates the awakening of the national consciousness of the modern Chinese in her reading of Lu Xun's autobiographical narrative, where he attributes his impulse to give up medicine and become a writer to the experience of watching some Chinese being humiliated on the cinema screen. See Rey Chow, *Primitive Passions* (New York: Columbia University Press, 1995).

14. Chow, *Primitive Passions*, 10.

15. Wang Jing, *High Culture Fever: Politics, Aesthetics and Ideology in Deng's Era* (Berkeley: University of California Press, 1996).

16. Wang Jing, *High Culture*, 134.

17. Laura Mulvey, "Visual Pleasure and Narrative Cinema," in *Movies and Methods*, vol. 2, ed. Bill Nichols (Berkeley: University of California Press, 1985), 303–15.

18. James Donald, *Imagining the Modern City* (London: Athlone, 1999).

19. James Donald, *Imagining*, 69.

20. Michel de Certeau, *The Practice of Everyday Life* (Berkeley: University of California Press, 1984).

21. Naficy, *Exile Cultures*; Edward Soja, *Thirdspace: Journeys to Los Angeles and Other Real-and-Imagined Places* (Cambridge, Mass.: Blackwell, 1996); Paul Wollen, "The World City and the Global Village," *Emergences: Journal for the Study of Media and Composite Cultures* 9, no. 1 (1999): 69–78.

22. James Donald, *Imagining*, 86.

23. Naficy, *Exile Cultures*.

24. Mayfair Yang, "Mass Media and Transnational Subjectivity in Shanghai: Notes on (Re)Cosmopolitanism in a Chinese Metropolis," in *Ungrounded Empires: The Cultural Politics of Modern Chinese Transnationalism*, ed. Aihwa Ong and Donald M. Nonini (New York and London: Routledge, 1997): 287–322.

25. Dai Jinhua, "Redemption and Consumption: Depicting Culture in the 1990s," *Positions: East Asia Culture Critique* 4, no. 1 (1996): 127–43.

26. Ulf Hannerz, *Transnational Connections: Culture, People, Places* (London: Routledge, 1996).

27. Michael Dutton, *Streetlife China* (Melbourne: Cambridge University Press, 1998).

28. Liu Xin, "Space, Mobility, and Flexibility: Chinese Villagers and Scholars Negotiate Power at Home and Abroad," in *Ungrounded Empires: The Cultural Politics of Modern Chinese Transnationalism*, ed. Aihwa Ong and Donald M. Nonini (New York and London: Routledge, 1997).

29. Anne McClintock, *Imperial Leather: Race, Gender, and Sexuality in the Colonial Conquest* (New York: Routledge, 1995)

30. See Wanning Sun, "Anhui Working Girls in Shanghai: Gender, Class and a Sense of Place" (paper presented to the workshop on Space and Place: Popular Culture in China, Hangzhou, China, June 18–21, 2001b).

31. For an analysis of the media representations of the *dagongmei*, see Tamara Jacka, "My Life as a Migrant Worker," *Intersections* 4 (September 2000), <wwwsshe.murdoch.edu.au/intersections/issue4/> (accessed November 2000); and Wanning Sun, "Indoctrination, Fetishization and Compassion: Media, Mobility and the Constructions of the Working Girl," in *On the Move: Women in Rural–Urban Migration in Contemporary China*, ed. Tamara Jacka and Arianne Gaetano (New York: Columbia University Press, in progress).

32. Mayfair Yang, "Mass Media," 300.

33. Liu, "Space, Mobility."

34. Dai Jinhua, "Behind Global Spectacle and National Image-Making," *Positions: East Asia Culture Critique* 9, no. 1 (2001): 161–86.

35. Ong and Nonini, ed., *Ungrounded Empires*, 13.

4

✛

Haggling in the Margin: Videotapes and Paradiasporic Audiences

On a trip back to China in late 1994—my first visit since leaving in 1989—my mother asked me whether I had seen *A Beijing Native in New York*. My mother lived in China and had at that time not been overseas. The show had been screened on Chinese television, and Wang Qiming, the protagonist of the drama, was a household name in China. I said that I had seen it on video in Australia. My mother went on to express her disbelief—and she claimed that her friends shared her disbelief—at the "un-Chineseness" and "meanness" of Wang's relatives. These relatives went to meet Wang and his wife at the New York airport. They then told Wang and his wife that they had arranged a job interview for Wang, rented a cheap flat for the couple in a basement, paid the bond for the flat, and then told Wang and his wife to take their time paying back the money. "Imagine doing such a thing to your relatives!" my mother commented. "Leaving them in a basement and telling them to pay back the money—and then simply taking off!" She added that most Chinese viewers were appalled. I responded that living in a basement was not necessarily degrading; and as for Wang's relatives' behavior, I thought it was quite reasonable and not particularly ungenerous. I added that I had never lived in New York, but that I would imagine the "basement scene"— discussed in detail in the previous chapter—to be quite plausible. I said, "It's hard to make you understand, but that's just what things are like over there." I kept mulling over this conversation I had had with my mother upon my return to Australia. I then tried my mother's question and response on my interviewees in Marrickville—an inner-west suburb in Sydney with a high concentration of Asian immigrants—to see whether they thought Wang's relatives were "mean" and "un-Chinese," and how they assessed basement living. Not surprisingly, they shared my reading. In addition, almost all of them added, as an afterthought, "It's hard for them to imagine what life is like here. Unless they have lived here, they will never understand what living here is like."

"They will never understand." This sounds like a throw-away remark, but for me it helps bring to light an epistemological gap between two Chinese interpretative communities. Behind this seemingly casual, though frequently made, remark, I sense a touch of mournfulness, a sense of loss, a pain occasioned by the loss of the ability to make oneself understood by people one holds dear. This, dare I say, grieving results from what Naficy calls an exile's unrealizable and insatiable desire to return to the homeland,[1] although this "return" is epistemological, not material, and what this remark seems to be lamenting is a kind of cultural, though not necessarily political or physical, banishment and homelessness.

The feeling of mournfulness and loss discussed here can sometimes be literal. A Chinese migrant now living in the United States published an article in the *Beijing Youth Daily* entitled "Return for the Funeral: The Grief of Chinese in America."[2] According to the author, one of the most frequently cited reasons for the sudden return to China by Chinese living in America is to attend the funeral of one's parents, family members, or relatives. The sadness of these returns is not so much due to the death per se, as to the failure to see one's loved one before he or she dies, partly due to the common Chinese practice of withholding news of sickness for fear of worrying sons and daughters far away, and partly due to the demands of work and life that make traveling to China at short notice difficult. The saddest scenario, which, according to the author, occurs regularly, is when the grieving person arrives at a Chinese airport only to be turned back because the traveler, in extreme distress and haste, has forgotten to secure a Chinese visa. Although these people are refused entry for purely technical reasons, they cannot be blamed for feeling a sense of betrayal and that their decision to give up Chinese citizenship—China does not allow dual citizenship—has had a punitive effect.

This sense of loss and an attending desire to compensate for it, I argue, are consistent themes running throughout the media production and consumption of this paradiasporic community. One of the few instances whereby a "return" is effectively realized is in *Our Lives as Overseas Students* (*Women de liuxue shenghuo*), a television series about Chinese students in Japan. The show was first broadcast on Channel 27 of Beijing TV in the winter of 1999 and became a success overnight. The station received numerous calls from viewers, complaining that they had missed the show due to poor promotion. The station responded by promising to repeat the show at once. The media in Beijing also reacted to the popularity of the show. *Beijing Morning News* (*Beijing Cheng Bao*) hosted a seminar of interested viewers to discuss the show, Beijing TV hosted a panel discussion on the impact of the show, and *Beijing*

Youth Daily (*Beijing Qinnian Bao*) gave generous coverage that profiled the main players of the production. Within the space of a few weeks, more than a dozen television stations outside Beijing requested permission to broadcast the program.

Zhang Liling and Zhang Huanqi, the producer and director of the marathon production, had both worked in television prior to leaving China and both obtained advanced degrees in Japan. According to them, the decision to make a documentary about the lives of Chinese students was motivated by a strong urge to record and communicate their experiences to people back home. "Ever since I arrived in Japan," Zhang Liling says:

> I have wanted to find a way to record the many things which happen around me. Some of these things are impossible to understand and cannot be accounted for with rational explanations. Yet they are true and vivid. I wanted to find a way of telling the stories of these uprooted Chinese, for the sake of folks back at home as well as for China's future generations.[3]

One example of the effectiveness of this attempt to communicate with domestic audiences is the story of Mr. Ding's—one of the Chinese students profiled in the documentary—life in Tokyo. A resident of Shanghai and a former sent-down youth, Ding worked as a kitchen hand in Tokyo for eight years and saved every penny he could, in order to secure a good education for his daughter in China. Throughout the story, Ding says that the sole meaning of his life in Japan lies in making enough money to provide for his daughter—a mentality and commitment little understood and appreciated by her, until she sees the video footage of her father struggling in Japan. Having shot the footage of Ding, the camera crew flew to Shanghai and showed the footage to Ding's wife and daughter of how Mr. Ding worked and lived. The crew then recorded Ding's wife and daughter crying freely into the camera, heartbroken to realize the extent of Mr. Ding's sacrifice over eight years. It is one of the few moments of fruitful exchange of experience between those who have left home and those who stay in the homeland.

Continuing the discussion of television dramas, I move the focus in this chapter to the diasporic consumption and, in doing so, highlight an irony in the production and consumption of this particular cluster of narratives: Both the Chinese who did "leave" and those who were "left behind" have had to rely, to a considerable extent, on the technologized images of television for the effective communication of the experiences of these "Chinese in the New World." In spite of the common remark that each migrant has a story to tell, when these stories are finally told, it is not usually done for the benefit of the migrants themselves, but rather for the benefit of nonmigrants or would-be migrants—and from their point of view. These individuals' experiences become validated and authenticated not in spite of, but because of, the electronic mediation afforded by the technology of mass media. Given this irony, it seems useful to unravel the various ways that a particular group of expatriate Chinese takes advantage of the "cultural trafficking" between the PRC and the diaspora, in attempting to articulate and reinforce a transnational imaginary specific to a group of former PRC Chinese. What constitutes the politics and process by which exiles voluntarily subject themselves to state "propaganda" by using cultural texts from "home"? In what way do their strategies and tactics of consumption contribute to the formation of a complex and ambiguous national imaginary? How can we account for a parallel but reverse process by which exiles actively struggle for the rights and opportunities to speak, rather than being spoken for, about their own experiences to the audiences back in the homeland?

The usefulness of these televisual texts in communicating one's experience to others is evidenced in the ways in which new migrants find themselves explaining and justifying the representation of migrant experiences in these products, although they usually have no control over or input into such representations. Diasporic audiences are often invited by friends and family in China to comment on and (dis)confirm these narratives, or, to put it another way, to authenticate these "New World" stories with their own experiences. This, to many expatriates, is often a fraught process. Sensing the difficulty, if not the impossibility, of being understood by folks back home, migrants find these mediated images of their lives a useful straw to clutch at in their attempts to establish some kind of epistemological affinity with those they have left behind. However, such attempts may ultimately be futile, since conversations with family and friends quite often end with something like, "It's hard to make you understand, but that's just what things are like over there."

Another significant dimension of the production and consumption of this cluster of television dramas is that the former Chinese nationals whose lives form the narrative fodder for these representations are also avid viewers of them. Here we see a good example of one consequence of the trend described by Appadurai as "increasing motion and mediation."[4] The relationship between electronic mediation and mass migration, according to Appadurai, is highly irregular and unpredictable because both viewers and images are increasingly in circulation globally. As a result of this trend, the negotiation of cultural identity through the use of cultural texts may take place in unlikely places and at unpredictable times. The globalization of cultural products and the technology of home video and, more recently, digital video technology such as VCD and DVD cooperate to give "the absent" access to "homegrown" products. The activity of watching the video or DVD versions of these television series about exilic experiences by exile audiences themselves is an interesting phenomenon—similar to someone catching a glimpse of him- or herself in someone else's mirror. If, as I discuss in the previous chapter, the visuality of the world cities depicted in these dramas invites the voyeuristic gaze of Chinese domestic audiences, the pleasure of consumption of the same products by the exilic community is much more complex. It is both exhibitionist—showing folks back home how we live—and self-reflexive, like gazing at oneself in a mirror, if we can consider the screen of television a mirror. Considering that the representations are neither produced by, nor intended for, this diasporic community, the pleasure deriving from this exhibitionism and self-reflexivity has an "illicit" flavor to it. In addition, while audiences in China who have never lived overseas may experience voyeuristic pleasure and vicarious travel, for these self-exiles, seeing their own lives represented on the screen is a crucially significant activity in the construction of an exilic intersubjectivity.

Here we have a curious scenario in which television not only provides a screen that projects their lives, but also holds up an imaginary mirror in which exilic audiences can look at themselves, wondering who is looking and who is being looked at. In this sense, the case I present here is similar to that on the use of video letters by Macedonian communities, described by Kolar-Panov,[5] in that it points to the usefulness of video technology in the formation of a diasporic imagination. It is, however, significantly different from her work, in that I not only look at a new genre of diasporic video, but more important, consider this genre a site of cultural negotiation and resistance, a site that enables both interpellation and counterinterpellation.

Migrant experiences, whenever they are constructed by the hegemonic voices of host cultures, tend to be stereotypical. However, it is not just the host cultures that subject these new migrants to hegemonic constructions. In the case of these television stories of the experiences of new Chinese migrants, their lives are also narrative fodder for state media in "the homeland." These representations have an ideological nation-building agenda, and, since migrants are not the intended audience, these representations are created in order to speak about, but not to, them. In this sense, the relevant question to ask in terms of representing the migrant experience is not so much what kind of images are represented, left out, distorted, or invented out of whole cloth or which discourses are privileged. Rather, it is whether these "less-than-patriotic" Chinese have any access to the means of cultural production or any control over the ways in which they are represented. Furthermore, if the answer is largely negative, what means and tactics do they have to communicate "the authentic migrant experience" to folks back at home?

Another dimension of the politics of representing migrant experience is that of consumption: Who gets to become the "intended" or "legitimate" audience, and hence have the "privilege" of being interpellated, to use Althusser's useful, albeit contentious, term?[6] To become a member of the "mainstream audience" in the host country, the migrant needs to possess language proficiency, knowledge of the host culture, and socioeconomic security. Although mainland Chinese students now living overseas, like any other migrant group, differ from one another on the previous indicators, there is little risk in saying that many of them are consumers of their host country's material goods more than of its cultural symbols. For this reason, migrants may, whenever possible, attempt to compensate for this lack through using cultural products from home—be they in the form of print materials, of video, or via other new technologies. However, homegrown products are sometimes viewed with suspicion by this group, either because they smack of state propaganda or because they are seen to lack artistic creativity.

MOTION AND MEDIATION

As Appadurai reminds us, world migration creates mobility not only of people but also of media images.[7] With China quickly opening up and Chinese television increasingly becoming a popular national pastime, this medium has had to find new ways of telling old stories or old ways of telling new stories. Many of the resulting drama series were produced by state-owned television, some local and others national, but many of them received considerable sponsorship from private companies, both domestic and overseas. *Broadway No. 100*, for instance, was a joint production by China's Shenzhen TV, the Shanghai-Los Angeles Culture and Recreation Company, and a Hong Kong bank. The production was also sponsored by a number of other business consortia from Macao, the United States, Shenzhen, Guangzhou, and Shanghai. The foreign money that goes into these state productions is bound to have an impact on the ways in which stories are told. The most obvious example is the controversy within the cultural sector in Japan that surrounded the making of *Our Lives as Overseas Students*, a television drama that was generously funded by a Japanese business company that allegedly had right-wing support.[8] It may well be for this reason that the show does not have a single reference to the uncomfortable history of the Japanese invasion of China, although, being a program about the contemporary lives of Chinese students, the documentary often refers to earlier interactions between the Chinese and the Japanese throughout history.

In addition, once other local and provincial television networks have bought these programs, they are free to sell their screening time to local businesses. In other words, when screened on Chinese television, these series were to varying degrees tied in with the advertising of particular products. An extreme example is *The New World*, which, when screened on Shanxi cable television, not only had the logo of Shanxi Chemical Industry onscreen, but also ran, simultaneously with the story, commercials for a provincial dental care hospital and a telecommunications company across the bottom of the screen.

The profits generated by these programs are not limited to China, although they are made primarily for television audiences in China. The reality is that despite these shows having domestic viewers as the intended audience, video copies of these marathon-length drama series usually find their way into Chinese-language video shops in the major cities of the world, where there are sizable communities of Chinese students. This means that within weeks of the first screening of these programs, Chinese overseas can see them locally at a very low cost. The videotapes become available quickly and cheaply because many are taped directly off Chinese television, most without acknowledgment of copyrights and usually with poor-quality recording. Sometimes it is even possible to tell which Chinese television stations the shows were taped from, because of the onscreen channel logos. Furthermore, once they are bought by Chinese-language video shops around the globe, these videos often advertise the business and products of the shops themselves.

As discussed in the previous chapter, what dominates these television dramas are the themes of dislocation and displacement, as well as the meaning of travel and mobility brought about by these processes. A common theme in these narratives is survival: making money, obtaining legitimate residential status, and struggling to find meaning in a liminal existence. Most series begin with some Chinese on their way to a particular world city—such as those on the Budapest-bound, trans-Siberian train in *The Danube and the Yellow Sun* (*Duo Nao He Huang Tai Yang*)—or, more often, arriving in a global airport, be it in New York or Los Angeles. Lin Yifan, the self-appointed ethnographer in *The Danube*, persistently asks himself in his diary, "Who am I?" "Why did I leave China?" "Why do I want to struggle in this foreign land?" "Will I ever return?" Although he finds that there is no easy answer, he cannot stop asking these questions. Reflecting on a seemingly unstoppable urge to go abroad, Lin points to a collective impulse that was experienced by a whole generation.

VOLUNTARY INTERPELLATION

Studying the Iranian exilic community living in Los Angeles, Naficy observes that exiles live in a "state of unbelonging," a "slipzone of indeterminacy and shifting positionalities."[9] Because of this, he argues, neither the host culture nor the home culture can easily interpellate them, for they move in a liminal space. Such freedom, however, is more often than not experienced as a threat: the fear of disappearing from both the homeland and the host culture. As a result, the exile develops a kind of fetish for things signifying the "absent home," very often via mass media such as papers in the mother tongue and television products from the homeland.

One existing study that functions as a relevant point of departure is Sinclair et al.'s inquiry into the uses of media among various Chinese communities in

Australia.[10] Their work in particular considers the role of SBS (Special Broadcasting Service) Television[11] in the lives of diasporic communities in Australia. My work resonates with theirs by addressing a common concern with the relationship between media and diasporic identity. For instance, I am told by my interviewees that SBS's relay of CCTV4 news at 6:30 A.M. every day is one of the few opportunities for overseas Chinese to find out what is going on in China. Although some comment on its "propaganda flavor," most agree that it is not so much the "truth" or news values they are after as an opportunity to keep abreast of the happenings in China. However, Sinclair et al. do not pay much attention to certain reading tactics and strategies that are deployed by one particular group of Chinese that consists of former PRC nationals who left China since the economic reforms and that, due to historical and cultural specificities, negotiates a different relationship to "China" than other Chinese communities do.

Conversations with some of these diasporic audiences indicate that a fetish for things Chinese among expatriates also derives from their overriding sense of lack. This sense of lack comes not only from a shortage of Chinese-language programs—apart from half an hour on SBS—but also from a lack of sympathetic and favorable perspectives when matters and issues pertaining to China are involved. This sense of lack is particularly acute when their "motherland" comes under the international media's spotlight. On May 3, 2001, for instance, SBS's *Dateline* host Jana Wendt[12] had an exclusive interview with China's arms control spokesman, General Sha Zhukang, discussing the incident that resulted in an American plane crash in Hainan.[13] Following a subsequent special screening to a focus group that consisted of eight Chinese now living in Perth, Western Australia, participants were asked to talk about their feelings about this program.[14] One said that he was proud of China for having such a competent spokesman; others expressed embarrassment about the white froth around Sha's mouth, but still unequivocally identified with him. A few of them were indignant over Jana Wendt's irreverent questioning manner, saying that she was "devious and calculating." Only one acknowledged that Western journalists sometimes asked tough questions even to their own country's leaders, while the consensus was that they tended to particularly do so to China's leaders.

The concept of embarrassment is worth noting here, as one only tends to be embarrassed when the gaze of the Other is felt to be present. Here I argue that for the paradiasporic audiences that watch media coverage of their "motherland," embarrassment is an emotion experienced on a daily basis. Although my interviewees thought that the froth on General Sha's mouth was natural—he was emotional and he had a lot to say—they were annoyed that *Dateline* had left it unedited. One interviewee recalled another occasion when he felt embarrassed with Australian ABC's news story of Beijing's attempt to spruce up the city to increase its chance as an Olympic bidder. According to him, ABC's camera lingered on the big brushes used by Beijing residents to whitewash the city walls. From what he could see, those brushes appeared very "primitive" (*tu*) and "unsightly" (*chou*), showing foreigners how unmodern and backward Beijing still was. He said that he was both embarrassed and annoyed—embarrassed because Beijing was shown to be so unmodern and annoyed that the television presentation of his host country was unsympathetic to the city that he called home.

The incident involving the crash of the spy plane, like the bombing of the Chinese embassy, is a hot button issue that is likely to stir up nationalism, on both the Western and the Chinese sides. American media—and the media in the Western world in general—tirelessly devote their attention to a repertoire of "Chinese problems," including China's abuse of human rights, the treatment of the Falungong cult, the controls on dissidents, the issue of Tibet, mining of internal organs for sale, environmental pollution, and issues relating to Chinese militarism and expansionism. This tendency to focus on the dark side of China is often a source of embarrassment and indignation for former Chinese nationals now living in Western countries, as well as a source of a diasporic Chinese nationalism.

At the end of the focus group's discussion, I put to my interviewees one final question: "How does it feel to watch this kind of program on television in the host country when you feel that China is unfairly portrayed?" One of them said, "Swearing can be cathartic" (*ma ren jie qi*), while another asked rhetorically, "There is nothing I can do about it, is there?" Contingent on the extent of their language competence, cultural awareness, and interpersonal skills, my interviewees,[15] rather than expressing the euphoria of freedom from interpellation by both home and host cultures, in one way or another express a profound sense of loss and even a perverse yearning to be interpellated. To be interpellated, after all, means in a sense to belong.

Gao is a forty-year-old Ph.D. candidate in computing science in an Australian regional university. He is a native of Tianjin and is now the single parent of a teenaged son. When asked whether he related to news and current affairs on Australian television, his answer was:

> News and current affairs on Australian television doesn't interest me. I'm mainly interested in news from China. If there's a choice between a story about Chinese ping pong players and one on East Timor, I'd stop eating to watch the former but not the latter. As for entertainment, comedy stuff on Australian TV, I don't like it because I don't understand it. It's too far from my life. I can never laugh when I'm supposed to.

Gao also spends a lot of time on the Internet, reading Chinese fiction, current affairs, and news. He professed that sometimes he reads materials in Chinese simply because he finds the form of "square-shaped" Chinese characters comforting. A number of respondents, when asked to nominate their favorite television programs of the host country, listed *Australia's Funniest Videos*, an entertainment program on a commercial channel. When asked why they prefer these programs, one of them answered, "Because you don't have to have good English to understand it."

Ye is a middle-aged female science researcher from mainland China now working in computer science in an Australian university. She is completing her Ph.D. degree in e-commerce and hopes to become a lecturer in computer science in Australia. Her English is less fluent than Gao's, and she has a smaller vocabulary. Ye also has a shyer, more retiring personality. When I asked her about her patterns of consuming Australian media, she said that she has become an "uneducated and uncultured person" from an English-speaking perspective (*mei wen hua de ren*) and has long since given up trying to relate to Australian media. Though she professed to spend a lot of time reading Chinese on the Internet and watching Chinese videos, Ye nevertheless emphasized that these activities could not compensate for the lack of firsthand culture from the homeland. "It looks like we have the choice between noodles and pizza, but in fact we don't have a choice."

I have also asked my interviewees whether Chinese-language products from Hong Kong and Taiwan compensate for a shortage of mainland cultural products, and the consistent answer is that these products may serve as substitutes up to a point, but they do not invoke "identification" (*rentong*). Mr. Liu from Newcastle, a small city two hours' drive from Sydney, says that he occasionally reads Chinese newspapers such as *Independent Daily* (a Taiwan-based Chinese newspaper), but seldom buys Chinese newspapers published in Australia, because they are usually "directly downloaded from the Internet or poorly edited." The quality of supplementary pages in these newspapers, he says, is also "not impressive." From these conversations with former PRC nationals emerges a consistent refusal to equate cultural products from Hong Kong, Taiwan, and other diasporic Chinese communities with "authentic" ones from mainland China. In fact, there seems to be a general reluctance to consider these places of "Greater China" to be genuinely Chinese. One interviewee said bluntly, "There is no real culture in Hong Kong, is there?"

What these people seem to be looking for is "home," and indeed Hong Kong and Taiwan, though their citizens speak Chinese languages, are not home. This desire to compensate for the lack of "authentic" home culture—a fetish for "signs" that stand for it—combined with the pleasure of identifying with these stories, sustains many hours of compulsive viewing of television dramas on video. In my partly social, partly ethnographic viewing sessions, I enjoyed these shows with my friends/research participants; observed their viewing habits, behavior, and patterns; and took part in many stimulating, though somewhat unfocused, chats about a certain plot or character. Tears and laughter were almost an integral part of the viewing experience, as was the consumption of home-cooked Chinese food and drinks. The tears and laughter of these transnationals are worth considering. They are, on the one hand, signs of empathy for, and identification with, characters like the transnationals themselves, who are trying to survive in a foreign land. The tears and laughter are also, on the other hand, evidence of the transnationals' desire and ability to be interpellated—at a bodily, as well as an emotional, level—by the state representations.

The first "Chinese in the New World" television series I watched with my friends/research subjects was *A Beijing Native in New York*, the earliest and most influential work to flow to the overseas market. The five people I watched the show with (in Lismore, a regional city in Northern New South Wales) voted it the most powerful and moving representation they had ever seen of the displacement and alienation experienced by self-exiles. A twenty-episode TV drama that followed *A Beijing Native in New York* was *The New World* (*Xin Da Lu*). Produced by CCTV's China Television Drama Production Centre (CTPC), *The New World* claims to be the first joint production between American and mainland Chinese partners. It is the story of mainland Chinese students who find themselves working for a Chinese restaurant in Chicago that is owned by a Hong Kong family. The characters are all from mainland China, all are dirt-poor, and none of them has a green card. The show is about how they survive in the shadows by whatever means are available, be it hard work, sham marriage, sexual favors, cheating insurance companies, dodgy business deals, pyramid marketing, gambling, and sometimes pure luck. To these people, nothing seems immoral, under the imperative of surviving in the New World. For them, neither the Chinese value system nor American law has any authority. Indeed, both systems prove to be more a hindrance than a help in the students' attempts to get where they want to be, for the simple reason that they are all mainland Chinese trying to make it in America. Although *The New World* is considered to be less impressive a production in artistic terms than *A Beijing Native in New York*, it is thought to be more "realistic" and more representative of the typical experiences of new migrants. After we finished viewing the show in two sittings—two long evenings interrupted only by a quick meal and an occasional visit to the bathroom, my fellow viewers—two former PRC women in their forties[16]—said that most of "us" are not Wang Qiming, and "our" stories are not as dramatic as his. "We" are more like those little people in the *New World*, trying to cope and survive in various ways.

I invited a Chinese family of four, living in Sydney, to join me to watch two other series in a friend's flat in Marrickville, a Sydney suburb. Xue is a middle-aged businessman. His English is almost nonexistent. Xue's wife was a surgeon before coming to Australia and now works as a casual in a garment factory. Their daughter (twelve years old) came to join them four years ago, and their two-and-one-half-year-old son was born in Australia. One of the shows we watched was *A Shanghai Native in Tokyo*, a twenty-episode series produced by

Shanghai TV. It has a similar flavor to *A Beijing Native in New York* and depicts the lives of several Shanghai students living in a group house in Tokyo. The show, which was also an instant success, was bought and screened by many other provincial TV stations in China and was quickly made available in Chinatown video shops in the major cities of English-speaking countries. At the end of the viewing, Xue mentioned casually that he had watched the show before—he started watching after his family went to bed and finished when they got up the next morning.

The other series we watched was *Broadway No. 100* (*Bei Lao Hui Yibai Hao*), another twenty-episode drama set in a Chinese group house in Los Angeles. This series, too, falls under the category of survival narrative, and like *A Shanghai Native* it adopts the narrative format of a soap opera. This storyline apparently has a basis in truth. Nevertheless, the "recycled" version of the same story—a series titled *Dignity* (*Zun Yan*)—was unanimously considered "crude" and reminiscent of state propaganda. However, remembering that Mrs. Xue had earlier recounted how her boss in the garment factory treated her poorly because she spoke no English, I quietly wondered if this "propaganda" had taken an unexpected turn of fate and ended up becoming a powerful source of identification for her.

These many sessions of viewing—of looking at ourselves reflected in someone else's mirror—and many subsequent attempts to explain, justify, and account for these representations have led me to conclude that in identity politics, interpellation may not simply be about "hailing" someone into place. It can happen in a more complex way; being interpellated may be voluntary and may bring the pleasure of recognition or even of acceptance. Hall's understanding of "identity" is useful here. He sees identity as

> the meeting point, the point of *suture*, between on the one hand the discourses and practices which attempt to "interpellate," speak to us or hail us into place as the social subjects of particular discourses, and on the other hand, the processes which produce subjectivities, which construct us as subjects which can be "spoken."[17]

Hall notes that "an effective suturing of the subject to a subject-position requires, not only that the subject is 'hailed,' but that the subject *invests* in the position."[18] Thinking of identity in this way—as the point of suture between the subject-position to which an individual is being hailed and the subject investing in that position—is crucial to my understanding of how an unintended interpretative community can end up being hailed. Exile audiences, though not spoken *to*, are nevertheless spoken *about* and *for*—although they may ultimately assume the role of unsolicited spokesperson for these narratives that attempt to depict the life of the exile. In other words, such audiences subject themselves to voluntary interpellation, a process by which they find themselves defending and justifying a representation—even though they are not its intended audience and have had no input into its production. Such a process is one of identification, in which exile viewers articulate a subject-position from which to speak of their own experiences, dilemmas, and desires—albeit through the characters in the fictional world of a television series. They see the usefulness of these mediated representations when they attempt the difficult process of communicating with folks at home what their lives are like "over there."

Voluntary interpellation is a symptom of an anxiety that resulted from loss. It is also a manifestation of a desire to be noticed and remembered in spite of one's absence. Being interpellated works in the way of confirmation of both the old self—I am represented, therefore I must exist; I am one of them, in spite of my absence—and the new self: I am Chinese, but I am different because I have been absent. Through interpellation, an exilic imagination is linked to the imagination of the nation from the homeland. A delineation of the self/other boundary, characterized by ambiguity and ambivalence, also becomes a pro forma, according to which the exilic population imagines itself in relation to both China and the West. A nationalism constructed within the national space of the PRC is transformed; it is displaced and dispersed into a diasporic space and thereby affords the collective pleasure of belonging—however ephemeral—to an otherwise uprooted community.

HAGGLERS AND RENTERS

However, the willingness to explain, justify, and defend a story that is not one's own, and hence to be interpellated into that story, does not mean that exiles are not making choices and negotiations. Exiles need to "haggle" because, according to Naficy, they are "liminars": they are neither here nor there; their identity is both partial and plural.[19] One important thing to haggle over is the "us" versus "them" position. A reluctance—or inability—to identify totally with the system of signification of either the official culture of their homeland or their host society, but the impossibility of distancing themselves completely from either, is a quotidian scenario that requires strategic positioning. By watching these state-sponsored Chinese productions about exiles in the West, exile viewers may allow themselves to be interpellated into a national imaginary that is constructed on the binarism of "us" versus "the West." However, by no means do they consider themselves to have a similar cultural position to that of audiences "at home." To them, Westerners are different from "us" because they have not lived in China; the Chinese at home are different from "us" because they have not lived overseas. An often-uttered remark in these viewing sessions—"They will never be able to relate to this; for them, it's just another story"—is a constant reminder and affirmation of this sense of difference.

Writing about his experience of watching movies in Third World contexts, Naficy realizes that "as movies interpellate the spectator, so, too, does the spectator interpellate the movie."[20] According to Naficy, the spectator does so by disrupting the normative spectator behavior and becoming a producer of the meaning of the movie, rather than a consumer of it. In the case of watching televisual texts produced by Chinese state television, haggling is made easy by the ready availability of video technology in domestic settings, which allows exile viewers a high degree of control over what they watch and how they watch. Remote control is also a powerful filter, since it allows viewers to take what they want and leave what doesn't suit them. Unlike domestic television audiences of these dramas, video viewers can, if they choose, use the remote control to skip the longish theme song at the beginning of each episode, fast forward through the "recap" of the last episode, cut the credits for a "fast food" version of the story, and pause, rewind, and repeat if they want to dwell on something of particular interest.

That exile viewers are hagglers is also clear from the fact that sometimes they watch a television drama only to disavow its purported representation of their lives. They may watch every episode, knowing all along that it is the product of state propaganda. Although enjoying these stories at one level—the comfort of consuming familiar Chinese signs—the exile can refuse to be implicated in the ideological position articulated within them.While my friends and I were watching *Dignity* in a Sydney home, our conversation frequently turned to Chinese propaganda. Set in Chicago, *Dignity* has an overtly nationalistic tone and resorts to a narrative formula and rhetoric that, to exile viewers, are reminiscent of the propagandistic pathos of the communist era. For instance, the audience is told by one character that Chinese students love their homeland, that they go to the United States to study Western science and technology with no intention of staying, and that in the end they return to China—something that the migrant, familiar with the decision by the great majority of students to remain abroad after the Tiananmen tragedy of 1989, finds comically unconvincing. Xue, a Beijing native now living in Sydney, seemed more impressed by the snow in Chicago than by the moral message of the series. Throughout the show, he consistently remarked on the severity of winter and the ubiquitousness of snow in that city. His comment at the end of the series was: "It looks like we've made a better decision by coming to Australia rather than going to the States. The weather looks horrible there." Xue does not seem to mind or notice the propaganda content of the show. His consistent attention, as a Chinese living in Australia who has never been to the United States, to the details of this mise-en-scène—what America looks like—again brings home the capacity of diasporic audiences to take what they need and ignore what they do not need.

In spite of the fact that the former PRC nationals constitute one of the most successful migrant communities in Western countries—many of them have secured professional positions—the televisual narratives of this group seem more interested in the downside of their struggle. In these shows, the desperate need to secure legitimate residential status, combined with slender prospects for gainful employment in a tight job market, results in many shadowy Chinese figures trying to survive in the margin. The characters in most of these narratives are hardly "heroes." Instead, they are members of a disadvantaged social group who have to engage in various petty tricks, maneuvers, and deceptions in everyday life in order to survive against the dominant system. Wang Qiming, in *A Beijing Native in New York*, has to abuse the trust of his former wife to poach a business deal from his American rival; the characters in *The New World* are variously engaged in sham marriage, insurance swindling, pyramid marketing, and gambling. Some of them even have to literally scramble whenever immigration officers appear.

Wedged between the meaning systems of homeland and host culture, neither of which is willing to validate their everyday practices fully, the exilic viewers of these programs resort to making their own meanings with someone else's stories. In this sense, they are what de Certeau refers to as "renters," who know how to insinuate their countless differences into the dominant discourses of their society.[21] Rather than joining in the intended disavowal of themselves and their lives that these narratives of tricks and deception embody, members of this paradiasporic community read them as validation— stories that normalize their not-so-dignified and less-than-noble behavior. One of my interviewees told me that when he first came to Australia, he had little money and no job. He bought secondhand furniture from flea markets when he arrived, but was too embarrassed to admit this to his Chinese friends since it was likely to be considered "shabby." He was therefore quite heartened and relieved to see Wang, in *A Beijing Native in New York*, bring used furniture off the street to furnish his home. "These shows make you realize that there's nothing embarrassing or scandalous about washing dishes in a restaurant or cleaning toilets in people's houses. You just have to do whatever it takes to survive."

In chapters 2 and 3, I show that the marginal and even phobic spaces inhabited by Third World migrants in global cities are invested with meaning, memories, and desires. I observe a number of ways in which a sense of place is crucial to one's feeling of belonging and this is often acquired through identifying either with or against a place. In theorizing place and identity, Gillian Rose shows that while some identify with or against a place, it is important to recognize that migrants in a new country tend to adopt the strategy of "not identifying."[22] Here I want to proceed from this position and add that this reality of living in the margin, hence "not identifying," is both spatial and textual. For instance, many ex-PRC nationals now living overseas continue to identify with cultural products from the "homeland," while identifying against hostile representations of China or not identifying at all. The metaphor of the renter allows de Certeau to conceive a text as a "habitable" space, like a rented apartment where the renter "furnishes the place with acts and memories."[23] This spatialization of the text is useful here because it allows me to consider these representations as having the function of "housing" the longing, nostalgia, and anxiety of a group that no longer has a psychological and emotional home. Viewing these series on video together with friends who have had similar experiences allows these needs to be performed and articulated; this has the effect of normalizing the anxiety, loneliness, and loss that inevitably come from displacement and dislocation.

The communal viewing pattern that is characteristic of exilic Chinese audiences allows collective memories to be easily activated. The consumption of nostalgia—yearning for the past and the absent home—often goes hand-in-hand with chatting in Mandarin and cooking and eating Chinese food, mostly in the family lounge room. Shared memories of jokes and events from another time; tacit knowledge of a historical ethos; the nostalgic or humorous invocation of familiar songs, music, or sayings in a new setting—all these experiences allow viewers to laugh or wax nostalgic collectively, in ways unintelligible to others. Like renters who make creative use of space in their rented apartment, these paradiasporic people make meaning of these representations in a highly creative way, generating jokes, memories, and cross-cultural observations that are only comprehensible to a specific community. In other words, this process of consumption lends itself to the possibilities of further cultural production, which occurs in a highly quotidian, mundane, personalized, and certainly undocumented fashion. For instance, in January 1999, while watching *Dignity* in a Sydney townhouse with some friends who were originally from Beijing, I found the conversation turning to the ubiquitous role of the law in American life. "In America, people like to settle their differences in court," said my friend. To the amusement of everyone present, he continued: "It's like us going to the Party secretary of our work unit to argue our case" (*jiang li*).

Exilic audiences believe that although they are not the intended audience, they get more out of these television representations of their lives than do their family and friends who are still in China. To start with, it makes the daunting task of narrating the "authentic" migrant experience to their folks at home a bit easier. Although exiles lament that mainland Chinese will never understand them, this gap between the "authentic" and the "represented" holds out the hope of finding a positive space in which genuine dialogues can emerge. There is irony in this: Increasingly, migrants' attempts to authenticate their unfamiliar experiences become possible mainly through—and not in spite of—the beguiling lens of the mass media. This happens in two ways. First, these representations offer a more vivid and realistic account of life overseas than what exiles could hope to deliver themselves. For instance, many mainland students, having read Qian Ning's work *Student Lives in the*

USA (*Liuxue Meiguo*), either in magazines or on the Internet, recommend it to their folks back home as a realistic account of their experiences.[24] A former *People's Daily* journalist and the son of China's foreign policy chief Qian Qichen, the author wrote about his observations during a few years' sojourn in the United States, providing one of the earliest, most influential firsthand accounts of student lives overseas. Second, the fictional narratives of the television series I have discussed so far function as catalysts: By commenting on, explaining, justifying, and (dis)confirming these accounts with their own experiences, exiles can enter, perhaps for the first time, into meaningful communication with their folks and friends at home about their lives in the New World. Third, it is possible that ex-PRC exiles who now live in various parts of the world and watch this particular televisual genre on video may identify with exilic experience transnationally and deterritorially. My own impulse to defend the basement scene in *A Beijing Native in New York*, despite my living in Australia and never having been to New York, derives from the fact that I share with the story's characters a similar experience of mobility and displacement. Translocal identifications in this case provide a telling footnote to an argument put forward by Ong and Nonini (1997): The locus of contemporary ethnography should be travel and movement itself, rather than spatially delimited and fixed places.

The exilic consumption of television dramas from the homeland is yet another example of how media texts and images are consumed in transition, in juxtaposition, and in betweenness. Due to this global trend, meaning-making has become a more complicated process, and it is in the unraveling of this dynamic process that the conventional distinction between domestic and international audiences, or intended and unintended viewers, comes undone. The implication of all this is clear: Identity politics needs to be investigated not just as a discourse of sameness and inclusion, but also in terms of the "smuggling tactics" of the excluded—a concatenation of performances and rituals—for it is in what Hall calls the "play of specific modalities of power"[25] that clues can be found to the ways in which exilic subjectivity is articulated, negotiated, and acted out.

ACTIVE HAGGLING: *OUR LIVES AS OVERSEAS STUDENTS*

The most direct and effective form of haggling takes the form of active participation in the production of the representations of exilic lives. Despite all these series being produced by state television, several of them have varying degrees of input from the exilic community itself, on matters ranging from funding and casting to scriptwriting and directing. An example is *The Danube and the Yellow Sun*, which was made by the TV Drama Production Unit of the Beijing Film Academy in 1997 and funded by several companies in Hungary.

The series was produced by Xue Fei, a former CCTV newsreader who, after the Tiananmen Incident, left China and went to Hungary. A target of political banishment—he was allegedly sacked as an anchorman for his behavior during the Incident—Xue has since become a wealthy entrepreneur in Hungary. Such participation may be read as the exiles' insistence on having their "Chineseness" recognized, as well as a strategy for gaining a degree of state validation of their liminal existence—an existence that had previously been frowned upon and left aside as an "untouchable subject matter," unsuitable for state-sanctioned and nationalistically motivated representation. Moreover, such validation comes not only through this newfound legitimacy as narrative fodder, but also through increasing recognition of the exiles as a group with a degree of financial and political clout of its own.

The most powerful example of active haggling is the broadcasting of the ten-episode show *Our Lives as Overseas Students* on Chinese television. Scripted, shot, and produced entirely by a group of Chinese students in Japan, this documentary, which focuses on the experiences of Chinese students, took four years to complete and had input from more than four hundred Chinese students in Japan. *Our Lives as Overseas Students* is an example of students who want to tell their story to Chinese audiences in their own way. At the time of conception, *A Beijing Native in New York* was being screened in China and was immensely popular. In spite of this, the producers opted for a documentary format. The outcome was a series of interviews with more than a hundred people about the lives of sixty-six people. To produce the film, the producers had to borrow capital, facilities, and resources and risk incurring cost without financial return because there was no guarantee of broadcasting from any television station. Although Zhang Liling, the producer, managed to mobilize support—through her personal connections—from both Fuji TV and Beijing TV, the documentary is an independent production whose copyrights rest exclusively with the Chinese students in Japan who participated in the production. In other words, these Chinese now living overseas actively haggled with both countries by taking and giving what they could. One example of such giving and taking is the role Zhang Liling played in setting up the infrastructure in Japan that allowed the satellite transmission of CCTV's Channel 4 into Japanese households. Her active liaising in the negotiation between China's CCTV4, Japan's Fuji TV, and the Japanese company that employs her allegedly resulted in landing CCTV4 in Japan at no cost to the Chinese side.[26]

Xue Fei's involvement in *The Blue Danube* and, more recently, Zhang Liling's involvement in *Our Lives as Overseas Students* signify the possibility of a turn in the direction of the movement of images. In these cases, exile audiences are no longer content to gaze at themselves through a borrowed mirror or to convey their experiences to Chinese audiences by borrowing someone else's stories. In authoring their own stories, they decide what stories to tell to Chinese audiences and control how these are told. After the show was screened on Chinese television, Zhang Liling and Zhang Huanqi, the producer and director of *Our Lives as Overseas Students*, went on Beijing television to share their experience of producing the documentary with the Chinese audience. Many of these stories unfolded in a multiplicity of locations, requiring camera crews to be present in China, Tokyo, and other places. In arranging this, the students negotiated a strategic relationship with the motherland and at the same time actively (re)shaped the ways in which the Chinese lives are imagined.

That being said, it is also clear that the exiles' relationship to dominant systems of representation—of both home and host cultures—is ambivalent. On the one hand, they want to escape interpellation, but on the other, they see the price that comes with such freedom: exclusion by, and disappearance from, both cultures. While the worry of being interpellated turns them into hagglers who must constantly negotiate new positions, the fear of banishment often makes them voluntary subjects of interpellation. Still largely denied access to the means of cultural production in mainstream culture, and rarely having direct control over or substantial input into representations of themselves, exiles inhabit a fugitive textual space, where any available tactics for appropriating and insinuating their difference into dominant discourses become crucial and effective maneuvers in constructing exilic subjective positions. It is in the dynamic process of moving in and out of these textual spaces that the complexity and ambiguity of an exilic transnational subjectivity can be appreciated. On the one hand, the exile aspires to be a global cosmopolitan who is capable of having multiple allegiances; on the other hand, the exile fears exclusion by the systems of signification and representation of both cultures, hence often opting for a strategically essentialist position of "Chineseness." As I argue in the introduction, one's engagement with the imagination of people in other places is an everyday activity that nevertheless contributes to the formation of a transnational imagination. Such engagement may take the form of both domestic audiences identifying with overseas Chinese and exile audiences identifying with domestic audiences. The circulation of television and video narratives and images of the global cities where many Chinese students have made their second home, as discussed in the previous and in this chapter, does exactly that.

NOTES

1. Hamid Naficy, *The Making of Exile Cultures: Iranian Television in Los Angeles* (Minneapolis: University of Minnesota Press, 1993).

2. Yi Min, "Going to the Funeral: The Untold Sadness of Chinese in America," originally published in *Beijing Youth Daily*, <www.clibrary.com> (accessed August 2001).

3. Quoted in Liu Fang, Liu Lishen, and Wang Wanping, *The Woman Who Chased a Dream* (*Zuei Meng Nuren*), Guangming Daily Press, 2000, 9.

4. Arjun Appadurai, *Modernity at Large: Cultural Dimensions of Globalization* (Minneapolis: University of Minnesota Press, 1996), 4.

5. Dana Kolar-Panov, *Video, War and the Diasporic Imagination* (London: Routledge, 1997).

6. Louis Althusser, *Lenin and Philosophy and Other Essays* (London: New Left Books, 1971).

7. See Appadurai, *Modernity at Large*, 4.

8. I obtained this information through personal communication with Professor Dai Jinhua in China in June 2000.

9. Naficy, *Exile Cultures*, 127.

10. John Sinclair, Audrey Yue, Gay Hawkins, Kee Pookong, and Josephine Fox, "Chinese Cosmopolitanism and Media Use," in *Floating Lives: The Media and Asian Diasporas*, ed. Stuart Cunningham and John Sinclair (St. Lucia: University of Queensland Press, 2000).

11. SBS Television was established in 1980. As one of Australia's public broadcasters, its purpose is to service various special ethnic, indigenous, and minority communities in Australia.

12. Jana Wendt is one of the most well-known Australian television personalities. She has interviewed a number of world-famous leaders and has a reputation for asking pesky questions and getting the answers she wants.

13. During half an hour's interview, Wendt was cool but persistent and Sha became increasingly irritable and rattled. He raised his voice, gesticulated wildly, and his mouth started to froth. Toward the end of the interview, he told Jana Wendt: "Don't blackmail China. China is a big country with five thousand years. It is not to be blackmailed by a country of two hundred years."

14. The viewing and the subsequent group discussion took place on June 1, 2001.

15. I conducted a number of person-to-person interviews and group discussions (a group usually consists of five to ten people) with a number of PRC Chinese now living in New South Wales and Western Australia in 2000 and 2001. Some were general interviews about their cultural consumption, others were based on their viewing of a particular program. Some of these interviewees have lived in Australia for more than ten years and had acquired residency or citizenship, while others were relatively recent arrivals studying on students' visas.

16. At the time of viewing, one of these women was trying to finish a doctoral thesis in computing. The other woman was in Australia to be with her husband, who was working as an engineer. They have since migrated to New Zealand, where they settled down permanently.

17. Stuart Hall, "Introduction: Who Needs 'Identity'?" in *Questions of Cultural Identity*, ed. Stuart Hall and Paul du Gay (London: Sage, 1996), 5–6.

18. Hall, "'Identity'?" 6; emphasis added.

19. Naficy, *Exile Cultures*, 8–10.

20. Hamid Naficy, "Theorising 'Third World' Film Spectatorship," *Wide Angle* 18, no. 4 (1996): 10.

21. See Michel de Certeau, *The Practice of Everyday Life* (Berkeley: University of California Press, 1984).

22. Gillian Rose, "Place and Identity: A Sense of Place," in *A Place in the World*, ed. Doreen Massey and Pat Jess (Oxford: Open University Press, 1995), 87–132.

23. de Certeau, *Everyday Life*, xxi.

24. Qian Ning, *Liuxue Meiguo* (Nanjing: Jiangsu Wenyi Chubanshe, 1996). For some sample chapters, see the following website: <www.shuku.net/novels/oversea/usa/usa.html> (accessed January 2000).

25. Hall, "'Identity'?" 4.

26. It is claimed that Zhang's involvement in setting up its transmission in Japan saved CCTV big money. See Liu et al., *The Woman Who Chased*.

5

✛

Fantasizing the Homeland:
The Internet, Memory,
and Exilic Longings

I have thus far looked at a number of ways in which a bounded notion of the territorial nation has been challenged by diasporic perspectives. Both the diasporic consumption of mainland Chinese television dramas and the domestic television audiences' consumption of exiles' self-presentation point to the fact that the project of imagining the nation, often problematic, is now, as Appadurai puts it, increasingly "plural, serial, contextual and mobile."[1] In other words, in an era of growing physical mobility and electronic mediation, neither viewers nor images remain fixed and stable. From the point of view of nation-building in contemporary China, these changes imply that more than ever before, one has to include a diasporic and exilic perspective in answering questions such as "What has become of national stories?" and "How do these stories continue to be told in increasingly deterritorialized spaces and in technological modes?" By implication, a different range of questions needs to be asked: What do the exiles do with their memory of Chinese history when they themselves relocate outside China? How does an ongoing involvement in the production and/or consumption of Chinese "national stories" serve exiles in the daily practice of exilic politics in their adopted country?

Talking about memory and subjectivity in the formation of a transnational imagination means confronting the inevitable disjuncture between a national culture, which, to use Anthony Smith's words, is "particular, time-bound and expressive,"[2] and a global culture, which is deterritorialized and memoryless. If one way of looking at the formation of a transnational imagination is to consider it a space where diasporic members seek identification "outside the national time/space in order to live inside, with a difference,"[3] then questions need to be asked as to whether or how well nationalist discourses serve those people now living in the trans/postnational condition. Consider the following paragraph, which was posted on a Nanjing Massacre site in 1995 to commemorate the fiftieth anniversary of the Japanese War:

> No matter how much conclusive evidence we have of the aggressive intentions of the Japanese people, many people still consider what I say to be raising a false alarm. Although today these people can ignore the clear and looming dangers, continuing to live and work in peace, when the day comes that our nation once again is conquered, there will be nothing we Chinese will be able to do to wipe away the humiliation and suffering of being an enslaved people. . . . Wake up! If you do not make a determined effort to strengthen our nation, we will soon be confronted with the death of our people and the destruction of our ancient civilisation.[4]

In terms of rhetoric and theme, the previous paragraph, written by Li Yongzhen, a twenty-year-old college student in Seattle, Washington, could very well have been written by someone living in war-torn China half a century ago at the time of the Japanese occupation. But how did such a distinctive narrative of the "imminent death of the nation" in the history of modern China make its way from the War of Resistance against Japanese Invasion waged six decades ago to this cyber-narrative of the Nanjing Massacre? The familiar trope of fear of losing one's freedom and sovereignty—effective in raising national consciousness and patriotism in the face of foreign invasion—sounds hollow and ill-fitting, in both temporary and spatial terms. For these readers and writers now living outside China, how is it possible to say, "Who is the 'we'?" "What constitutes 'our nation'?" and "Where is it?" If "we" refers to Chinese who mostly hold Australian or Canadian passports or American green cards and many of whose offspring barely, if at all, speak Chinese, what action should "we" take when "we" "wake up" to the danger facing the "nation"?

Here we see an intriguing process, whereby cyber-identity, supposedly memoryless and deterritorialized, is grafted onto a territorial notion of China—a nation united by a common past and defined by territorial borders. It also points to the disjuncture between a displaced, fractured materiality of migrants and their ways of imagining "our nation," which operate according to a spatial and temporal reality that precedes their displacement and fracture. Migrants may become more possessive on issues of national sovereignty than do their compatriots at home, in spite of the fact that for these migrants, a peopled and territorial nation called "China" is becoming increasingly a fantasy space. The intensity and urgency that mark the ways in which the "motherland" as a real place is fantasized seem to grow, not in spite of, but precisely because of, the physical estrangement of the diasporic and exilic body from China. Ironically, it is cyberspace, a virtual place, that is critical to sustaining and disseminating these fantasies. Contrary to their material identity, which is partial, contradictory, and strategic, their discourses of the nation tend to be totalizing and firmly anchored in (pre)modern notions of place and time. It is somewhat ironic that in trying to come to terms with an increasingly fragmented material reality, the exilic imagination is maintaining some kind of strategically essentialist discursive position that corresponds with the PRC's official discourse of the nation. In other words, falling into the crevices between commonly evoked markers of identity such as "exile," "diaspora," and "migrant," this paradiasporic group, being both transnational and transitional, negotiates an ambiguous, as well as an ambivalent, space between itself and the homeland. This example testifies to an important point that Appadurai makes about the formations of a post/national imaginary. Although postnational movements challenge the monopoly of the nation-state as guardians of national identities, they are nevertheless trapped in the linguistic imaginary of the territorial state, due to the lack of a separate repertoire of images, idioms, and symbols. For Appadurai, this constitutes the contradictory nature of diasporic subjectivity: "Displacement and exile, migration and terror create powerful attachments to ideas of homeland that seem more deeply territorial than ever."[5]

It is here that the relationship between historical memory and new technology becomes crucial. The Internet may provide a forum for such powerful attachments to be maintained in spite of time and distance, but it may also slow or even prevent the formations of diasporic imaginaries that may more adequately address the needs and desires arising from myriad forms of fracture and displacement. The question, therefore, is: To what extent does this global cultural form—technological, timeless, and placeless—enable or inhibit the articulation of postnational "nomadic subjectivities"?

The relationship between history and nation is a complex one. Contemporary politics of nation-states require suppressing, or even erasing, memories of certain collective traumas in order to reconcile with former enemies. However, suppressed memories do not simply disappear. They retain the capacity to be mobilized in new political contexts. Pointing to the importance of historical memory in community building, Duara suggests that historical conceptions of political community have relied on a process of radical "Othering" and that these processes are kept alive in historical memories and periodically reenacted to "mobilise the new community."[6]

Much has been written about how electronic media have transformed our understanding of temporality, spatiality, and a sense of who we are as individuals.[7] Critical studies remind us of the materiality behind the virtual reality, in terms of both gender and race.[8] Naficy's work on the use of video images of trauma and torture by the Iranian diasporic communities is relevant,[9] and so is more recent work[10] on the ways in which Croatian ethnic communities use VCR technology for the purposes of reproduction and consumption of nostalgia. Other works, set in the context of the Indian diaspora, look at whether or how the new spatiality and temporality of cyber-technology transform ways of imagining diasporic identity.[11] The power of the Internet in connecting, forging, and enhancing diasporic awareness is also clearly demonstrated in the role that Huaren[12] played in promoting global Chinese outrage over the rapes and atrocities committed against ethnic Chinese women in the Indonesian riots in 1998. In this chapter I continue to address my concern with the ways in which the movement of people and images have an impact on the formation of transnational imagination of a particular group of former PRC nationals now living overseas. Moving from film and television to the Internet, I seek to unravel the relationship between history, new technologies, and the postnational imaginary by assessing the role of new technologies in sustaining a sense of identity in diasporic contexts.

FANTASIES OF THE HOMELAND

The size of the mobile population worldwide is increasing. It consists of refugees, migrants, guest workers, transnational academics and professionals, business people and workers sojourning in foreign countries, and illegal aliens. These people deal with, on a daily basis, not only the question "Where do I come from?" but also the question "Where is my home?" For the diasporic, unrestrained by ideas of spatial boundary and territorial sovereignty, these questions are raised and answered at both the personal and the collective level. Global population movements are producing a growing tendency for bounded territories to give way to diasporic networks, nations to transnations. This tendency encourages some to argue for a "democratic cosmopolitanism" as a goal for an "emerging international civil society." These arguments also make clear that the study of the formation of post/trans/national imaginaries needs to consider diasporic yearnings and subjectivities in discursive spaces, as well as postnational movements and organizational activities of migrants. Bonnie Honig, for instance, points to both the necessity and the absence of myth, which is crucial in political movements of a transnational nature.[13] Werbner's inquiry into the south Asian settlers in Manchester suggests that the diasporic public sphere remains "a sphere of illusions" because of the "futility" of "highly localised, parochial battles" among the diasporic members.[14] I want to suggest, through the examination of a particularly influential and visible Chinese diasporic group, that such illusoriness of the diasporic public sphere may also be a result of the fact that diasporic imaginaries are largely exilic in nature and somewhat trapped in a discourse of place and time that is *national*, rather than *postnational*.

Alongside these postnational movements and migrant organizations, members of exile communities are increasingly active in seeking the means to reconnect with the homeland that they have, voluntarily or by force, left behind. This is certainly the case with the Chinese scholars, students, and business people who left China for the West prior to and since June 4, 1989. Since the 1980s, and particularly since June 4, 1989, many young intellectuals left China for political, educational, and economic reasons, most going to the United States, Japan, Canada, and Australia. Although these expatriates, particularly the political dissidents among them, remain critical of the Chinese government, they have by no means stopped identifying with China. In fact, the relative political stability and the economic boom during the years since June 4, 1989, have enabled many of these expatriates to travel freely to China; many have found professional or business opportunities there; and their personal and emotional ties with home and family have in many instances been strengthened.

In short, this group of people confronts a complex situation in a diasporic public space. On the one hand, their professional competence and ability to interact successfully with their peers abroad may afford many a comfortable or even cosmopolitan lifestyle. On the other hand, they may still find themselves in a national space—be it in the United States, Canada, or Australia—whereby their racial difference, "foreignness" of accent and behavior, or simply what Ghassan Hage calls "a third-world looking" exteriority places them in a space of marginalization on a daily basis, often in mundane, yet profoundly alienating, ways.[15] This in-between position renders many diasporic people particularly susceptible to what Appadurai calls the "anguish of displacement" and the "nostalgia of exile." In the case of this group of former mainland Chinese, absence increases their desire to see China take a more assertive position on the international stage. Indeed, as some Chinese living in the West often remark, they have become more "Chinese" since leaving China. The desire of these people to maintain some kind of connection with China can be seen in their regular consumption of cultural products from mainland China. The viewing of videotapes of Chinese television drama series by former mainland Chinese now living overseas, as discussed in the previous chapter, is a good example of this hunger for connectedness. For a community to form a sense of identity, two things are necessary: a shared memory of the specific events that have significance for the entire population and access to cultural locations that enable these memories to be continuously refreshed and articulated. In the case of many exile communities, the issue of coming to terms with the local–global nexus is more urgent, if not desperate, since their identities are premised upon a nationalism without a nation, a sense of loss, or lack, that makes them more intent on preserving whatever cultural resources they still possess. The result is an inevitable sense of displacement, manifest in the presence of a portable "memory bank." The bank, which stores memories of shared histories of national traumas and tragedies, as well as of the proud achievements and glories of the nation in the history of human civilization, is carried in the diasporic (sub)consciousness, regardless of how dispersed and displaced the diasporic body may be. Therefore, the central issue here is: If the construction of nationalist discourses relies on both the powerful emotions of patriotism and the everyday comfort of "feeling at home," how does a group of people removed from country and "home" maintain this "nationalist" feeling?

CND—A VIRTUAL COMMUNAL HOME

Three factors suggest that a good place to look for some answers to this question is the World Wide Web (WWW) pages maintained by the formerly Chinese scholars and professionals now living in diaspora. First, formerly mainland Chinese communities are increasingly strong forces to be reckoned with in the plethora of contending Chinese identities; second, their doubly "outsider" position—marginalized in their host countries in racial terms and in their homeland in political terms—creates in them a desire to negotiate a new space in which to assert their Chinese identity; third, scholars and professionals affiliated with academic and professional institutions of their host countries (United States, Canada, Australia, Japan, Europe), far more than their counterparts in mainland China, possess access to and knowledge of new computer technology, including the Internet and the WWW sites, although this gap is closing rapidly. These factors combine to make the enactments and mobilizations of certain cultural memories about China's past in these pages a significant phenomenon to study.

One of the most prominent sites maintained by this particular group of former PRC nationals is the Chinese News Digest (CND), a news distribution organization in the computer network. Founded by a group of mainland Chinese students and scholars in the United States and Canada in 1991 in the wake of the Tiananmen events, CND readers can be found on all continents, in sixty-three countries and regions, including mainland China, Taiwan, and Hong Kong. Since 1996, CND has developed from the original English service to CSS (Chinese Students and Scholars) in the United States and Canada into a news digesting and information distribution service of different sections that is customized toward readers in Canada, Europe/Pacific, the United States, and China. In addition to the English regional services, three times a week the CND-Global section provides China-related news of interest to all readers around the globe. CND also disseminates the first network-based Chinese language periodical, *Hua Xia Wen Zhai*.

Since 1995, CND has been officially registered as a nonprofit organization under the name of China News Digest International, Inc., with headquarters in the State of Maryland, U.S.A. In 1996, CND obtained tax-exempt status from the U.S. Internal Revenue Service. CND, after nearly a decade, continues to maintain its voluntary and nonprofit nature and to provide news and other information services to readers who are concerned with China-related affairs. CND editors estimate the total number of CND readers at 150,000, although the exact figure is unknown, since most people access CND publications via WWW and print-out copies, rather than through CND's mailing lists. As a community-based free service, CND is maintained by some forty active volunteers, who are "mostly overseas Chinese students and scholars" and who, according to its editorial board, donate on average twenty hours a week to keep the services running. The editorial board constantly encourages its readers to donate money or offer volunteer work. When asked what attracts them to work for CND, the board of directors says, "Not the money—that's for sure, since there is none. People join CND to volunteer for various reasons. . . . CND volunteers are either established professionals in their own careers or students working on their graduate degrees."[16]

The diasporic communities' desire for connection is, of course, not unique to the Chinese experience. Many diasporic groups in the contemporary global context use the Internet for community-building. Mitra's work on Indian diasporic websites points to the use of the Internet to express marginal voices, as well as highlights the tension of addressing in-group visitors and out-group browsers. He identifies an array of textual strategies, format, language, images, and links—in negotiating the problem of plural address. Similar issues and textual strategies apply to Chinese diasporic sites. The distinction between the intended audience and casual browsers is made primarily through the differentiating use of language. Many sites use only Chinese and even among the Chinese visitors, the choice between simplified Chinese (GB) and traditional Chinese (big5) further distinguishes Chinese who are migrants from the mainland and Chinese who live or migrate from Taiwan, Hong Kong, and elsewhere. In addition, some websites, although available to everyone and addressing the global Chinese population, have explicitly localized concerns. *Huaren*, for instance, states that although its vision is "global," it is particularly concerned with situations relating to discrimination against ethnic Chinese by local governments and people in Southeast Asia.[17] Furthermore, certain subject matters may resonate among one particular group of Chinese who share similar historical experiences, but not with others, hence setting these groups apart. For example, anecdotes and jokes about how fate played tricks on individuals during the Cultural Revolution are clearly intended for, and resonate particularly with, mainland Chinese who migrated since the 1980s.

A further technologically derived difference is between those who can use and have access to Chinese software and those who do not, as GIF allows those who do not have Chinese software to read the Chinese language as images, rather than as data. The use of images in these pages also plays an important role in allowing diasporic members to live with a split identity. *Feng*

Hua Yuan is a very popular electronic magazine in CND that is maintained by Chinese professionals and students in Canada (FCSPC). Unlike the American-based *Hua Xia Wen Zhai* (which literally means "Chinese reader's digest"), the literal translation of *Feng Hua Yuan* is "maple flower garden." The name operates on dual symbolism, maple being the symbol of Canada, and *hua*, which means both "flower" and "China." The creativity of this symbolism of a dual allegiance, which negotiates the tension between "where you are from" and "where home is now," is further evidenced in the image of maple leaves on top of the Great Wall, which serves as the magazine's logo.

"THE SPECTACLE OF DYING"—THE NANJING MASSACRE MEMORIAL

Apart from regular news bulletins and supplements (*Zengkan*), in both simplified and traditional Chinese, of essays and literature written by Chinese writers, CND also maintains a number of permanent virtual museums of the three most profoundly traumatic events in twentieth-century China—that is, the Nanjing Massacre, the Cultural Revolution, and the June 4th Incident in 1989. Remembering these three events provides an occasion for the paradiasporic community to critique the Chinese government—albeit for different reasons—as well as discursive spaces in which an ambiguous and ambivalent relationship to the Chinese state is played out. An important component of these sites is visual, in the form of photo archives, which provide "documentary" accounts of violence and atrocities that the official Chinese history has shunned or downplayed—as in the case of the Nanjing Massacre—and suppressed, as with the Cultural Revolution and the June 4th incident.

CND began its 1998 Global News Bulletin with a special issue on the author of *The Rape of Nanking*, the number 1 book on CND's Virtual Bookshelf. The special issue includes a feature story about the book, which is claimed to be the first English book ever written on the 1937–1938 Nanjing Holocaust. This is complemented by an exclusive interview with the author, Iris Chang, a young American Chinese freelance writer; a feature story on the publication and distribution of her book; and messages to the discussion group. Website visitors, mostly overseas Chinese and some Westerners, praise Chang for her work and express their rage at the Japanese atrocities. A best-seller, *The Rape of Nanking* provides a powerful and highly contested source of information to those wishing to educate themselves about the history of that particular event, so much so that it became a patriotic act among the Chinese communities to buy the book and give it to others or donate it to the local library. In spite of the existence of some well-researched works on the issue of the Nanjing Massacre prior to the publication of Chang's book (some in the Japanese language), it is Chang's book that touched off a plethora of publications in English on the same subject matter.

What does it mean for CND visitors when they find themselves, intentionally or not, taking a trip down memory lane to the nation's traumatic past? If nations are imagined through narration and, as Anderson points out eloquently, the narratives that sustain communities are to be distinguished not by their falsity or authenticity, but by the style in which they are imagined,[18] then what do these sites reveal about the Internet as a tool for the national imagining of certain communities? I suggest that in their bid to provide a collective virtual address, these sites hone in on the most repressed collective memories in China's modern history. This new space of Chineseness is a virtual communal home to many Chinese. As such, it is necessarily fraught with ambiguity and tensions—fact versus fiction, truth versus narrative, virtual versus real, image versus reality, self versus Other. Painful as they are to recall, the trips down these virtual memory lanes compensate the estranged visitor—both in the geographic and cultural sense—with a sense of belonging, in which one's Chineseness is affirmed through an act of articulation or participation. In this sense, these sites testify to the arguments[19] that point to the potency of cultural memories associated with shame, trauma, and humiliation as active agents for the redrawing of the self/other boundary. In other words, trauma and memories of atrocities become perverse catalysts for a postnational pride and consciousness, which fosters collective identification. Writing about the nature of Chinese nationalism, Peter Gries[20] points out that a sense of Chinese superiority, evidenced in the "5,000 years of civilization," is easily turned into anger when this sense of superiority is challenged or national pride is hurt. This Janus-faced, affect-determined nature of Chinese "face nationalism" encompasses both pride and humiliation. This view, Gries argues, accounts for the ambivalence in Chinese perceptions of the Sino-Japanese relationship. According to Gries, Sino–Japanese relationships, from the Chinese perspective, should be marked by a relationship that is best described as a teacher–student or older brother–younger brother relationship. "Many Chinese see themselves as the moral superior in a hierarchical relationship with Japan, not as Japan's equal." The anger and the sense of humiliation directed at the Japanese government and the Japanese in general over issues of Japan's war atrocities, as demonstrated by Chinese communities in both China and the diaspora, point to the enduring potency of anger and pride as emotional tenets of Chinese nationalism. In an age of increasing mobility—in terms of both people and images—it is the Internet, by rendering distance relatively less relevant, that continues to articulate these time-bound and location-specific sentiments.

To unravel these complex issues regarding the relationship between history, memory, and new technologies, I will examine the online Nanjing Massacre Memorial, a permanent historical archive maintained by CND. Why did CND create this particular website from the many themes/subjects/events it could have selected, given that the history of modern China has been full of violence and trauma, as well as moments of victory and elation? The privileging of the

Nanjing Massacre over colonial wars against the British (the Opium War), civil wars with the GMD (Nationalists), and international war with the Americans (the Korean War) reveals how Japan has best served as the archetype of otherness in the Chinese national psyche. The Japanese military invasions and atrocities carried out during WWII have been most frequently constructed in the nationalist and anti-imperialistic discourses in modern Chinese history. Unlike the "British" or the "Americans," casting the "Japanese" in the image of a historical enemy appeals to the widest array of Chinese communities, including those in Taiwan, Hong Kong, Southeast Asia, and Oceanic countries. It may be for this reason that the Nanjing Massacre also features prominently in other Chinese websites, such as *Huaren*, a site that caters mainly to ethnic Chinese in Southeast Asia.

Furthermore, unlike the website on the Cultural Revolution and the June 4th Incident of 1989, which seem to consolidate a sense of community among those members of the diasporic Chinese from the PRC who lived through these periods, a website on the war against the Japanese invasion more than half a century ago may also serve to soften the boundaries between PRC Chinese and various Chinese diasporic communities in terms of origin, dialect group, and generation, as well as social-economic position. At the same time, like the Tiananmen Incident in 1989 and the Cultural Revolution, the Nanjing Massacre hardens the boundary between Chinese and non-Chinese communities. In other words, by practicing both inclusion and exclusion, this website signals, first, the formation of a new diasporic Chinese identity that for particular political, historical, and psychological reasons remains wedded to a "nationalist" discourse of China, and second, the desire of this particular diasporic group to seek a culturally based identification with other diasporic Chinese communities by mobilizing the memory of a historical national trauma that is capable of eliciting emotional engagement across the broadest identification of Chineseness.

While a number of factors contribute to a renewed sense of urgency in the international arena in demanding apologies and compensations from the Japanese government for Japan's wartime atrocities,[21] some additional factors account for the emergence of a collective desire among various Chinese communities to re-revisit these issues. These reasons include a less censorial stance of the Chinese government on the population's spontaneous anti-Japanese outbursts at different times since the late 1980s and 1990s and the emergence of more diverse and pluralistic discursive spaces that articulate a collective desire for the truth about the Japanese war atrocities.[22] This is evidenced in the popularity, among Chinese readers—both domestic and diasporic ones—of publications such as *China Can Say No* (*Zhongguo Keyi Shuobu*)[23] throughout the 1990s, in which Japan, together with the United States, was the target of the anti-imperialistic discourses of China's urban nationalism. Prior to that, criticism of Japan in China was largely limited to protest—mainly in official media outlets—against the Japanese government and right-wing nationalists' unrepentance, as seen in such acts as prime ministers' visits to the Yasukuni Shrine and attempts to revise textbooks to downgrade or eliminate discussion of such Japanese war atrocities as the Nanjing Massacre and the enslavement of the "comfort women." From the early 1990s onward, narratives about Japanese war atrocities started to appear in the entertainment-oriented mass-appeal press, opening hitherto tabooed topics such as the crimes committed by Unit 731, which conducted biological warfare experimentation on Chinese civilians; the Japanese army's forced prostitution of "comfort women" from Asian countries, including China; and the use of Chinese and other slave laborers in Japan during the war.[24] Discussions on the number of civilians killed during the Nanjing Massacre and the nature of cruelties perpetuated by the Japanese army also reentered the public consciousness.

In other words, the desire of diasporic Chinese communities to revitalize memories of the Japanese war atrocities, as evidenced in the Nanjing Massacre websites, are by no means isolated or local initiatives. In calling for people to confront historical truths, these initiatives, on the one hand, draw inspiration and moral strength from the discourses of human rights and justice that are gaining momentum in the international arena and, at the same time, add ammunition to international demands for the Japanese government to officially apologize and redress the issues that resulted from the war. Similarly, these initiatives, by resonating with the anti-Japanese, anti-imperialistic sentiments that were palpable in urban China throughout the 1990s and by making available materials that the Chinese government may be wary of publishing in official media for fear of damaging "national interests," these sites accommodate and thus validate a collective Chinese desire to approach the issues of Japanese war crimes in an affective and emotional manner. Having said this, I should also point out that for this geographically dispersed Chinese community that consists of former PRC nationals, the telling and retelling of stories about Japanese war atrocities has another function. Similar to efforts to remember the Cultural Revolution and the Tiananmen Incident, these online narratives are part of the ongoing process of articulating and reiterating a paradiasporic position. Indeed, these paradiasporic Chinese, in spite of their displacement from China and geographic dispersal across the globe, are able to practice and perform a particular kind of Chineseness in a virtual space created by cyber-technology.

In short, the project of maintaining the Nanjing Massacre website that was undertaken by these ex-patriots from the PRC is an ambitious one, for its politics of identification seems to operate on a yearning that is both cultural—a desire deriving from a general self-awareness of being Chinese—and nationalist, which is more politicized and location-specific. This is made even more complex by the fact that this nationalist project, which has its emotional anchor in mainland China, is in part in contestation with the PRC's official memory of Japan and the Anti-Japanese Resistance War.

The Chinese Communist Party (CCP) uses a strategy of cultural diplomacy in playing two themes alternately in its treatment of Japan's past—namely, cultural affinity, premised, of course, on the perception of Japan's cultural indebtedness to China; and war guilt.[25] Throughout the 1980s, the Chinese government's desire to secure low-interest government loans from Japan resulted in the Chinese government consistently discouraging its people from dealing with the emotional trauma of events like the Nanjing Massacre in an organized, cathartic manner—in particular, from making public demands or filing suit against Japan. The difficulty of coming to terms with collective traumas is also closely linked to the (im)possibility of using language and technology effectively in the remembering process. Reading representations of the Jewish Holocaust, Juchau points to the importance of a history that "acknowledges its fragmented construction, which points to its gaps and absences and its silences in representing the past."[26] She cautions us that historical representations tend to, ironically, forget three things: The process of rendering the past into an account in the present is inevitably characterized by an intrinsic lack, an absence of the originating moment or event. In addition, historical discourses often adopt an "unquestioned and undefined position," and the "we" is seldom identified or placed in a social, moral, and political context. Furthermore, narratives of past events are often driven not so much by truth as by desire and are concerned not so much with the past as with the present and the future. Such a history, argues Juchau, is necessarily awkward—showing "seams and lacunae that fracture many historical representations"—and noncathartic, since it needs to "testify to its own limits of expression." Remembering deploys language to represent death, and, confronted by the Holocaust's profound madness and catastrophic scale, language is found wanting and gives way to the profusion of images, which are brought in to relieve words from the burden of representation. Implicit in such practices of visuality is an epistemological faith in pictures.

To appreciate the anger and the magnitude of the catastrophe conveyed by the Nanjing Massacre website, it is useful to visit its main menu where you are greeted by NANJING MASSACRE: 300,000 CHINESE PEOPLE KILLED, 20,000 WOMEN RAPED . . .[27] There are hypertext links to a Nanjing Massacre photo archive, with warnings of the "extremely gruesome pictures"; basic facts on the Massacres and the Tokyo War Crimes Trial; and a list of other Massacre-related pages.

Those who have spent some time browsing through the Internet know that items in this menu merely provide a list of starting points, whereby visitors can, with a click of the mouse, easily connect to a plethora of other related sites. The route of each visit could be different and is often navigated by whims and desire. Nevertheless, there is a certainty about visiting these sites: No matter how long one lingers and how widely and randomly one roams, one is likely to return feeling angry, humiliated, or sad—emotionally stirred. This is precisely the goal of the Web page. Rather than attempting to weigh conflicting interpretations of the historical event, the site is marked by an absence of perspectives that may contradict, challenge, and interrogate the claims. For instance, works that dispute the veracity or accuracy of Iris Chang's account—both discursive and pictorial—of the event in her *The Rape of Nanking* are not included in the site.[28] The implication of this is clear: Although the Internet may be hypertextual and nonlinear, the routes of such cyber-journeys may not be totally unpredictable.

China's modern national literature, born in the throes of imperialism, has long been characterized by a desire for justice.[29] This desire to seek justice results in modern Chinese intellectuals investing in the trope of suffering, an investment that aims to expose social injustice. These tropes of shame and suffering continued to be potent in history writing of the Mao era, which, according to Fitzgerald, drew on the rich repository of "remembered grievances" and "cultivated glories."[30] Along with shame and suffering, another mobilizing trope in Chinese history writing is the fear of the death and disintegration of the nation. This fear of the death of the nation, according to Fitzgerald, has played a critical part in China's identity as a historical community throughout this century, informing political intention and behavior, much as personal memory informs individual action.

Contrary to the official noncathartic approach identified with contemporary China's official memory of Japan's war crimes, the narratives on the Nanjing Massacre website have the definite effect of playing up, rather than playing down, anti-Japanese feelings. This is not due to a lack of information on how to access researched works that provide more dispassionate, balanced, or comprehensive accounts of the controversy and its place in historical memory.[31] Rather, it may be due to an inherent hierarchy of representation on the Internet, which tends to privilege pictures over words. The most attention-grabbing, indeed gut-wrenching, parts of the page are the "museum," "gallery," "memorial hall," and "archive," which contain graphic and sensational details of the Massacre—a baby on the tip of a Japanese soldier's bayonet, a close-up shot of the naked lower part of a female body with a dagger stuck into the vagina, civilians being forced to dig graves for themselves to be buried in. By clicking the mouse at "entrance," "exhibition halls No. #," visitors are ushered to these virtual spaces, where they are free to linger, go back and forth, and, again with a click of the mouse, make any of these many pictures become as big as your computer screen. In this sense, cyberspace, with its own dimensions of space and time, allows a particular Chinese diasporic community to challenge the PRC's official narratives by facilitating a discursive shift from verbal to visual, mind to body, rational to emotional, restrained to cathartic. In other words, the capacity of cyber-technology to present virtual evidence allows the narration of the Chinese nation to bypass the CCP's current politics and policies on Japan and run recourse to shame and suffering—the more primordial, though still culturally constructed, elements of nationalism.

Take, for example, the site of "Japanese Imperialism and the Massacre in Nanjing," one of the sites provided in the main page. Even without clicking on the title of each chapter to read the gruesome details, it is possible to fathom the degree of humiliation and outrage:

Table of Contents[32]
Preface: Translator's Introduction
Chapter I: Nanjing Prior to the Occupation
Chapter II: Two Blood-Stained Paths
Chapter III: Cruel Slaughter along the River
Chapter IV: Slaughter in the Outskirts of the City
Chapter V: The Campaign to Clear the Streets
Chapter VI: Killing Games
Chapter VII: Killing Competitions
Chapter VIII: Killings Committed by Military Police
Chapter IX: Corpses on the Roadside
Chapter X: Widespread Incidents of Rape
Chapter XI: Brutal Killing Committed by the Japanese Invasion Force in the Safety Zone
Chapter XII: Raping and Pillaging Committed by the Japanese in the Safety Zone
Chapter XIII: A People Who Will Never Submit
Epilogue: Li Yongzheng, "A Half-Century of Humiliation: Thoughts on the 50th Anniversary of the Victory in the War of Resistance against Japan"

A common sentiment expressed over and over in these narratives is that the PRC government has failed to act firmly in response to Japan's refusal to apologize for its war crimes, in spite of the fact that the Japanese government has at various times apologized. The demand for apology in the case of Japanese war crimes is consistent with other outbursts of Chinese nationalism, such as one that followed an incident in which the shadowing of a U.S. spy plane ended in the death of a Chinese fighter jet pilot in 2001. In these incidents, whether the "enemy" is "to apologize or not to apologize," becomes a major point of contention, thereby sustaining and even fueling anti-American or anti-Japanese sentiments.

Another popular sentiment expressed in these narratives is anger at the Japanese government's frequent relapses into unrepentant rhetoric about the war. This is evidenced in Guo Peiyu's virtual gallery, one of the many sites visitors can "enter" with a click of the mouse. Guo is an art student from Shanghai who now resides in Japan. In the introduction to his virtual gallery, Guo recounts the failures and frustrations he met with in Japan while attempting to exhibit his work (which details Japanese war crimes).

As a last resort, Guo turned to cyberspace, where he displays 3,000 faces in clay; these, according to Guo, represent 300,000 Chinese who were massacred at Nanjing:

> There are 3,000 clay faces exhibited in the museum. They express the souls of the 300,000 victims who still do not rest peacefully. For the remaining 297,000 faces, I would like to make them agents to cooperate in reforming the Japanese conscience. Please come to my museum, and let's make a society where such tragedies will never happen again.[33]

Guo's account of his desire and frustration as an artist in Japan points to an important dimension of the nature of cultural memory. Although memory is about things past, the enactments and mobilizations of them are engendered by the conditions and constraints of the present. Guo's artwork in cyberspace is premised on his material experience of marginalization as a Chinese artist living in Japan. For this reason, remembering the past is not only important in the name of the "truth," but is also useful as an intellectual exercise, because it allows him to assert his identity in both racial and professional terms. In other words, Guo's own otherness in Japan may have contributed to the hardening of self/Other boundary that marks his work. In this sense, Internet technology plays an empowering role, as it enables him to continue to articulate a culturally autonomous and patriotic position—a crucial exercise in effectively negotiating a diasporic identity. This strategy is in sharp contrast to his like-minded compatriot Feng Jinhua, who was arrested in Japan for painting anti-Japanese graffiti on the Yasukuni Shrine.[34]

AWKWARD HISTORY AND POSTNATIONAL IMAGINARY

The purpose of this discussion is by no means to suggest that the Massacre never happened, or that these photos were simulacra—the uneasiness that comes from the fear of giving such an impression has always haunted me. Rather, I want to argue that in an attempt to provide an "authentic," spectacularized version of the historical event, many important questions are elided. The use of photographic images as "evidence-and-witness" is, as Rey Chow argues, often problematic. This is evidenced, for instance, in the contestation surrounding the real meaning of two photos used in Iris Chang's book. In a number of websites, the veracity of photos, together with her facts and figures, is called into question and found wanting.[35] One picture, for instance, showing images of Chinese women and Japanese soldiers walking, has a caption, in Chang's book, that says that thousands of women were gang-raped and forced into military prostitution. It was later admitted by a Japanese historian who had originally used the photo that the picture was intended for a

Japanese news magazine and had as its caption "a group of women and children returning home from field work with the guard of our soldiers." The irony in the controversy surrounding these photos lies, however, in the fact that both those who want to condemn Japan for its war crimes and those who defend it had recourse to the visual. Visual images provided powerful ammunition, but in the attempt to mobilize them, their power appeared to have been both revered and abused. The reuse of photos and pictures is even more problematic when images are transferred from a "hard copy" onto a virtual space, given that computer technology makes it easier to both reproduce and manipulate images, thereby making it more difficult to ask critical questions as to who took these pictures and what the narratives behind these images are. It thus can be seen that there are some structural contradictions in post-national identity formations on the Internet. On the one hand, the hypertextuality of the WWW technology problematizes the notion of authorship, as well as the activity of reading as a linear process. In addition, the possibility of linking to other pages makes the direction and intensity of the page visitor's movements largely unchartered. "Wandering" from the museum to the gallery, "browsing" readings in the virtual library, the visitor's itineraries may differ from one another, as well as differ each time she or he makes the visit. However, instead of this, the Internet has produced a group of self-appointed "cyber-historians"—artists, writers, and academics who consider photos and images to be much more telling and authoritative evidence of historical truth than documentary sources are. In other words, in spite of cyber-technology's textual capacity to destabilize and fragment the notion of history of both the reader and the writer—indeed, sometimes they are both reader and writer at once—the narrative presented in this cyberspace seems to encourage a view of history that is in fact linear and totalizing. Lavish use of historical photos, which are usually associated with historical/journalistic credibility, seems to be premised on an authoritative, modernist notion of visuality.

The ease with which computer technology produces cyber-historians, as well as images of suffering, has also resulted in the proliferation of images of the violation of Chinese women's bodies by Japanese perpetrators during the Massacre. Here we see an instance in which cyber-technology consolidates, rather than disables, a long-established complicity between an anti-imperialist discourse and a masculinist point of view. Confronted with these pictures, visitors to the virtual galleries are told that to download, print, or see these pictures enlarged on the screen, they simply have to "click the mouse." The visualization of the violated female bodies and images of their suffering in this case is, I argue, deeply problematic. Most of the people who visit the Nanjing Massacre website are bilingual, professional, and probably predominantly male. In the same way that desirable female bodies (or body parts) are recruited as objects of men's desire in advertising discourses in the service of consumption, the images of violated female bodies, as many have pointed out, may also be used either as a metonym in representing the traumatized nation in anti-imperialist discourses or as a metaphor for the oppressed in class-struggle narratives.[36] For this reason, any analysis of the recruitment of images of suffering and shame needs to start with interrogating, not eliding, questions of the materiality of the producers of these images. This is because even though these cyber-historians consider that it is their Chinese *tongbao* (compatriots) that were victimized, their status is not identical with that of the people whose images we are looking at. In this sense, Internet technology, in spite of its capacity for hypertextuality and fusion of authorial and reader's position, normalizes, rather than highlights, the absence of a critical consciousness. These Chinese professionals and scholars' use of the Internet in reproducing images of cruelty and pornographic acts is not dissimilar to Algerian-born scholar Alloula's use of picture postcards of Algerian women in his critique of the European phantasm of the Oriental female, which, according to Chow, exhibits Algerian women as the silent objects represented not only by the French, but also by Alloula's own anti-imperialist discourse. In other words, anti-imperialistic narratives, whether on the Internet or not, run the risk of perpetuating, rather than dismantling, the "pornographic apparatus of imperialist domination" by "crossing over the images of native women as silent object."[37] Chow's point about the Third World male historians' and writers' visualization of the female in anti-imperialistic discourses becomes even more relevant in the age of the Internet.

There also seems to be an incongruity between a continuous use of familiar narrative style and an absence of the ritual of collective participation that sustains such traditional pathos. People who grew up in mainland China in the 1960s and 1970s—in other words, many of these page visitors—when "class struggle" was the privileged political discourse, should remember the ritualized act of "speaking bitterness" (*su ku*). Model workers or peasants spoke to organized crowds about how hard life was under the oppression of the Guomindang (the Nationalist Party) and feudal landlords before the CCP liberated China. These mass rituals were conducted in a spirit of "lest we forget." The speaker usually showed the audience some material objects as evidence of hardship and oppression, and his or her talk was regularly and ritualistically interrupted by emotional, tearful audiences shouting, "Never forget the past bitterness!" (*bu wang jie ji ku*). Although the "speaking bitterness" ritual ended with the disappearance, for the most part, of the discourse of "class struggle" following Mao's death, its rhetorical techniques of achieving emotional engagement and maximizing audience participation seem to be still at work in these virtual memorials. In lieu of raising fists and shouting slogans, the emotionally charged cyborgs facing the computer screen have recourse to nothing other than expletives to express their anger. This is one reason why "flames" and the Internet are inherently linked. Among the six recent cyber-attacks launched by angry Chinese hackers, two of them targeted

Japanese websites—including official ones—in protest of the Japanese Education Ministry's attempt to revise the history of Japanese aggression in Japanese textbooks and some Japanese websites that carried materials that denied the truth of the Nanjing Massacre.[38]

This is mostly seen in the style and content of the accounts of the Nanjing Massacre by individual survivors and witnesses of the event, which, once publicized, acquired a collective significance. The combination of the close-up visual presentations of traumatized bodies in virtual photo archives and emotionally charged personal accounts detailing atrocities culminates in a surge of anti-Japanese feelings for website visitors. However, although they may have bodily and emotional responses to these images, in the absence of a ritualized collective catharsis, they can only resort to the virtual by entering their names in the guest book of the website or "posting" their responses on the message board as a way of voicing their moral support. In a similar way that cyber-historians have no access to the bodily experience of addressing an empathetic audience, as was formerly the case in the *su ku* setting, these addressees—website visitors—are denied the opportunity to participate and interact in a bodily fashion. In other words, cultural signs are still deployed, but are at once disabled by a lack of signifying context. CND, like other diasporic websites, is a mediated space, whereby a deterritorialized site *about* China is substituted for a territorial nation that *is* China. Instead of going back to the PRC, providing technical support, or donating money to people in the homeland, these displaced Chinese maintain their connection not just with China, but increasingly with things Chinese, by offering their volunteer work and donations to CND. As the CND editorial says:

> Many of them (CND volunteers) . . . work co-operatively through the computer network. As the years pass by, groups of CND members have held joyful mini-gatherings whenever they have the chance. Still many of them have never met their colleagues in person.[39]

It is thus clear that partly through cyber-connections, this communality is maintained. Here we see a highly complex and ambiguous scenario: Cyber-technology is embraced by a group of dispersed Chinese wanting to maintain some kind of collective sense of belonging, and the Internet, as a deterritorialized space, makes it possible by overcoming space and time. However, the mode of address on the Net, which is marked by a body/text split, also seems to heighten, rather than overcome, the sense of absence.

Many of the Chinese scholars and professionals now living in the West are self-exiles who left China before and after the June 4th Incident of 1989. While some have succeeded, even brilliantly, in their professional or academic pursuits, they, as well as their less successful nationals, may have lived a peripheral and alienating existence in their adopted countries. Meanwhile, the culture of the natal country continues to change, transform, and develop in ways that the migrant may not be able to anticipate or even understand. The experience of double marginalization—that is, from both their natal and adopted countries—may generate a complex array of divided loyalties and systems of reference. Many members of these diasporic communities, like other newcomers, have experienced disorientation, alienation, and loneliness. The constant traversing of borders between inclusion and exclusion, the familiar and the strange, here and there, us and them, can result in a somewhat liminal existence—what I refer to as the unbearable lightness of being in-between.[40] Websites like CND's highlight a contradiction between a tendency toward an increasingly displaced and fractured postnational identity and an essentialist discourse of national Self and Other. Because of its deterritorialized nature, cyber-technology makes such contradictions not only possible but also intrinsic.

CYBERSPACE AND DIASPORIC PUBLIC SPHERE?

In what way is exilic subjectivity formation dependent on shared histories? How is history constantly tapped to construct an identity of dispersal and displacement? Are these new forms and strategies of narrating the (post)nation, which are inspired and enabled by the new technologies, or is it simply that new technologies are reproducing the existing national pathos? The very existence of the Nanjing Massacre pages, as well as those on the Cultural Revolution and June 4th Incident, suggests that in the enterprise of using history as a source of appropriation, partial forgetting, and selective remembering, cyber-technology is not fundamentally dissimilar from other forms of representation. Estranged from their "homeland," members of the diasporic communities tend to hold on to a sense of history, as collective memory is one of the few things that they have in common with their increasingly imaginary homeland. Under these circumstances, cyber-technology, with its capacity to transcend distance, is likely to continue to be regarded as empowering to those whose desire for cultural affinity with China comes from the material reality of not being "there." This geographic lack will continue to be compensated for through the growing importance of memories—memories of the past that are portable, potent, patriotic, and available for constant and repetitious retrieval.

The "radical process of Othering"—indispensable to the nationalist discourses in the history of the modern Chinese nation—is clearly continuing in the identity politics of cyberspace. The softening and hardening of the self/Other boundary is determined not only by images of collective identities circulated in mass media, but, more important, by their individual experiences of being "othered"—in terms of race, ethnicity, gender, and/or class— in their adopted countries. In these circumstances, cyberspace may become a

new space to accommodate a reorganized hierarchy of ignorance and preju-
dice. This is most poignantly evidenced in the heated and sometimes hostile
discussions posted on the Nanjing Massacre Virtual Monument Guestbook.
Internet communications, unlike other forms of mass media, are decentralized, nonlinear, and interactive, and for this reason, they seem to herald new
possibilities of democratic and rational public debate. One may also hope that
the organic body, specifically located in the prevailing hierarchy of race, gender, age, class, and socioeconomic status, may be hidden by a computer terminal, allowing all to become "equal." However, communications between
visitors to the virtual monument chat room are clearly not equal, let alone rational. One visitor, for instance, calls a fellow visitor "arse-kissers of Jap
dwarf" for defending the Japanese invasion, while another calls those who op-
pose boycotting Japanese products "shameless." Although name-calling is a
way of venting anger and frustration, others resort to more subtle put-downs
to mark their intellectual, moral, and political superiority. A visitor is advised
by a fellow visitor to write in Chinese instead of English, in order to make
himself understood, and is told by another visitor that his English is a bit
"rustic." Reading the "(post)nation" and its Other on the Nanjing Massacre
sites, as well as on their many related pages, seems to suggest that nationalism is becoming less an ideology of the nation-state and more a personal project motivated and sustained by the desires of postnational diasporic individuals. In the constant articulation of one's position, the self/Other boundary is
subject to constant shifting. A related change is that Chineseness becomes
less an unproblematic and privileged marker of identity for those living in the
mainland and more a free-floating signifier whose ownership is up for grabs
among those who have left China. Furthermore, though history is still written and rewritten to "let the past serve the present, the foreign serve China,"
the totality and singularity of the official history of modern China are open
to new forms of challenge, with its repressed memories mobilized elsewhere
in the formation of new Chinese communities. Cyber-technology, with its capacity to transform spatiality, temporality, and embodiment, provides an enabling matrix—for those who have access to it—under which conflicting narratives of the national past contest one another.

Writing about the experience of migrants, Madan Sarup observes that for
migrants, identity is about becoming, not "being," and expressing nostalgia and
loss is part of that becoming.[41] This process of becoming, according to Trinh
Min-ha, is a process of ongoing articulation.[42] This constant articulation of
what one has become or what one is becoming in postnational contexts also
constitutes an important part of Bhabha's "narration of the nation."[43] In the
case of Chinese scholars now living in North America, Japan, and other Western countries, in order to remain Chinese, one has to keep telling stories of being Chinese. Collective memories of China are kept alive by these self-exiled
Chinese, not only by the constant retelling of familiar national stories, but also

by the repetitive deployment of familiar forms and strategies of storytelling. Unlike many Chinese living inside China, for whom foreign places such as New York or Tokyo constitute the stuff of their fantasies, these Chinese who have left China now find themselves on the other side, fantasizing a sovereign, territorial China under the siege of an imperial Other. This fantasy is sustained by constantly renewing, rediscovering, and regenerating a collective sense of humiliation and anger for the enemy from the past. The Internet and cyber-technology, more than any other forms of mass media, enable such a project to take place in a displaced and deterritorialized fashion.

Cyberspace, in this sense, becomes a vitally significant space for the telling and retelling of national stories. In the same way that remembering the past is motivated by the politics of the present, condemnation of the historical Other may say as much or more about the fear, insecurity, and desire of the contemporary self than about the Other. For those Chinese *hai wai you zi* (Chinese descendants wandering overseas), the Internet and WWW technology will continue to activate Chinese memories, a history of "remembered grievances and cultivated glories." In addition, it would be wrong to equate the formation of transnational imagination only with the articulation of desires and fantasies and to leave out the loathing and hatred for the Other that the Nanjing Massacre website reveals so starkly. Furthermore, fantasies about the self and the Other hinge on imagining the future—collective dreams—but equally significantly, on remembering the past, collective nightmare.

What seems uncanny is that in spite of, or perhaps because of, the tension between new technology, which is memoryless and deterritorialized, and memory, which is bound by a specific notion of time and place, the Internet and its attendant cyberspace prove to be hugely enabling in articulating a strategically "pure" collective subjectivity. Here we see an interesting reversal of the argument concerning identity and the Internet. While, as Turkle argues,[44] role playing in MUDs (Multi-User Dungeons) allows individuals to take on an identity that is more multiple, heterogeneous, and fragmented than in real life, on a collective level the Internet can be used by translocal members of a particular community to negotiate an essentialist identity position as a way of coming to terms with an identity that in material life is marked by difference, multiplicity, and fragmentation.

However, postnational identities, characterized with "translocal solidarities" and "cross-border mobilisations,"[45] are still stuck in a discourse of the nation rooted in the nation-state. Postnational discourses still deploy both a sublime and a mundane sense of nationalism, which not only inherit a notion of place based on territoriality, but also are trapped in a nation-state's memory of the past. In addition, discourses of the nation continue to use a patriarchal trope of masculinity, male honor, and the female body.

Internet technologies seem to highlight, rather than resolve, the predicaments of dispersal and displacement. This lack of a political language explains the contradictions, tensions, and ambiguities that I identify here. While Internet technology can overcome traditional notions of time and place, it nevertheless also highlights, rather than compensates for, the limitation and inadequacy of the existing discursive resources in diasporic identity politics. As we head toward a postnational diasporic public sphere at the beginning of the new century, we see that the uncertainties of its constitution suggest that a "diasporic public sphere" will not be truly possible unless and until diasporic communities find themselves a political "voice" that best serves the interests of the postnational identity. Internet and computer-mediated technology may "amplify" that voice once it is found, but should never be expected to substitute for or produce that voice per se.

NOTES

1. Arjun Appadurai, *Modernity at Large: Cultural Dimensions of Globalization* (Minneapolis: University of Minnesota Press, 1996), 176.

2. Anthony Smith, "Towards Global Culture," in *Global Culture: Nationalism, Globalisation and Modernity*, ed. Mike Featherstone (London: Sage, 1990), 178.

3. James Clifford, "Diasporas," *Cultural Anthropology* 9, no. 4 (1994): 308.

4. Nanjing Massacre Site, <museums.cnd.org/njmassacre/njm-tran/njm-ch14.htm> (accessed September 2001).

5. Appadurai, *Modernity at Large*, 177.

6. Presanjit Duara, *Rescuing History from the Nation: Questioning Narratives of Modern China* (Chicago: University of Chicago Press, 1995), 51.

7. For example, see Sherry Turkle, *Life on the Screen: Identity in the Age of the Internet* (London: Phoenix, 1995).

8. For cyberspace and race, see Cameron Bailey, "Virtual Skin: Articulating Race in Cyberspace," in *Immersed in Technology*, ed. Mary Anne Moser (Cambridge: MIT Press, 1996). For cyberspace and gender, see Donna Haraway, *Simians, Cyborgs, Women: The Reinvention of Nature* (New York: Routledge, 1991).

9. Hamid Naficy, *The Making of Exile Cultures: Iranian Television in Los Angeles* (Minneapolis: University of Minnesota Press, 1993).

10. For example, see Dana Kolar-Panov, "Video as the Diasporic Imagination of Selfhood: A Case Study of the Croatians in Australia," *Cultural Studies* 10, no. 2 (1996); and Zatko Skribis, "Making It Tradable: Videotapes, Cultural Technologies and Diasporas," *Cultural Studies* 12, no. 2 (1998).

11. On the Internet and the Indian diaspora, see Ananda Mitra, "Marginal Voices in Cyberspace," *New Media and Society* 3, no. 1 (2001); "Diasporic Websites: Ingroup and Outgroup Discourse," *Critical Studies in Mass Communication* 14, no. 2 (1997); and "'Nations and the Internet': The Case of a National Newsgroup, 'soc.cult.indian,'" *Convergence: Journal of Research in New Technologies* 2, no. 1 (1996). On the Internet and the exilic communities from Iraq, see Ella Shohat, "By the Bitstream of Babylon: Cyberfrontiers and Diasporic Vistas," in *Home, Exile, Homeland: Film, Media, and the Politics of Place*, ed. Hamid Naficy (New York: Routledge, 1999). Shohat's work also discusses the possibilities of the Internet in the formation of a multicultural feminism.

12. *Huaren* is a website <www.huaren.org/> maintained by the World Huaren Federation. News of rapes of ethnic Chinese women by Indonesians in May 1998 was widely publicized by the site. For a republication of "Tragedy and Technology Makes Overseas Chinese Unite," from *The Straits Times*, August 8, 1998, see <www.straitstimes. asia1.com/pages/cyb1_0820.html>.

13. Bonnie Honig, "How Foreignness 'Solves' Democracy's Problems," *Social Text* 16, no. 3 (1998): 1–27.

14. Pnina Werbner, "Diasporic Political Imaginaries: A Sphere of Freedom or a Sphere of Illusions?" *Communal/Plural: Journal of Transnational and Cross-Cultural Studies* 6, no. 1 (1998): 11–32.

15. Ghassan Hage, *White Nation: Fantasies of White Supremacy in a Multicultural Society* (Sydney: Pluto Press, 1998).

16. See website <cnd-board@cnd.org> (accessed October 2001).

17. See *Huaren*, <www.huaren.org> (accessed May 1988).

18. See Benedict Anderson, *Imagined Communities: Reflections on the Origins and Spread of Nationalism* (London: Verso, 1983).

19. For example, see Lucien Pye, *The Spirit of Chinese Politics* (Boston: Harvard University Press, new ed., 1992).

20. Peter Hays Gries, "'A China Threat?' Power and Passion in Chinese Face Nationalism," *World Affairs* (Fall 1999), <www.findarticles.com> (accessed August, 2001).

21. In a talk at the University of Toronto on September 28, 2001, Mark Selden noted a number of reasons for this new wave of demands for apologies and war reparations among some Asian countries and the United States. Among the reasons cited are the growing momentum of the international human rights movements, the emergence of transnational feminism, the end of the Cold War, and, increasingly, U.S.–Japan tensions.

22. The role played by the Chinese media in keeping the memory of war alive will be discussed in greater detail in the section involving the Koei Incident and the JAL incident in chapter 7.

23. *China Can Say No* (*Zhongguo Keyi Shuobu*), by Song Qiang, Zhang Zangzang, and Qiao Bian (Beijing: Zhonghua Gongshangliang Chubanshe, 1996).

24. The stories of Liu Lianren, a Chinese national who went into hiding in the mountains for many years in order to escape forced slavery during the war, for instance, was extensively covered in these mass-appeal papers in the early 1990s.

25. See Hidenori Ijiri, "Sino–Japanese Controversy since the 1972 Diplomatic Normalisation," *China Quarterly* 124 (1990): 639–61, for an account of the cultural diplomacy; and Wanning Sun, "People's Daily, China and Japan: A Narrative Analysis," *Gazette: The International Journal for Mass Communication Studies* 54, no. 1 (1995): 198–207, for the role of the Party media in such cultural diplomacy.

26. Meirelle Juchau, "Forgetful Memory: The Holocaust, History and Representation," *The UTS Review: Cultural Studies and New Writing* 2, no. 2 (1996): 70.

27. See the Nanjing Massacre site <museums.cnd.org/njmassacre/> (accessed October 2001).

28. For an example of such perspectives, which contradict and repudiate Iris Chang's claims, see websites such as <www.jiyuu-shikan.org/nanjing/contents.html> (accessed October 2001), which are run by Japanese ultra-nationalists whose mission it is to defend or deny the war atrocities committed by the Japanese army.

29. Rey Chow, *Writing Diaspora: Tactics of Intervention in Contemporary Cultural Studies* (Bloomington and Indianapolis: Indiana University Press, 1993); Pye, *Chinese Politics.*

30. John Fitzgerald, "'Reports of My Death Have Been Greatly Exaggerated': The History of the Death of China," in *China Deconstructs: Politics, Trade, and Regionalism,* ed. David S. G. Goodman and Gerald Segal (London: Routledge, 1994), 23.

31. For instance, the CND lists a number of titles that belong to this category. See works by, for instance, Katsuichi Honda, Timothy Brooks, Joshua Fogel, Laura Hein, and Mark Selden, among others. The listing of these titles in the website, though a valuable source of information, does not lend itself to "good" visuality. To many cyber-browsers hungry for a quick feed—or a quick tour—online galleries and museums, with their visuality and immediacy, stand a much better chance of having more impact.

32. See <museums.cnd.org/njmassacre/njm-tran/index.html> (accessed September 2001).

33. See <museums.cnd.org/njmassacre/njm-tran/njm-ch14.htm> (accessed September 2001).

34. See my introduction for an account of Feng and chapter 7 for online reactions to Feng's arrest.

35. For instance, see <www.members.tripod.com/~funkytomoya/massacre/sample01. htm> and "doctored" photos in <www.jiyuu-shikan.org/nanjing/contents.html> (accessed October 2001).

36. For the female body and the Chinese nation, see Lydia Liu, "The Female Body and Nationalist Discourse: Manchuria in Xiao Hong's Field of Life and Death," in *Body, Subject, and Power in China,* ed. Angela Zito and Tani Barlow (Chicago: University of Chicago Press, 1994). For the violated female body as a metaphor in class struggle narratives, see Meng Yue, *"Nuxin biaoxiang yu minzhu shenghua"* ("Representations of the Female and National Myths"), *Er shi yi shi ji* (The 21st Century) (April 1991): 103–12.

37. Chow, *Writing Diasporas,* 41.

38. See <www.clibrary.com/digest/0108/13026.html> (accessed October 2001).

39. See <www.cnd.org> (accessed October 2001).

40. Here I appropriate the title of Milan Kundera's well-known book *The Unbearable Lightness of Being,* about the position of intellectuals in the Communist regime.

41. Madun Sarup, "Home and Identity," in *Travellers' Tales: Narratives of Home and Displacement,* ed. George Robertson, Melinda Mash, Lias Tickner, Jon Bird, Barry Curtis, and Tim Putnam (London and New York: Routledge, 1994).

42. Trinh Min-ha, "Other Than Myself/My Other Self," in *Travellers' Tales: Narratives of Home and Displacement,* ed. George Robertson, Melinda Mash, Lias Tickner, Jon Bird, Barry Curtis, and Tim Putnam (London and New York: Routledge, 1994).

43. Homi Bhabha, "Dissemination: Time, Narrative, and the Margin of the Modern Nation," in *Nation and Narration,* ed. Homi Bhabha (London: Routledge, 1990).

44. Turkle, *Life on the Screen.*

45. Appadurai, *Modernity at Large,* 177.

6

✛

Eating Food and Telling Stories: From Home(land) to Homepage

A number of anecdotes emerge from my conversations on food consumption with some former PRC nationals now living overseas. One participant told me that in the place where she used to live in New Zealand, prior to coming to Australia, wild chives (*jiu cai*), a favorite vegetable of the Chinese, used to be a weed that grew ubiquitously and in abundance, until the Chinese arrived there in large numbers. Another anecdote concerns the gradual decrease of carp (*li yu*) in Lake Burley Griffens, a large manmade lake in Canberra, the capital of Australia. Carp are considered to be unclean and inedible there, and because local fishermen tended to throw them back whenever they were caught, there was an overpopulation of carp in the lake, until the Chinese in the city discovered them. Still another common remark was that some landlords were reluctant to rent accommodations to Chinese students, worrying that a lot of frying in the kitchen would create excessive grease and smoke. If I have, in the previous chapter, conjured up a scenario of a displaced and dispersed Chinese community consisting of "surrogate travellers of cyberspace,"[1] going back in time to fantasize about returning to a motherland that is territorial and sovereign, the previous anecdotes are a reminder that these virtual travelers—in both a spatial and a temporal sense— also have a body, which smells, touches, hears, tastes, and, above all, is kept alive by eating food. Physical displacement from the homeland means that the exiled body has to negotiate what the stomach likes to eat and what is available in the host country. These anecdotes, which are circulated among the Chinese about eating in exile, also articulate an awareness of what the presence of the corporeal bodies of exiles like themselves do to a locality. Although displacement can to some extent be compensated by frequent virtual journeys to the imaginary homeland, the question of what the displaced body eats in a foreign land remains. As Morse puts it plainly: "Travellers on the virtual highways of an information society have, in fact, at least one body too many—the one now largely sedentary carbon-based body resting at the control console that suffers hunger, corpulence, illness, old age, and ultimately death."[2] Here Morse reminds us of the corporeal materiality of cyber-travelers and argues that "what cyborgs eat" in the electronic culture is by no means a mundane or trivial question.

While Morse is right to remind us of the materiality of the cyborg—defined as part-human, part-cyberian—I want to, as a matter of urgency, add that this materiality consists of a racial, social, and gendered, as well as a biological, dimension. For this reason, it is important to go further than Morse's question as to "what cyborgs eat" and to address a number of other questions. First, what happens to the migrant's palate and memory of eating in the transnational spaces, where people not only eat different food, but also eat food differently? Second, how do "ethnic" cooks serve, eat, and, equally important, talk about food in their "multicultural" host countries, in ways that allow them to articulate a particular kind of transnational subjectivity? Finally and most important, how do the Internet and its attendant cyberspace—a placeless space—keep memories of sensory experiences, which are time-bound and location-specific, alive and fresh?

Talking about food and eating in the context of place and transnational imagination produces a new angle from which to study the intersection of food and subjectivity, for it represents a step beyond the "you-are-what-you-eat" thesis[3] and "you-are-where-you-eat" thesis.[4] It also goes beyond the food-ethnicity coupling. Narayan's work, for instance, looks at the ways in which curry is located within cultural spheres and across boundaries separating colonial India and imperial England. She observes that "ethnic food" is used in England in ways that reflect the practice of "food colonialism."[5] When the intersection of food with ethnicity is discussed,[6] it is usually dealt with from the point of view of the "mainstream" and tends to focus on the ethics of ethnic eating. Hage's study of Australian multiculturalism, for instance, points out that ethnic food serves as a metaphor of cultural diversity, but that such diversity is displayed to "enrich" the lives of white Anglo cosmopolitans.[7] In other words, the ethnic is assigned the role of the "feeder," not the "eater." Susan Sheridan's work on the *Australian Women's Weekly*'s culinary interests, for instance, suggests that the social-symbolic value of food lies in its capacity to embody the fantasy of consumers who wish to mark themselves as being different from the "Other" in class and ethnic terms by eating the food of the Other and by consuming the notion of difference, thus eating the Other.[8]

Food is also seen to have a close relationship to national identities. Roland Barthes writes about food and Frenchness, and Nietzche is known to argue that nations are the product of the food they ingested.[9] A distinctive cuisine, a shared food vocabulary, and cooking practices are perceived to be essential elements in defining a nation.[10] It is for this reason that both travel guides to foreign countries and anthropologists who study "other cultures" prominently feature the cuisine of the country. Food, more than housing, dress, and language, plays an indispensable part in sustaining the body and functions as a cultural practice that sets insiders apart from outsiders. Given that food has been talked about in the context of national identity, and eating exotic food is often associated with mobility, it seems surprising that a largely unexplored perspective concerns the unique ways in which food, as well as discourses surrounding food and eating, articulates a sense of the self and a sense of belonging to a particular place. Equally surprising is an underdeveloped understanding of how practices and discourses surrounding food assist or inhibit the formation of transnational imagination, as do watching television or visiting virtual museums on the Internet.

So what do watching images of foreign places on television and eating exotic food have in common? To start with, watching a television program about a foreign city—as in the case of Chinese viewing images of New York on Chinese television dramas—is akin to eating ethnic food in one's home or the local ethnic restaurant. Both offer a representation or images of faraway places. Both the viewer and the diner partake of some kind of virtual travel via the mediation of these images. It may well be for this reason that recipes for cooking ethnic food are sometimes described as the guides in "kitchen table tourism,"[11] whereby the eater/tourist gets a sampling of foreign cultures through their food, without really engaging with knowledge of the food practices of the ethnic communities. David Harvey argues that due to time-space compression, images of ethnic food travel faster than the migrants of ethnic groups, so much so that the world's cuisine can be assembled in one place in a similar fashion as images of the world are screened on TV on any given night.[12]

In addition, although images are made to represent foreign places, while food is made to embody them, there is a structural asymmetry and unevenness in the ways in which both the media images of, and food from, foreign places are represented and consumed. When those from the "center" consume images of, and food from, the periphery, it represents a desire, as Hage observes, to enjoy the alternative and diverse lifestyle that is essential to the definition of cosmopolitanism. Such cosmopolitan tastes involve the appreciation of the traditional, the earthy, the exotic, and the authentic. In contrast, those in the "periphery" consume images of, and food from, foreign countries often to partake in fantasies—including both fear and desire—about being modern and Westernized. In other words, in spite of the fluidity of international cuisine and global images, the definition of "ethnic" remains rigid and largely reserved for the description of underdeveloped places and areas. Furthermore, in the same way that media images and narratives from home are consumed by exilic audiences in articulating fantasies, desire, loss, and nostalgia, food is consumed by exiles who yearn for "home produce," and for this reason, food eaten by the "ethnic"—rather than ethnic food—performs a reverse function to "kitchen table tourism," in that it allows the exiled body to "go home" in spite of being away from home.

I have so far in this book argued for a concept of the exile that is not only political, but, more important, is cultural and epistemological. This concept of exile is central to the paradiasporic position. This cultural and epistemological excommunication includes, of course, an everyday sense of sensory estrangement, a feeling of being out of touch with the smell and taste of "home," encapsulated most tangibly in the practices and discourses surrounding food and eating. Since eating is so basic a human need, yet is also an entrenched cultural practice to the extent that one may be branded a culinary chauvinist or food fundamentalist, might it also be useful, I ask, to entertain the possibility of the concept of a gastronomic exile?

While ethnic eaters can engage discourses of race or citizenship to argue against the imperialistic discourse of food, they are compelled to decide what food to put in their "ethnic stomach." Answering my question about whether they have a stubborn "Chinese" stomach, one of the respondents (a middle-aged man now working in the IT industry in Australia) said that his stomach is not stubborn enough to reject all non-Chinese food, but it is certainly "attracted" by Chinese food. When asked how he would choose between "mediocre Chinese food" and "good-quality" Western food, his answer was "I don't have a problem choosing either, but unfortunately, I have never had high-quality Western food." Although some respondents think that preference for Chinese food is cultural, rather than natural, many believe that their bodies are too used to Chinese food to be able to change. This is evidenced by their common observation that their children are born and brought up in the West and they love pizza and spaghetti—some, of course, would argue that both foods can claim Chinese origin—because their bodies don't have memories and therefore are not as "stubborn."

One of the most important themes in theorizing diasporic realities is that of displacement, and in no other way is displacement more tangible than in the way food is consumed. What happens to the migrant, who has rejected, or is rejected by, the homeland in a political or even an emotional sense, but who is still trapped in a body that yearns for the "authentic" food from home? In light of these issues, the activity of cooking is a quotidian practice of appropriating local food and "making do," hence providing rich fodder for the study of subjectivity and individualized uses of material consumable items. For instance, while white, Anglo, and cosmopolitan Australians "dine out" to consume multiculturalism, cultural pluralism, and hence an attractive lifestyle through choosing to eat "Japanese" or "Chinese," the "ethnic," who wants to eat food that agrees with his or her palate, is more likely to "dine in." This is because most "ethnic restaurants," from the perspective of migrants, cater to the culinary expectations of the mainstream clientele and are therefore considered less "authentic."

Sometimes it is not so much authenticity as flavor that is the issue. Many former PRC nationals, for instance, observe that most ethnic Chinese restaurants in the West cater to the Cantonese palate—or southern Chinese, for that matter—which is often too sweet, oily, and sometimes not spicy enough. To a certain extent, this hegemony of Cantonese food as the "ethnic Chinese" food in the West is under threat, with the arrival of mainland Chinese in many Western cities. Northern Noodle Restaurant, for instance, a small café-like eating place outside the Chinatown in Sydney, is run by a couple from Beijing. Featuring Lanzhou hand-made noodles, Beijing dumplings, and homemade spicy and sour cucumber salad, the place, since its opening a dozen years ago, has been featured on the food page of the *Sydney Morning Herald*. My favorite dishes are cold-cut beef with chili and peppers (lots of them!) and spring pancake (*chun juan*), with savory fillings such as wood ears, vermicelli, sprouts, and bukchoy, wrapped in pancake-like pastry. During my interview with the chef, Mr. Sha, who is the master of hand-made noodles, he told me that he had spent his childhood in Xinjiang, a predominantly Muslin region, and liked spicy and peppery food. He said that when the restaurant first started, he was careful and moderate with the amount of chili, pepper, and vinegar so as not to turn away first-time diners. As he surely and gradually built his clientele—many of whom, like myself, have become regular diners there—he was able to become more bold with seasonings, the stuff that marked his food as being different from most other Chinese restaurants in Chinatown. The success of Mr. Sha's business strategies seems to depend on the sophisticated palates of cosmopolitan local diners, who are looking for Chinese food with a difference, as well as on the sizable numbers of mainland Chinese living in the global city. Since I moved to Perth, the capital of Western Australia, almost two years ago, I have been searching for the holy grail—a replica of Northern Noodle Restaurant—and the quest continues.

The Chinese-language websites maintained by Chinese now living outside China—the former *liuxuesheng*—hold on to two types of memory: important and tragic events in Chinese history such as the Nanjing Massacre, the Cultural Revolution, and the June 4th Tiananmen Incident; and the mundane topic of food and the activity of eating. Throughout the previous chapter, I argued that for a collectivity to form a sense of identity or continue to articulate a sense of identity, two things are necessary: a shared memory of the specific events and things that have significance for the entire population and access to the cultural forms that enable these memories to be continuously refreshed and articulated. Here I add that a body-home-community-city-region-nation-global configuration, used by some cultural geographers in the scaling of place,[13] is a useful way of considering how the previous two things are maintained. In other words, in unraveling the formation of transnational imagination, the most apt place to start is the body and the home. Given the dispersed and displaced nature of the exiled body, in no other places are shared memories of somatic and sensory experiences most effectively activated and articulated via the Internet.

SENSORY MEMORY AND GOING HOME

From childhood to adulthood, from south to north, the best things in my memory are always associated with food. When I was a toddler, living in No. 8 Qijiaqiao Street in Nanjing, a nice old man would come to sell rice pudding (it is called "jiu niang" and made from glutinous rice soaked in the wine which fermented rice produces) from time to time. His arrival was always announced by the sound of a wooden clapper. So whenever I heard the "bang bang" sound, I would rush to either Mum or Grandpa, pleading. Sometimes Mum would say, "OK go and get some." Looking back, snuggling against Grandpa's long white beard and savouring the sweetness and aroma of fermented rice has got to be the best thing in my childhood. . . . In 1984, I became a teacher in Xi'an. There is a lot of rain in that ancient town, especially between autumn and winter. When it rained, it really rained. With the rain came gusty wind and flying sand. I would impatiently wait for the rain to stop, and then jump on my "golden rooster" (bicycle), and rush to "Mr. Ma Lamb Dumpling House" in the western part of town. I would order two pies (fried and with thinner pastry than western pies) with beef mince filling and a bowl of boiling hot shelled wheat gruel. The steam of the gruel would rise and blind my eyes, and all I could hear was the sound of hearty slurping and cheerful shoutings of more orders, and in the meantime I would demand waiters to give me more chili! Upon finishing, I would wipe the perspiration off my face, blow my running nose, let out a belch and a happy fart before making my way out. What bliss![14]

The reminiscences quoted here, written by Han Xuan, a mainland Chinese now living in the United States, appeared in *Hua Xia Wen Zhai*, the same magazine that hosts the Nanjing Massacre Virtual Monument Guestbook. This electronic magazine includes weekly news and current affairs, mainly about China, and also runs features and opinions from freelancers. Former mainland Chinese now living overseas are both the intended audience and the writers. Han Xuan's piece quoted here is a common narrative. These accounts of eating are marked with a vivid memory of somatic delights and bodily pleasures. Moreover, they are tied to a specific place—there—and time, then. I showed this story in my interviews to a dozen people and asked them if they also had a story to tell. My favorite one comes from Zhou, a man in his mid-forties, now a sports scientist working in a regional university in a country town in northern New South Wales, Australia:

During the cultural revolution when I was a young worker, I went to the wedding ceremony of one of my colleagues. High-quality food (meat, etc.) was very limited at that time, so everyone took the opportunity of the wedding ceremony to satisfy their unused taste buds. The host would do his/her best to get enough meat (at least half a pig and/or sheep, the fatter the better, 10–20 chickens/ducks, etc.), oil, wine and vegies. The banquet normally consisted of at least 8 dishes. As far as I can remember, there must have been (this was in western China) zhouzi (pig elbow), kourou (stewed pork), liji (a kind of chicken), tofu, a fish, stewed lamb, etc. About 10 people around a table, and there were 15–20 tables of guests. Everyone pretended to be modest, but the fat dishes were emptied quickly. The most exciting part was the fist games for drinking spirits.[15]

How can these people remember so clearly and vividly what they ate more than two decades ago? What makes the experience of eating what seems to be fairly simple food such a memorable experience? Where do pleasures of the body and feelings of bliss and excitement come from, if this entire generation grew up underfed and malnourished? What do these stories—and storytelling—tell us about identity, desire, and diasporic imagination?

Clues to these questions lie in the things that unite this particular group of Chinese. In spite of the different motivations behind their decision to leave China—some political; others professional, economic, or personal; and others a combination of these factors—they have at least four things in common. First, they were mostly born and raised in the 1950s in China and therefore either witnessed and suffered, as children, the nationwide famine of the early 1960s, in which millions of people died from this manmade starvation[16] or lived through the consequence of that famine, by enduring the subsequent quotidian reality of food shortage and malnutrition. Second, they all experienced the Cultural Revolution, during which time many of them were sent to the countryside for part or all of a decade and hence had experienced various privations. Third, they left China during the 1980s, mostly in their twenties and thirties, before the arrival of commercialism, consumerism, and materialism, which have given free rein to the long-suppressed carnal and gastronomic appetites and fantasies of the entire nation. It is common knowledge that when members of this diasporic group of people visit folks back in China and witness wondrous scenes of gastronomic orgy, whereby people everywhere seem to be eating whatever flies in the sky, moves on the ground, and swims in the water, they are told by their folks that they look very *tu* (provincial, premodern) and that they behave like peasants. Many have found themselves "strangers" in their homeland. Fourth, having voluntarily or involuntarily left their country, members of this group of people have nevertheless been unable or reluctant to assimilate into their respective host societies or have found it difficult to do so.

What distinguishes this group from other Chinese migrants from Hong Kong or Taiwan and from second- or third-generation diasporic Chinese in

Southeast Asia or elsewhere is a collective memory of mainland China prior to their migration and a common will to enact or sustain that memory in both bodily and symbolic ways. In spite of their geographic dispersal and stratification in terms of gender, professional level, and socioeconomic status, these Chinese, having lived through numerous famines in the twentieth century, including the 1960s famine, and experienced the food scarcity and rationing throughout the Cultural Revolution period, share a deep understanding of the psychological and cultural impact that famine and hunger can make on the national psyche and human relationships.[17] This shared history and experience give this group a common cultural idiom built around food, which, through language, reflects the centrality of food in their cosmological understanding. It is no surprise that only the mainland Chinese are known to greet each other with the question: "Have you eaten yet?" (*chi guo le ma*). It is therefore easier for them than for other diasporic Chinese, for instance, to appreciate why the Chinese character for "eating" (*chi*) consists of two radicals, with the left one meaning "mouth" and the right one meaning "begging." In the same way that some Western discourses have a tendency to sexualize the representation of social relations, a preoccupation with food results in the "gastronomization" of the discourses of social relations in a Chinese context. Consequently, people eat not only food, they also "eat" inedible things, including "eating vinegar" (*chicu*—becoming jealous), "eating bitterness" (*chiku*—enduring hardship), "eating loss" (*chikuei*—receiving unfair treatment), "eating fragrance" (*chixiang*—gaining popularity), "eating beancurd" (*chi doufu*—taking liberties with women), *chi bukai/ chi dekai* (being unpopular/popular), *chibuxiao* (being exhausted), *chibuzhu* (being unable to bear something), *chijin* (being hard pressed), and *chijing* (being shocked or amazed).

Han Xuan's and Zhou's stories point to a crucial, yet understudied, area: the relationship between identity, desire, and exilic imagination. Living in the English-speaking world, both storytellers, like thousands of other ex-mainlanders who end up in the United States, Canada, Japan, Australia, and New Zealand, have to feed their "Chinese" stomach with what is available locally. Most mainland students were in their late twenties, thirties, or even forties when they left China, and many profess that they are too old to change their palate. Are they too old to change the palate, or are they too old to erase memory? Or do they really want to forget? Or does Chinese food simply have few, if any peers, in its variety and quality? Here I argue that rather than wanting to forget history, the migrant both needs to and wants to remember it because it is in this constant mobilization of a collective memory bank that an exilic imagination begins to take shape. This is evidenced in the perennial circulation of memoirs and reminiscences— the Nanjing Massacre during World War II, the Cultural Revolution, the Tiananmen Square Incident in 1989—among the Chinese students and scholars who left China to live overseas during the last two decades.[18] The 1958–1962 famine, in which 30 million Chinese died of starvation, is certifiably the most traumatic, yet the least publicly commemorated, loss experienced by the Chinese population. When Jasper Becker announced in an overseas Chinese-language newspaper his intention to write a book on the famine and invited readers to share their memories, he received hundreds of responses, ranging from a few lines to many pages of still "fresh memories."[19]

The memories of food and of eating food back home are intensified by a perennial sense of loss: In spite of the increasingly varied and sophisticated Chinese restaurants and Chinese grocery shops that are widely available in most world cities, for many migrants these cannot substitute for the "real experience." In other words, although the past offered little material comfort and few culinary delights, it becomes memorable in the migrant's imagination because it was a special time, a time before he or she turned "ethnic," and when food was associated with bodily satisfaction, rather than a signifier of ethnic desire. Note how the sheer joy of physical sensation permeates the following reminiscence from Liu, a native from Tianjin now living in Sydney with her Caucasian partner:

> I like hot chilies. Mum always cooked some hot chilies dishes to go with whatever meals. Mind you, she liked hot food too. No matter what food I ate, I would eat more if I could have the hot chili dish at the same time. Eating or chewing the hot chili, you have the burning hot feeling in your mouth, at the same time, the chili taste seemed to stimulate the appetite.

Both Han and Liu evoke a strong sense of taste, touch, and smell, and through these details, a nostalgia for the past—childhood or youth. Writing about the relationship between exile and memories of childhood, Naficy says:

> Sometimes a small gesture or body posture, a particular gleam in the eye, or a smell, a sound, or a taste suddenly and directly sutures one to a former house or home and to cherished memories of childhood. Sometimes a small, insignificant object taken into exile becomes a powerful synecdoche for the lost house and the unreachable home, feeding the memories of the past and the narratives of exile.[20]

Although nostalgia is hardly the exclusive domain of the exile—many people are prone to this sentiment—details from the past are particularly powerful when the person remembering the past is in exile. Margaret Morse's work on home and emotional identification through sensory association is useful:

> Since "home" is not a real place, feeling at home is, in essence, a personal and culturally specific link to the imaginary. Feelings and memories linked to home are highly charged, if not with meaning, then with sense memories that began in childhood before the mastery of language.[21]

Morse argues that it is not until one leaves home that the need to imagine being home becomes urgent, for then home becomes associated with place of birth, a house, a family, a locality, and a nation, all of which are abundantly visible in Han's reverie of eating in childhood and youth. What both Han and Liu perhaps express is not so much the yearning for the taste of beef mince dumplings, fermented rice pudding, or hot chili, as a desire to go back to that fantasy space called "home." This desire to "go home" also manifests itself in remembering the social context in which eating took place. Storytellers evoke not only the sensory and bodily experience of eating—note the sound of wooden clapper and the touch of "grandpa's" beard in Han's piece—but also the feeling of warmth and fuzziness that "my grandpa," Mum, or colleague workers brought to bear on such occasions. In other words, the migrant remembers not only a time when he or she was "home," but also a time when he or she "felt at home"—eating took place in a familiar, (extended) familial, or "natural" habitat. In remembering his childhood and his young adulthood in China prior to migration, via the eating of food, Han Xuan sublimates a desire to satisfy a biological bodily need such as eating and drinking into the pursuit of a pleasure that comes from his nostalgic reconstruction of another, or even "better," era. In this sense, Han's reverie about eating in the past and remembering his bodily reactions to food are induced not so much by a desire to recapture the authentic taste of Chinese food, as by a desire that Naficy describes as "fetishistic"—a feeling of lack resulting from physical displacement and a pathological yearning for an impossible return (in both a spatial and a temporal sense).

Diasporic people live in what Naficy calls the "liminal slipzone," between "here and now" and "there and then."[22] In other words, remembering eating becomes a mediated and vicarious way of going back in time and space and reliving the "authentic" past, not in spite of, but precisely because of, the Spartan conditions and sensory deprivation of the era of collectivism. For the Chinese who left China, daydreaming about eating "authentic" Chinese food may not be as appealing as the real experience of eating it, but it is the only one possible. In this sense, these diasporic fantasies are those of the typical modern consumer. However, what sets Han and his fellow expatriates apart from the "typical modern consumer" is that while this modern consumer yearns for pleasant experiences that have not yet been experienced, the migrant is governed by nostalgia, a longing for the past and for experiences already lived, yet impossible to repeat. Mr. Liu, a chemical engineer in Western Australia, for instance, is a native of rural Qingzhou County, Shangdong Province. He goes into great length and detail in describing the indigenous food and cooking on his Web page, including the minutia in preparing the famously pungent and hearty "Shangdong pancake with spring shallots" (*Shangdong jianbing juan dachong*) and millet gruel (*xiaomi xifan*). "I have travelled to many places in the world and tasted many fine cuisines. What I really want, however, is to again taste a mouthful of the shallot pancake and millet gruel."[23]

For Han, the pleasure of remembering the bodily may also come from gaining a sense of solidarity, community, or new sense of belonging. Although the experience of Han is personal, it is nevertheless likely to strike a resonance with, or even invite identification by, fellow expatriates who lived through the years of collective economy under Mao's regime, when material goods were far from plentiful. The great famine of the 1960s, in which millions died; the period of the Cultural Revolution, during which everything—including eggs, sugar, rice, and flour—was rationed, and when few died of starvation, but nobody had enough to eat. However, precisely because of the scarcity, any gastronomic delights that the era could afford became ingrained in people's memory because they were aberrations in an otherwise harsh somatic landscape. And yet the world that both Han and my interviewees inhabited seems simple and more "fun," uncorrupted by the rampant consumerism that one witnesses in China and abroad today. As most students left China in the 1980s—when consumerism was about to take off in a big way—their expectations and desires were shaped by pre-reform experiences. The potency and intensity of Han's intimate account of his bodily pleasure comes from its capacity to tap into a collective consciousness of a group of people who, due to migration, have become self-imposed exiles not only geographically, but also epistemologically.

What is also interesting to note is that such attempts to keep memories of pleasures alive—memories that are embodied, location-specific, and time-indexed—are made possible largely by new media technology, which is known for its ephemerality, deterritoriality, and amnesiac qualities.[24] Equipped with a Chinese-language Web browser and computer, one does not have to linger too long in the most frequently visited websites, maintained by and for Chinese students now living in diaspora, to realize the extent to which food is central to the formation of the diasporic imagination within these groups. Some websites specialize in interweaving Chinese recipes with anecdotal accounts of cooking, giving intense attention to the sensual dimension, including smell, taste, touch, and sound. Some of these accounts have appetite-whetting pictures of the dish in question.[25] Another genre is that of the memory of food or the remembering of eating experiences, mostly nostalgic reminiscences of which Han's piece, quoted earlier, is typical. Like recipe narratives, these kinds of narratives are also strongly evocative of the sensual pleasures of eating. Such remembering usually takes the form of "time travel" or "stepping back into the past," whereby memories of eating take one back to another space, another era. "Going home" is a fantasy constantly evoked through these rememberings, only to be displaced onto the virtual space of a homepage, which in turn creates a sense—however ephemeral—of "feeling at home." During my interviews with some diasporic Chinese on the issue of watching the Sydney Olympic Games in Australia (chapter 8), Mr. Liu, a most generous and friendly person living in the industrial town of Newcastle outside Sydney, invited me to "drop" by if I

happened to be in Newcastle. Living on the other side of the Australian continent (three hours' time difference), I realized that the chance of my dropping
by was slim. I, however, accepted his invitation to visit his homepage and have
become a frequent visitor.[26] A great proportion of his homepage is devoted to
food and talking about eating, with other topics that focus on traveling and
"playing" (*wan*).

EATING IN BETWEEN

Just because the exiles' stomachs are "stubborn" does not mean that they have
to live with daily gastronomic deprivations in the mainstream society. Cultural engagement via food takes place in a wide range of sites, ranging from
the ubiquitously present "sinified" restaurant in the English-speaking
world—particularly in monocultural country towns, where "Chinese food" is
sweet and sour pork, honey prawns, beef in black bean sauce, and sizzling
Mongolian lamb—to numerous *yum-cha* venues serving "phoenix claws" (*feng
zhua*, chicken feet), "red hue" (*zhu hong*, pig blood pudding), and many other
exquisitely cooked delicacies. Migrants, for instance, are regular shoppers in
ethnic groceries that sell fresh and packaged cooking ingredients, as well as
utensils, many of which are imported from home countries. Information is
thus shared among friends as to where to buy the best Chinese cleavers—
some Chinese claim it is impossible to prepare Chinese food without a
cleaver—or which Chinese butchers sell the best pork (another complaint
among Chinese students in Australia is that pork from mainstream supermarkets smells "weird"). Ten years ago, when I was living in Canberra, a Chinese friend offered a most practical piece of advice on how to cook without
Chinese rice wine (*huang jiu*): Use dry sherry, which is cheap and available
from supermarkets. Cooking methods also need to be modified or sometimes
improvised to suit new kitchen facilities. For instance, stir-frying requires intense heat, something that the Western electric stove is ill-equipped for. Hot
plates, both gas and electronic, are not designed for a wok, a most frequently
used cooking utensil in a Chinese kitchen. Some people observe that a frying
pan is adequate for stir-fry, but it is never the same. Among the most memorable Chinese meals described to me by my interviewees were served in a
generic Chinese restaurant in Bathurst, a small country town in New South
Wales, Australia. The interviewee lives there for work reasons, and since he
does not speak much English and has difficulty understanding the menu in a
"foreign" restaurant, he figures that his best chance of getting a good deal
while eating out is to go to a local Chinese restaurant. He usually goes in and
chats with the waiter in Chinese, makes some inquiries about what is available in the kitchen, and proceeds to order a few dishes, none of which is on
the menu. His favorite orders are stir-fried tofu in freshly ground pepper and

chili with pickled mustard roots; a whole steamed bream with rice wine, es-
chalot, and ginger; baby Shanghai bukchoy stir-fried with sun-dried mushrooms in honey and garlic, and hot sour soup with vermicelli and pickled
wombuk (Chinese cabbage, similar to *kimchi* in Korean cuisine). My interviewee also offers the following advice, "That's the only way to get decent
food when you eat out, but it can be done, you know. After all, the chef is
Chinese. He just has to know who he is cooking for."

Experiences of cooking and eating are freely exchanged among exiles and
also are regular topics in online discussions. Note the following observation:

> The trip back to China left me with an indescribable taste in my mouth. I really
> had mixed feelings. I had been away from China for too long. Since I travelled
> with my grandmother, we were wined and dined non-stop for a whole week. For
> a "hungry ghost" from America such as myself, it was like breaking a long-time
> fast. Travelling along the Guangzhou-Shantou Highway, we stopped by the
> roadside for lunch. Upon walking into the place, we saw many types of coral fish,
> shell fish and seaweed. They were all kept—alive—in plastic tubs, waiting to be
> chosen. Although this was a seafood restaurant, its menu also boasted many
> other things, ranging from what flies in the sky—turtledove, egret, and pheas-
> ant—to what crawls on the ground—poisonous and non-poisonous snakes, sand
> worms, turtles and tortoises. The strangest sight was a dirty donkey tethered
> outside the place. I wondered to myself whether this was also for food, since
> southerners seldom use donkeys for farming purposes. That same evening, I saw
> on local television that a plague was spreading locally due to the eating of dis-
> eased donkeys, and on the screen were horrid pictures of a bloody, dissected don-
> key. I couldn't help picturing the horrified expressions on the face of my Amer-
> ican friends if I were to tell them the donkeys' misfortune.[27]

Readers of this online anecdote are presented with a spectacle whereby an
appetite, whetted by consumerism, has run wild. If the author had not identified herself as a mainland Chinese now living in America, the previous pas-
sage might well have been written by a Western journalist, travel writer, or
anthropologist. This is because the story invokes the gaze of an outsider,
someone who goes into the "tribe" to observe the material life of the "tribal
people." The finding is simple: Chinese not only eat all the time, they eat just
about everything, and they are, by implication, cruel, gluttonous, and licen-
tious. In other words, they are strange and different. To Ma Ya, the writer,
this difference is frowned upon, rather than understood or celebrated. The
orientalizing process seems to be completed when the "tribal people" and
their voracious appetites and uncivilized eating practices are brought under
the gaze of the imaginary gaze of "my American friends."

However, such an ethnographic account is not without its ambivalence and
tensions. Although the author has "mixed feelings" about strange people eating strange things, having been away for too long and acquired American taste
buds and aesthetic sensibilities, she has not forgotten the pleasure of eating

Chinese food or stopped yearning for it. Readers are told that the author, through living in America, has become a "hungry ghost." Of course, she is not talking about material starvation. Rather, she is referring to a perpetual lack, a symbolic hunger for sensuality and bodily pleasures that only Chinese food can deliver. In other words, the undertone of disapproval that is evident in her ethnographic account of eating in contemporary China is as much a lament for having become too "American" as it is an indication of her realization of the impossibility of returning to the China she used to know. She is frustrated because a homecoming in the physical sense no longer guarantees that she can relive her childhood memories and alleviate the sense of lack she chronically feels in America.

I like Ma Ya's story because it echoes my own sentiments of loss and even evokes a touch of mournfulness. Here, what is lost is not so much a "nonethnic" identity as a premodern habitat in which life was regulated by rituals, symbolism, and cultural memory—a life-world in which food had rich cultural meanings, and eating was always anchored to a particular cultural and social context. To this day, some foods evoke vivid memories of the ambiance and atmosphere of my childhood in China. Take, for instance, *zhongzi*, a fist-sized pyramid of glutinous rice wrapped in reed leaves. Eaten either as a sweet, with dates and red-bean paste inside the rice, or as a savory snack, with sun-dried mushrooms and stewed lean pork, *zhongzi*, once cooked, can be eaten either warm or cold. As a child, we had *zhongzi* once a year since it was associated with the *Duanwu* festival. Because my mother had never mastered the knack of making *zhongzi*—she complained that her *zhongzi* tended to leak, and rice would come out when they were cooked—she would usually invite a couple of women friends to help her out. These "aunties" would gather around a big bucket of glutinous rice and a big bunch of reed leaves. To this day I can remember the clear, sharp smell of the freshly cut leaves. Of course, kids were never trusted with such a delicate and complicated task, although we were an integral part of the ritual, having to answer the obligatory annual question put to us by the adults: Why are we eating *zhongzi* on this day? I remember answering, year after year: "*Zhongzi* comes from the story of Qu Yuan, the great poet exiled by the emperor in ancient times, who threw himself into the Miluo River in protest against the despotic ruler. People loved him and wanted him to live on, so they made *zhongzi* each year on the day Qu Yuan committed suicide, to feed the fish in the river. That way, the fish would be well-fed and would leave the body of the poet alone." Such proof of remembering would bring me the reward of freshly made *zhongzi* and, of course, a knowledge of the folklore that is passed on in such a typically informal and familial fashion.

Another food that is strongly evocative of the ritualistic and rhythmic nature of life is moon cake (*yuebing*), a cake made with all sorts of sweet things inside the pastry—almond kernels, lotus seeds, sesame seeds, and many other flavors. They are eaten during the mid-autumn festival, on the fifteenth day of the eighth month of the Chinese calendar, when the new autumn moon is expected to be at its brightest. To me, moon cakes were associated with autumn leaves, a full moon, and crab meat, since the family gathering on that day usually featured these. Unlike *zhongzi*, most moon cakes were bought from shops, rather than homemade, and a most popular gift for relatives and friends around the time of the full moon was a box of moon cakes bought from a prestigious shop. For those who haven't seen moon cake, all moon cakes—if they are made in the traditional style—have a small square piece of paper on the top. As a child, my parents would ask me each year if I remembered the story of the paper on the cake. Keen to get my hands on the moon cake, I always had the answer ready: "A peasant leader in ancient times decided to rebel against their cruel rulers and planned a coup. He needed to let his people know of his decision but had to do it secretly since the risk would be death. He therefore thought of a clever way of passing on the message, by writing the time of the planned coup on the pieces of paper attached to the moon cakes that were to be distributed to each household." Or something like that.

Most of my knowledge of Chinese folklore and legends—which is as deeply ideological as folklore and legends elsewhere—was acquired in this way. I am grateful to my parents for insisting on educating me like this, although I am certain that they were only doing what many other parents did. Such a way of passing on knowledge, however, seems to be disappearing fast in China, in part due to the rampant spread of consumerism, in part through the displacement of education from family and teachers to the media, both global phenomena. Nowadays, *zhongzi* and moon cakes are readily available in shops all year round. Mass-produced and retailed, they are bought and eaten as everyday foods, without much ritual or remembering. Like the delicacies on the menu of the roadside restaurant that Ma Ya patronized on her trip to China, they have become just another food product. Readily available or even in excess, these foods signify an absence, rather than a presence, of cultural memory. The delicacies on the menu are signs that stand for nothing else but the power to consume. Rather than being a bearer of cultural meaning and knowledge, they become advertisements of the eater's status and a metaphor for the stupendous appetite of the modern consumer. I wonder, with this dissociation of food from the traditional cultural calendar, whether alternative ways of passing on a knowledge of history and folklore are likely to arise. It may well be due to this dissociation that the paradiasporic Chinese community has formed a persistent desire to remember, as evidenced in its regularly produced narratives on the Internet, about both traditional food and the ritualistic context of eating traditional food.

Although many migrants travel back to China, they find that it is difficult, if not impossible, to relive the past. China, and the way people eat in China, has changed beyond recognition. This puts expatriate Chinese in the position of cross-cultural food ethnographers when they go back to China. The ethnographic gaze, however, is not focused exclusively on the Chinese folks back home who have been driven to tribal and primitive eating practices by the rise of the market economy and conspicuous consumption. It is also often directed toward the "locals"—Europeans living next door to the Chinese migrants. Like the Chinese folks at home, the "Americans," "Australians," or *gueilos* in general are both familiar and strange in the eyes of the migrant. Note the following account:

> The Germans eat not only with the mouth, but also with the eyes. To put it simply, the mouth eats the content, while the eyes eat the form of presentation. Presentation includes what sorts of plates, glasses and cutlery to use. There are many other distracting things on the table, such as candles, flowers, and huge napkins. These things take up most of the space on the dining table, and when it comes to the actual food, there is usually only one meat dish and one vegetable dish. The vegetable dish can be a raw salad, or it could be vegetables which have been boiled beyond recognition. As for the meat dish, it is usually a piece of beef or chicken. The surface of the meat may have some flavour, but as for the inside, it all tastes like wood, to quote many of our fellow expatriates. When the Germans want to go up one notch in formality, there might be a soup before and a dessert after. The way to eat is also weird: you eat yours, and I eat mine.[28]

Interestingly, the class distinction, which Bourdieu delineates through the aesthetic presentation of food,[29] is flattened out in these cross-cultural observations. How do we read this conflation of class-based difference with a race-based one? Is it that the migrant tends to have a "working-class" taste and aesthetic, or is it that migrants, regardless of their prior social, economic, and cultural capital, have, by default, moved downward in the social ladder by dislocating themselves? Here I suggest that such a conflation of class with race can be read in at least two ways. First, it carves out a strategically essentialist position from which to hail various forms of Chineseness. "Germans," in Yang's writing, are all the same, regardless of gender, class, and regional differences, and ultimately they function only so much as to signify racial difference or cultural superiority; the Chinese may be less concerned with the aesthetic surroundings of food than are some cultures, but their cooking certainly has more sophistication and finesse than many, and the Chinese have a more subtle palate. To be sure, since food is a tangible, regular source of affirmation of the "superiority" of Chinese culture, an occidentalist discourse on the China/West difference[30] inevitably has recourse to Chinese cuisine: You may have democracy and freedom of speech, but I have good food, and at the end of the day, you can't eat democracy and freedom.

Another way of making sense of these clearly ethnocentric observations by a group of self-appointed gastronomic anthropologists in this way is to establish their connection to a memory of the body politics of the pre-reform era, in which the Chinese state featured prominently. Yang Xiaohong's privileging of content over form, substance over formality, which Bourdieu identifies as distinctively "working class" in the context of French society, does not so much reflect a class position. Rather, it is an instinctive reaction of a politicized body, which, in the communist era of political fervor and material scarcity, was forced to demonstrate faith in socialism even though socialism failed to fill one's stomach. In other words, observations about eating in "other" cultures say not so much about the host societies as about the migrant's own fear and desire, stemming from past experiences. Ma Ya's ethnographic account of her gastronomic trip in China embodies both a desire by former mainlanders now living in diaspora to remain Chinese and a desire to negotiate a Chinese position that sets her apart from other forms of Chineseness. While sameness is evidenced in a common obsession with food and a preoccupation with the topic of eating—hence the famous saying that "Westerners eat to live, whereas the Chinese live to eat," or "Food is to the Chinese what sex is to Westerners"—difference manifests itself in the divergent ways in which food and eating are talked about. The constant traversing between inclusion and exclusion, the familiar and the strange, here and there, now and then, us and them, results in the diasporic impulse to be intrinsically ethnographic: While being the object of the gaze of both Chinese at home and Westerners—and other ethnic groups—"next door," the migrant is also an everyday anthropologist, returning the gaze of the gazer. Such an ethnographic impulse takes the form of constant discursive articulation: of what one has become or what one is becoming in postnational contexts. Crucial to the ethnographic impulse is not the state of "being," but that of "becoming," and nowhere else is the articulation of "becoming" more appropriately located than in the utterances and expressions of tension and ambivalence, as well as of nostalgia and loss, which is experienced daily by the migrant.

MOUTH TO MOUSE—*YUM CHA* AS A METAPHOR

I began this chapter by suggesting that media images and food may have more in common than we usually assume. Throughout the chapter, I have looked at a number of ways in which narratives and discourses surrounding food and eating play a pivotal role in articulating an exilic sense of the self and one's belonging to a place. In doing so, I have carried Morse's question "What do cyborgs eat?" one step further and have shown that these Chinese "cyborgs" not only eat food, but also write about food and eating in a manner that allows them to continue to be Chinese in a new way. In doing so, I have, by implication, lent support to the argument that links eating and writing. Terry Eagleton, for instance, observes that both food and language are "cusped" between nature and culture, and that in the same way that language is at once a material fact and rhetorical communication, eating combines biological necessity with cultural significance:

> Food is what makes up our bodies, just as words are what constitutes our minds; and if body and mind are hard to distinguish, it is no wonder that eating and speaking should continually cross over in metaphorical exchange. Both are, in any case, media of exchange themselves.[31]

Evidence of "the metaphorical exchange" between food and text to which Eagleton refers can be seen, for instance, in comparing fast food and take-out to cliché or computerese, and in describing, for instance, Samuel Beckett's texts as "anorexic." If the dialogically metaphoric relationship between food and writing put forward by Eagleton is valid, and if food practices and textual practices can be perceived as the metaphor for one another, I am then tempted to ask this question: Is there an apt metaphor or embodiment for a technologically enabled cyber-discourse of a displaced and deterritorialized Chineseness, as evidenced in both the cases of the Nanjing Massacre virtual monuments and memories of eating? Here I suggest that there is and venture to look at *yum-cha* as a possible example of such a metaphor. In other words, in a number of ways, a material practice such as *yum-cha* shares certain attributes with a discursive practice such as visiting Chinese websites.

First, both *yum-cha* and a cyber-discourse of Chinese nationalism constructed by the former PRC nationals are globalized, deterritorialized, and displaced signs that stand for the absent China. In the last chapter, I showed that Chinese websites such as the CND are a mediated space, whereby a deterritorialized site *about* China is substituted for a territorial nation that *is* China. I also point to the fact that instead of going back to the PRC, these displaced Chinese maintain their connection not just with China, but increasingly with things Chinese. Similar to the CND, *yum-cha* is also both a mediated space and a virtual place. A truly globalized phenomenon, the practice of *yum-cha* is found in Chinese restaurants (called *dim-sum* in North America) in most of the major global cities. It is a Cantonese way of serving dim sum that has become a most popular culinary pastime for Chinese communities in English-speaking countries.[32]

In addition, *yum-cha* is always a hustling and bustling place and, like the Chinese websites, is the testing ground for cultural legitimacy and the negotiation between the insider and outsider. Since the dishes, contained in hundreds of little bamboo steamers, are displayed to the patron every few minutes, *yum-cha* operates as much through the visuality of the experience as on the senses of taste and smell. In the websites, the use of Chinese language has a function of both excluding and including, and the decoding of historically specific jokes functions to bond, as well as to alienate. Among *yum-cha* patrons, *gueilos* (Cantonese for "white ghosts"—foreigners) are usually recommended "safe" dishes, such as prawn dumplings, barbecue pork buns, and spring rolls, and not, for instance, pork and century egg congee, which is a rice gruel with shredded pork and pieces of "foul-smelling, hideous-looking" (my *gueilo* friend's words) marble eggs. Those few *gueilo* individuals who embrace chicken feet and ox tripe are praised by the Chinese for their exemplary bravery, but may be perceived to have gone "native" by their own kind. Waiters and waitresses may have learned that *gueilos* are less likely to choose these dishes, having seen too many wincing faces when these dishes are presented. "Illegitimate" or "weird" food is consumed un-self-consciously side by side with the "tasty, exotic, but acceptable" food, giving each person what he or she wants. At the same time, perceptions of "other" cultures, through visual presentations of food, are both challenged and reinforced. Thus, solidarity is reinforced through the sharing of "nice food." When I asked one of my respondents, who now lives in the U.K., about whom she prefers to go *yum-cha* with, her answer was

Yes, I like *yum-cha* very much. Would prefer to eat with Chinese people, as when nice food is to be shared with people who like it as well, it tastes even better. I don't feel apologetic or rude, but if they don't enjoy it that much, we find something else that we can enjoy together.

Furthermore, one can even venture to suggest that while conventional restaurant dining, a most "intensely structured affair,"[33] is similar to reading a traditional text, following a linear and sequential order—entree-main-dessert in eating versus introduction-body-conclusion in reading—*yum-cha*-ing is akin to net surfing, in that there are no rigid rules of order to follow. Net surfing, the activity consisting of "point and click," and *yum-cha*-ing—the activity involving "point and lick"—are both nonlinear, interactive, and, dare I say, hypertextual. Similarly, to reverse the metaphoric exchange, a "click" may well be a cyber-lick—a bodily impulse to get "in touch" with the absent home.

Ultimately, if *yum-cha*, like Chinese websites, can be read as a metaphor for the globalization of Chineseness, then its practice is also metonymic of the unevenness of, and disparity within, Chinese transnationalism. While patrons are presented with "quintessentially Chinese" food, little is made of the fact that *yum-cha* is really a southern cuisine that originated in the Cantonese communities in Hong Kong, Taiwan, and Southeast Asia. In other words, rather than being a showcase of diasporic hybridity, *yum-cha*—a Cantonese expression that means "drinking tea"—is a triumph of the cultural and economic interests of some Chinese communities over others. The arrival of ex-mainlanders at the *yum-cha* scene in the Chinese restaurants of major cities in the West is a humble one. It is well-known that when students from the PRC first came overseas, they had little money and no residential status. Many of them ended up working in Chinese restaurants run by the older-generation

Chinese, for long hours and below-minimum wages. Since many students worked illegally, they were prepared to put up with this exploitation. These restaurants also reserved for women the lowest-paid, most menial, and onerous jobs.

If mainland students' participation in the production of Chinese food symbolizes the uneven relationship between different classes of Chineseness, the consumption of *yum-cha* is a powerful indication of the malleability of "Chineseness" in the face of a more urgent need to carve out a racially based difference. By equating *yum-cha* with Chinese food and categorizing customers in terms of Chinese or non-Chinese, what is erected is a position of strategic essentialism, as well as a tactic of appropriation. As relative newcomers to the diasporic space, the mainland Chinese who went overseas during the reform era naturally sought strategic alliances with established Chinese communities by latching onto, or "piggybacking" on, the more-established Chinese communities, which possessed more cultural and social capital than those less-established Chinese diasporic communities.

THE EXILED EATER, CONSUMPTION, AND TRANSNATIONAL IMAGINATION

If, in the previous chapter, I have looked at the strategies of activating a shared memory of the traumas of the national body, this chapter outlines a number of ways in which "long-distant nationalism"[34] can also be cultivated in a more everyday and individual manner through food practices. The notion of exile could be extended to include a somatic, as well as a political and cultural, dimension, because political or social displacement or banishment may lead to alienation of the body, as well as of the mind. Remembering bodily experiences that are associated with eating provides crucial clues to the relationship between memory, pleasure, and translocal subjectivity. Although I have thus far focused on eating and food narratives in the context of former PRC exiles now living overseas, the close relationship between food discourses and a sense of home, place, and belonging is also true of other migrant groups, including those internal ones. During a June 2001 field trip in China to research internal migration, I sat on an overnight Shanghai-to-Chongqing train with mostly rural migrant workers from Sichuan, who were going back to their villages for a brief visit. I was told again and again that they were beset with homesickness, that the food in the factory canteen in Shanghai was never spicy enough, and that once a week they would spend some of their hard-earned money to treat themselves to some real Sichuanese food in a restaurant run by their country fellows (*lao xiang*).

In addition, I have discussed a number of ways in which virtual spaces provided by the Internet and new technologies function to keep memories of the somatic and sensory experiences—the stuff out of which transnational imagination is based—alive and fresh. Finally, this seems to bring to light an irony of reversal in the formation of a transnational subjectivity: While a Chinese media consumer living in China may yearn to leave China—either physically (through migration) or vicariously (through consuming foreign images and foreign food)—the exiled Chinese lament the impossibility of a return.

NOTES

1. Margaret Morse, *Virtualities: Television, Media Art, and Cyberculture* (Bloomington and Indianapolis: Indiana University Press, 1998), 125.

2. Morse, *Virtualities*, 125.

3. Donna Gabaccia, *We Are What We Eat* (Cambridge, Mass.: Harvard University Press, 1998); Beverley Kingston, "Are We What We Eat?" in *The Abundant Culture*, ed. David Headon, Joy Hooton, and Donald Horne (Sydney: Allen & Unwin, 1995).

4. David Bell and Gill Valentine, *Consuming Geographies: We Are Where We Eat* (London and New York: Routledge, 1997).

5. See Uma Narayan, *Dislocating Cultures: Identity, Traditions, and Third-World Feminism* (New York: Routledge, 1997).

6. Cherry Ripe, *Goodbye Culinary Cringe* (St. Leonards: Allen & Unwin, 1993); Sneja Gunew, "Feminism in the Politics of Irreducible Differences: Multiculturalism/Ethnicity/Race," in *Feminism and the Politics of Difference*, ed. Sneja Gunew and Anna Yetman (Boulder, Colo.: Westview, 1993).

7. Ghassan Hage, *White Nation: Fantasies of White Supremacy in a Multicultural Society* (Sydney: Pluto, 1998).

8. See Susan Sheridan, "Eating the Other: Food and Cultural Difference in the Australian *Women's Weekly* in the 1960s," *Journal of International Studies* 21, no. 3 (2000).

9. Shannan Peckham, "Consuming Nations," in *Consuming Passions: Food in the Age of Anxiety*, ed. Sian Griffiths and Jennifer Wallace (Manchester and New York: Manchester University Press, 1998), 171–82.

10. Bell and Valentine, *Consuming Geographies*; Deborah Lupton, *The Food, the Body and the Self* (London: Sage, 1996).

11. Bell and Valentine, *Consuming Geographies*, 5–6.

12. David Harvey, *The Condition of Postmodernity* (Oxford: Blackwell, 1989).

13. For instance, see Neil Smith, "Homeless/Global: Scaling Places," in *Mapping the Futures: Local Cultures, Global Change*, ed. Jon Bird, Barry Curtis, Tim Putnam, George Tobertson, and Lias Tickner (London: Routledge, 1993).

14. Han Xuan, *Shi Zhile* (The Joy of Food) (*shi zhi le*, my translation), <www.cnd.org/HXWZ/CM99/cm9908a.hz8.html#3> (accessed August 2000).

15. The interviewee, like a few other interviewees who participated in my research, told the story in English. I try to preserve the flavor of the original conversation, with only occasional editing for grammatical reasons.

16. For a detailed and confronting account of the famine, see Jasper Becker's book *Hungry Ghost: China's Secret Famine* (London: John Murray, 1996).

17. For a recent work on eating and hunger in modern China, see Yue Gang, *The Mouth That Begs: Hunger, Cannibalism, and the Politics of Eating in Modern China* (Durham, N.C.: Duke University Press, 1999).

18. See my previous chapter on the websites on the Nanjing Massacre.

19. Jasper Becker, *Hungry Ghost.*

20. Hamid Naficy, "Framing Exile," in *Home, Exile, Homeland: Film, Media, and the Politics of Place*, ed. Hamid Naficy (London and New York: Routledge, 1999).

21. Margaret Morse, "Home: Smell, Taste, Posture, Gleam," in *Home, Exile, Homeland: Film, Media, and the Politics of Place*, ed. Hamid Naficy, 63.

22. Hamid Naficy, *The Making of Exile Culture: Iranian Television in Los Angeles* (Minneapolis: University of Minnesota Press, 1993).

23. You can read Mr. Liu's Web page on food at <www.meltingpot.fortunecity.com/sudan/47/> (accessed October 2001).

24. Mike Featherstone, ed., *Global Culture: Nationalism, Globalism and Modernity* (London: Sage, 1990).

25. For an example of this kind of website, see <www.cnd.org/huazhao> (accessed October 2001).

26. To visit Mr. Liu's homepage, go to<www.meltingpot.fortunecity.com/sudan/47/> (accessed October 2001).

27. Ma Ya, "On Eating a Donkey" (my translation), <www.cnd.org/HXWZ/CM00/cm0004c.hz8.html#7 (accessed October 2001).

28. Yang Xiaohong, "Eating All the Way" (my translation), <www.cnd.org/HXWZ/CM00/cm0005c.hz8.html#9> (accessed 2001).

29. Pierre Bourdieu, *Distinction: A Social Critique of the Judgement of Taste* (London: Routledge & Kegan Paul, 1984).

30. See Chen Xiaomei, *Occidentalism: A Theory of Counter-Discourse in Post-Mao China* (New York and Oxford: Oxford University Press, 1995).

31. Terry Eagleton, "Edible Ecriture," in *Consuming Passions: Food in the Age of Anxiety*, ed. Sian Griffiths and Jennifer Wallace (Manchester and New York: Manchester University Press, 1998), 207.

32. For the benefit of those who have yet to experience *yum-cha*, the service usually starts in the late mornings and finishes in the early afternoon. Waitresses push their trolley around, parading hundreds of types of dishes—usually very small in size—in front of you. You can stay there for hours eating many dishes, or you can be there for five minutes eating next to nothing. Chinese tea is always generously supplied and your teapot is promptly refilled. *Yum-cha* is particularly busy over the weekend, when it is common for popular restaurants to have many customers waiting outside to get a seat.

33. Bell and Valentine, *Consuming Geographies*, 131.

34. Arjun Appadurai, *Modernity at Large: Cultural Dimensions of Globalization* (Minneapolis: University of Minnesota Press, 1996).

7

+

Fragmenting the National Time-Space: Media Events in the Satellite Age

The electronic landscape outlined so far in this book suggests that the formation of a fluid, multidirectional, and multilayered mosaic of transnational imagination is dissolving the boundary between a domestic "image space"[1]—inside China (*guonei*)—and one outside China (*guowai*). In the same way that railways, planes, or dirt roads (in Ermo's case) transport people from one place to another, media technologies such as the Internet, new video technologies, and television allow images to travel, thereby figuratively transporting people from one space to another. The notion of mediascape, connoting a fluid, ever-changing, and unstable scenario of circulation[2] of, and interface between, people and images is central to understanding the formation of transnational imagination. More important, a crucial place where one witnesses the fluidity of the mediascape and the formation of a transnational subjectivity is the private space of individual citizen/audience/consumer. In other words, for someone living in transnational spaces, "home" is often where a television set, computer terminal, or DVD player is.

No other form of technology is more enabling than the satellite in overcoming the tyranny of distance in reaching many people. In some cases, developments in satellite technology have meant that many people can bypass state-regulated mechanisms to interact with people and images from afar, through, say, satellite conferencing, e-mail correspondence, and virtual travel on the Internet. In other cases, however, the advent of satellite technology has meant that the state has been able to carry out ideological work in the homes of private citizens more effectively than before. "Sentiments of nationhood pre-date the arrival of modern electronic media—but TV and radio

159

have nevertheless instituted new relationships between the state and the people," Moores writes in the European context.[3] Similarly, one important implication of the arrival of new media and communication technology into individual homes, including both domestic and Chinese audiences now living overseas, is this: The domestic space can no longer be easily separated or distinguishable from the public space. Nor can it shut its door to the presence of either globalization or the state. Starting from the first half of the 1980s in China, satellite transmission has progressively linked families to the central state. This is most clearly seen in the Chinese government's persistent attempts to maximize the appeal of the live transmission of the Spring Festival Eve Gala on national television. The annual event can be seen as a "happy marriage between an ancient Chinese ideal and a modern Western technology," whereby happy family gatherings are turned into grand "national reunions."[4]

With China increasingly connected to the outside world in various ways, the Chinese government has seen the potential of satellite technology for reaching spectators outside China, as well as national audiences. An example that well embodies the effectiveness of live transmission is the press conference held by U.S. President Bill Clinton and Chinese President Jiang Zemin during Clinton's visit to Beijing in 1998. Allowing questions and answers between journalists and the most powerful figures in the world to air live and unedited sent a powerful message to the international community about China's willingness and ability to participate in the global political and economic order. It also spoke to the Chinese students, scholars, and professionals living overseas about the Chinese government's more relaxed attitude toward students and the intelligentsia. The fact that Chinese embassies in some countries either freely handed out videotapes or organized screening sessions for overseas Chinese students during or after major Chinese media events, such as Hong Kong's handover ceremony in 1997 and the fiftieth-anniversary Tiananmen parade in 1999, suggests that the staging of these media events allowed the state to move propaganda offshore and penetrate the private space of the Chinese living overseas, as well as that of domestic audiences.

This does not mean, however, that the technology of live transmission has given the Chinese government the ultimate panacea for carrying out ideological work in the era of growing globalization. Tensions abound. Reading best-sellers, street and sports advertisements, and TV commercials in contemporary China, Dai Jinhua points to the ambiguous position of the Chinese state.[5] On the one hand, the ruling elite opts for nationalism to promote social harmony and cohesion, but on the other hand, it embraces with open arms the advent of transnational capitalism. This, according to Dai, creates a strange and ambiguous scenario in which China is saying "yes" and "no" to the West at the same time. Dai goes on to point to the complicity between these postures of Sinocentrism and Americanization: Both discourses have the effect of rendering class difference invisible and class analysis inarticulate. In the light of these tensions, the media have to negotiate a fine balance between wanting to hark back to China's colonial past in order to activate an anti-imperialistic trope for nation-building and at the same time trying to adopt a "forward-looking" global perspective. This means giving attention to events and issues that may incite patriotic feelings in the audience, but at the same time running the risk of provoking resentment against transnational processes.

That Party journalism[6] manipulates the spatial and temporal dimensions of news to suit the state agenda on critical issues is widely known, for, after all, the dictum of "using the past to serve the present and using the foreign to serve China" governs the daily judgment of newsworthiness. In fact, launching media campaigns to coordinate and complement official posturing, directives, and policies of the government on general matters, as well as on sensitive issues and incidents, is the "trademark" of Party journalism.[7] Although the Chinese government still does not refrain from launching media campaigns when it deems necessary, as evidenced in its handling of the Falungong cult, this practice is becoming less and less effective due to three factors. First, with the proliferation of sources of information about national and international events through the Internet, e-mail, and other forms of technologized access, it becomes increasingly hard for the government to manipulate images and facts. The plurality and diversity of news, current affairs, and views in, for instance, sina.com, the first commercial Internet news and information service sanctioned by the Chinese government, is a powerful testimony. Second, new media technologies and the globalization of communications processes result in the government having to use modern technologies to expand its reach beyond national boundaries. Television, which offers immediacy through live transmission and direct audience engagement through visuality, becomes an integral part of official media and nation-building. Third, the state has to live with a vibrant commercialized media sector, which is increasingly attentive to people's feelings about the issues arising from transnational processes in China. Narratives from the mass-appeal media, particularly print publications such as monthly magazines, weekend supplements to daily newspapers, and the tabloid press, use a benchmark of newsworthiness that may be different from the one used by CCTV or the *People's Daily*, thus fragmenting and dispersing the cohesiveness of national space and time that is created by the official media.

In other words, at least three implications arise from this fragmentation and dispersion of the national space and time, or the reconfiguration of the Chinese mediascape.[8] The adoption of live transmission of media events may be changing the ways in which "China" is imagined in spatial and temporal terms; news values practiced in some segments of the Chinese media may contest or undermine the significance of the officially defined national time.

As well, the coexistence of conflicting temporalities between various sectors of the Chinese media may change the texture and contour of transnational imagining, as well as reinforce the complicity between nationalist discourses and transnational processes in contemporary China.

While I focus here on the media events staged on Chinese television, the next chapter looks at the ways in which global media events that happen outside of China are produced for and interpreted by Chinese audiences, including both mainland Chinese and diasporic audiences. The juxtaposition of the two scenarios shows that while satellite technology allows exiled and diasporic audiences to access images and sentiments from their motherland, it proves to be equally enabling to the Chinese government in packaging and moving its propaganda project offshore. In pursuing this argument, I hope to provide a timely reminder of the pervasive and enduring presence of the Chinese state, which seems to remain firmly in place not in spite of, but probably because of, adopting new media formats and technologies.

MEDIA EVENTS, POLITICAL SPECTACLES, AND NATIONAL TIME

If the June 4th Tiananmen Incident in 1989 has taught the Chinese authorities one lesson, it is the importance of the camera in cultivating a "good" image for both the nation and the world. In hindsight, the government realized that in the business of manipulating the international media for internal political outcomes, the students at Tiananmen Square were far shrewder and more savvy.[9] One effective way to use media technology for nation-building is to stage what Dayan and Katz call "media events"[10]—national events, rituals, and ceremonies in which national unity, strength, and prosperity can be visualized for television audiences, both at home and abroad. The celebration of Hong Kong's return to mainland China in July 1998 was one such extravaganza. The commemoration of the fiftieth anniversary of the founding of the People's Republic of China on October 1, 1999, was another. Since 1997, Central Chinese Television (CCTV) has hosted a number of spectacular media events, including the opening of the Yellow River Xiaolangdi Dam and the completion of the construction of the Three Gorges Dam Project. In light of the domestic and international controversies surrounding both irrigation projects, live transmission of these ceremonies clearly had the intention of showcasing to the Chinese people and the world the wisdom and competence of the Chinese government.

"Media events," according to Dayan and Katz, entail the "interruption" of routine, in that they intervene in the normal rhythm of broadcasting—and of audiences' lives. They are also "live": The events are broadcast as they occur in real time. Above all, media events take place outside television studios, in "real" settings. What qualify as media events, argue Dayan and Katz, are events that, on the one hand, are live and remote from television audiences and, on the other, are interruptive, but preplanned.[11] These events celebrate reconciliation, not conflict; speak to very large audiences; and are necessarily "hegemonic."[12] Furthermore, media events follow three basic "scripts"—contest, conquest, and coronation—although the authors emphasize that many media events fall somewhere between these types. Examples of media events include the funeral of John F. Kennedy and the wedding of Prince Charles and Lady Diana, as well as Diana's funeral and the first human landing on the moon. Dayan and Katz make a distinction between "media events" and "news events," in that the latter are not preplanned, but are "newsworthy."[13] To exemplify the distinction, they argue that while the assassination of Kennedy was a "news event," the funeral was a "media event." Others, however, note the difference, as well as the similarity, between the two news genres. "News events," for instance, are routine news and differ from "media events," in that there is more of a ritualistic sense of heightened involvement in the latter. At the same time, they are similar, in that the practice of their production is equally shaped by the central structuring principle of news as narrative.[14] Narrativity aside, the difference and similarity between the two news genres can be noted. For instance, although "news events" are highly unusual and expected stories, newsmakers still try to find routine ways of dealing with the nonroutine. In other words, like "media events," nonroutine newswork does not operate differently from routine coverage. Instead, both of them depend on mobilizing strategies from the everyday routine of news-making, although there is an element of negotiation and improvisation in nonroutine work.[15]

Both "media events" and "news events" feature prominently in the Chinese mediascape[16] and bear a close relationship to one another. Whereas the Tiananmen Parade in 1999 and the Hong Kong handover ceremony were media events, since they were preplanned events with a highly ritualistic dimension that were carried in live transmissions, the U.S. bombing of the Chinese embassy in Kosovo in 1999 and the collision between a U.S. spy plane and a Chinese fighter jet in the international airspace over Hainan Island China in 2001 were "news events." Yet however sudden or unexpected, these events, too, were constructed within the existing and "usual" structures, formula, and procedures. Decisions in news-making, which include initial situation-defining, narrative framework, sourcing, discursive strategies, and subsequent editorializing, were mostly made within the parameters set by the official spokespersons, whose guiding principle in forming media responses lay in the perceived need to maintain the balance between social, political, and economic stability, on one hand, and to tap nationalist and anti-imperialistic sentiments, on the other.

In the case of Chinese media, both media events and news events provide good opportunities to use images of sorrow and tragedy to stir up nationalistic sentiments. The state television's coverage of the U.S. bombing of the Chinese embassy in Belgrade in May 1999, in which three Chinese journalists were killed, is one example. Chinese television gave lavish coverage to anti-American demonstrations in Chinese cities and presented tearful stories of the trauma and devastation experienced by relatives of those killed. Although the authorities cautioned against demonstrations for fear of internal social unrest and instability, their intention to create an external "Other" and to orchestrate public opinion to cohere with their foreign policy was obvious. This tendency was repeated in the media's coverage of the crash of the American spy plane over Hainan Island in early 2001 and the Chinese government's subsequent demand to the U.S. government for an official apology for the loss of the life of a Chinese pilot in the incident. Once again, issues of territoriality and national sovereignty featured prominently, and the Chinese population was seen to be on the side of the government in protesting against the imperialistic behavior of a world power. Although the Chinese government allegedly adopted a less sensational and cautious approach in covering the spy plane incident, in both cases the technology of the visual provided a powerful way of narrating the shame and sorrow that had been inflicted on the nation by the evil, imperialistic West.[17]

Media events and news events are common media genres practiced by many modern nation-states, including both state television and private networks, and the behavior of the Chinese media, in times of unexpected incidents and happenings, should also be understood in this context. This is particularly the case with issues and incidents of a politically sensitive—and potentially divisive—nature, such as the story of the immolation of the Falungong members on Tiananmen Square in early 2001 or the "firecracker incident."[18] When an explosion occurred in March 2001 at an elementary school in Jiangxi Province, claiming the lives of forty-two schoolchildren and teachers, the Chinese press and Internet websites published conflicting stories. However, the media's investigations were quickly quashed when Premier Zhu Rongji stated the official line—that is, the explosion was an accident and did not indicate a general absence of duty of care for schoolchildren. On occasions such as these, all media are likely to be brought into line, and the media campaign strategies of the pre-reform era remobilized, leaving little room for negotiation and improvisation.

The ubiquitousness of the media and their global reach in the age of satellite transmission means that wherever newsworthy events are anticipated, the media are present, although not always to provide live-to-air coverage. Wark's inclusion of the Gulf War in 1990,[19] the Tiananmen Incident in 1989, and the fall of the Berlin Wall in 1989 as "global media events" demonstrates the elasticity of "media event" as a concept. This elasticity is more clearly evidenced in the live and round-the-clock coverage by CNN, ABC, and others of the September 11, 2001, terrorist attacks on the World Trade Center in New York and the Pentagon in Washington and their aftermath.

The televised ceremony marking Hong Kong's return to the PRC was scripted to symbolize the "vindication" of the injustices done to the Chinese by British and other colonial powers over the past century and to mark closure of the historical British aggression against China.[20] The flag ceremony, in which the Chinese flag was raised to replace the British one over Hong Kong, was both a literal and a metaphorical reclaiming of Hong Kong from British colonialism. The ceremony can also be read as the triumph of the "one China, two systems" policy, as well as of China's desire and capacity to live with or even embrace transnational capitalism. Hong Kong, after all, has long been a hub of global capital flow and an archetype of transnational capitalism. The live transmission of China's jubilation over the return of Hong Kong sent a clear message to the world that China is a safe, stable, and investment-friendly place.

The military parade on October 1, 1999, to commemorate the fiftieth anniversary of the founding of the PRC, was also scripted as a narrative of "contest" and "conquest."[21] The intention to extract as much political mileage as possible from this anniversary is obvious from the government's elaborate preparations several months before the event. Stories of the preparations were newsworthy per se,[22] and books dealing with this subject also sold well.[23] To the Chinese government, the anniversary was an opportune time to instill pride and cohesion in the nation, but, more important, to reassure the international community that the Chinese government was in firm control and that transnational processes would continue to benefit from China's stability, prosperity, and openness. Apart from the imminence of the new millennium, October 1999 was a momentous time for China. NATO's invasion of Kosovo and the U.S. bombing of the Chinese embassy in Belgrade, the recurrent tension across the Taiwan Strait and renewed talks of military action, and the imminent return of Macau to China from Portugal were all making headlines at this time. Anti-American feelings were running high. Domestically, there had been unrest in the Muslim regions of Xinjiang, and Falungong was denounced by the Chinese authorities as an illegal and subversive sect. More important, economic restructuring in the state sector had begun massive layoffs of factory workers, creating a palpable sense of insecurity and discontent. The ceremonial marching of army, navy, and air force troops and the display of "sophisticated" technologies, as well as the parade of weapons, were intended to imbue domestic audiences with a sense of national cohesiveness and function as a muscle-flexing exercise to the international community.[24] It is estimated that as many as 1,800 journalists—both foreign and Chinese—were invited to attend the celebration, which was budgeted to cost 13 billion yuan, roughly equivalent to U.S.$1.6 billion.[25]

The fiftieth-anniversary celebration ceremony, however, also had an element of coronation. Three years after the death of Deng Xiaoping, CCP President Jiang Zemin was eager to consolidate his power base. Jiang, whose understanding of the usefulness of the media to increase his popularity had been evident in his media performance during his U.S. tour in 1998, was keen to exploit the potential of televisual technology and the power of media events as a genre. By scripting the military parade as an "inspection," the ceremony established Jiang Zemin as the authoritative and legitimate leader. As inspector of the parade, Jiang is seen standing in a taxiing "Red Flag"—a limousine produced in the PRC—waving his hand approvingly to his soldiers and regularly greeting them by shouting out ritualistically: "Hello, comrade [*tongzhimen hao*]," "You have been working hard, comrades" (*tongzhimen xinku le*).

While his posture in a taxiing limousine appropriates the authoritative image of Mao, his words also continue the trope of a top-down leadership rhetoric that is typical of the communist era. The "coronation" element, however, is not complete unless it is witnessed by the masses. According to CCTV's report, the entire ceremony was attended by 20,000 "distinguished guests" (*jia bin*) from both China and overseas, and altogether 500,000 people participated in viewing the parade. The "coronation" motif continued throughout the mass parade, which formed the second half of the media event, particularly in a gigantic float carrying a portrait of Jiang.

The fiftieth-anniversary parade was received with mixed feelings. It was described as showy and empty by former mainlanders now living in the West and was considered a wasteful extravaganza and a propaganda stunt by many Chinese.[26] When asked about the coming television event, some ordinary citizens in Beijing are quoted as saying, "It's got nothing to do with *us*—we are just ordinary people."[27] This does not mean, however, that the parade staged on the fiftieth national day had no impact on Chinese spectators, both domestic and overseas. Eric Ma's reflective account of watching the parade as a post-handover Hong Konger offers an intriguing example in which the spectacle of the army's "physical strength" and "discipline" instilled in viewers like himself a "strange" and surprising sense of solidarity, collectivity, and community.[28] Online postings on the diasporic Chinese websites—to be examined in detail in the next chapter—also indicate a certain interest in the event.

Staging media events live on national television has to take into account that more and more "national" audiences are on the move and live outside of what Hartley refers to as the "national semiosis."[29] This has an important implication: In the era of globalization and migration, when staging media events to national audiences, which requires the audiences to "be there" as witness of the events, media producers have to consider alternative strategies of "being there" on the part of those absent members of the national audiences. In other words, propaganda that promotes patriotism or state ideology may need to move offshore as the targets of propaganda move. A tangible example of this is with the freely distributed VCD copies of the CCTV's propaganda materials "Falung Gong—The Killer Cult" through overseas Chinese embassies. Similarly, Chinese embassies in cities that have sizable Chinese student populations sometimes organize screening sessions or freely distribute copies of the CCTV's annual Spring Festival Gala. Former PRC students in the United States, Canada, Australasia, and Europe are invited to come to the premises of the embassies on numerous occasions to participate in the collective viewing of national media events, such as the Hong Kong handover ceremony and the Tiananmen Parade.[30] These state attempts at reenacting national media events in foreign locations are also sometimes assisted by the willingness of overseas Chinese students to participate in such "propaganda activities" (*xuanchuan huodong*). This is an interesting phenomenon. While it seems to point to the fragmentation of the national time and space, it is also a powerful reminder that in the life of a migrant, the presence of the Chinese state, as well as the tenacious hold of national history, continues to loom large and real. Furthermore, an in-built aversion to the state propaganda may also be supplanted by a desire to be spoken to and hailed—the interpellated—by the propaganda messages from back home.

While the televising of the parade exemplifies key aspects of media events as described by Dayan and Katz, it also points to the danger of assuming the effects of media events in understanding media, nation, and citizenship in non-Western countries such as China. To start with, the dynamics between organizers, media producers, and audiences—what Dayan and Katz call the "three contractual partners" in the production of media events in the West[31]—are missing in China. Consequently, the assumption that typically comes with these dynamics—that each partner is a free and independent agent and that the production of a media event is a process of negotiation between the three parties—cannot be upheld, in spite of the rapid pace of commercialization of some dimensions of Chinese television.[32] In other words, Chinese television producers' participation in a media event of national significance is sometimes mandatory, rather than voluntary. Although Chinese TV producers and presenters now have more freedom than before, their participation in the making of media events may still be the result of submitting to higher orders, instead of voluntary involvement. Of course, they might be quite willing partners with the government on some occasions—for instance, televising the Hong Kong handover, transmitting the Sydney Olympic Games, or conveying the joyous celebration of Beijing as the host of 2008 Games, particularly since collaboration with the state agenda is indispensable in gaining high ratings and increased advertising revenue. However, at other times their collaboration may be an act of strategic compliance. Although individual journalists may not accept the official line on the issue of Falungong cult, they still need to obey orders or they will suffer heavy consequences. For another example, although campaign-like commemorative activities that inundated the CCTV around the time of the CCP's eightieth anniversary meant boring television programs and low ratings throughout

June 2001, television had no option but to submit to the will of the Party.[33] Compared with television, print media, especially the more commercialized segment of the media, have more leeway.

More important, while many events in China fit Dayan and Katz's definition of media events, there is a danger in assuming that media events such as the Hong Kong handover ceremony and the fiftieth-anniversary parade offer definitive clues as to the ways the media participate in constructing national space and time. Economic reforms and the subsequent processes of globalization and commercialization have resulted in what Zhao Yuezhi calls an uneasy coexistence between the "Party line" and the "bottom-line," or what Zhao Bin sees as the tension between "mouthpiece and money-spinner."[34] The growing stratification in the structure and function of Chinese media means that in asking about the relationship between the media and national time, it is increasingly difficult to assume the dominance of only one cultural calendar or of only one way to commemorate a particular national time. On the one hand, news and current affairs that are politically sensitive or have national significance are still produced under state surveillance in electronic media such as CCTV and its provincial and local subsidiaries; on the other hand, there has been a burgeoning print—and, recently, online—media sector that is profit-seeking and entertainment-oriented and has strong popular appeal. This bifurcated structure has implications for the media's creation of national time. While media events, as Carey says, reconfigure the attention of the nation by disrupting the regularity of the routine activity of reading and viewing,[35] print and online media are more about "regular imagining,"[36] in which the news often deals with "a slice of life"—in both temporal and spatial terms—and in a "banal," "prosaic," and "quotidian" manner.

MEDIA STORIES, UNOFFICIAL TIME, AND "REGULAR IMAGININGS"

The task of looking at how regular imagining is conducted has become particularly significant in the Chinese mediascape, due to the emergence of weekly papers, monthly magazines, and weekend supplements of many existing dailies in China since the early 1990s.[37] These publications cater to a readership that consists mainly of urban residents and youth.[38] Here I argue that the "banal" space created by entertainment and popular media should be watched carefully, not independently of, but in conjunction with, the spectacles created by state-controlled electronic media. To obtain a clear picture of the dynamism and complexity of China's mediascape, we need to study not only the production of spectacles, but also the production—and consumption—of incidents, phenomena, or even moods and sentiments that would otherwise remain the province of individuals in their daily lives, were it not for intervention, promotion, or endorsement by the popular media. The former warrants close analysis, as it reveals some of the ways in which "thought work" (*sixiang gongzuo*) is done in state representations[39] in an age of increasing globalization and technological convergence. The use of television to reach the home—both domestic and diasporic—embodies the desire and preferred approach of the Chinese government to "link the state with home."[40] The latter warrants study because this is where some real possibilities for democratizing the media lie. The two need to be studied together because only when they are juxtaposed can we see patterns of possible ideological divergence and convergence in the Chinese mediascape. The contradictory and ambiguous status of "Party media" and "popular media" is best summarized in the following:

> The Chinese press is undergoing a process of rapid transformation. This transformation is messy, protracted, confusing, and confused, littered with odd, even counterintuitive institutions, structures, and practices. Most party organs have gained financial autonomy from the state and become profit-making operations. Lively mass-appeal papers and sensationalist tabloids have flourished on urban newstands. Market competition has become very intense in some sectors. Exposure of official corruption has become standard daily fare. The party, however, has shown no signs of retreating, and old and news mechanisms of control—are firmly in place.[41]

The difference and the relationship between the Party press and the mass-appeal papers outlined here is crucial. As Zhao also makes clear, in China, media's initial commercialization and subsequent conglomeration occurred under the institutional umbrella of the Chinese state and the Party, not independently of it. Given this, there is as much danger in conflating the "state" and the "mass appeal" media as there is in dichotomizing the two. For want of a better term, I call these events, issues, and phenomena generated and promoted in the mass-appeal press "media stories," in order to highlight that they, unlike media events, are ordinary, rather than spectacular, and that they are usually stories that either fail to fulfill the routine test of newsworthiness in Party journalism in terms of significance and impact, or are deemed inconsistent or contrary to the state's agenda. In addition, they probably would not have entered public consciousness or acquired popular relevance without the media's recognition of the lives of ordinary people as a potential "selling point." Furthermore, I use the term to make a distinction between events that are televised *live*, deploying a collective temporality and spatiality, and issues and incidents that involve a sense of time and space that is shaped by the activities of the everyday—working, playing, and spending money.

The Koei Incident

I turn now to a media story that embodies this sort of "everydayness": the Koei Incident.[42] The story is a typical "slice of life" narrative, about some ordinary individuals going about working and living. Koei Software is a wholly Japanese-owned computer software company that has a few sub-branches in Beijing, Shanghai, and Tianjin. In May 1996, four young Chinese digital designers employed by the Tianjin branch of the company were assigned to produce a computer game called "The General's Decision" (*Ti Du De Jue Ze*). Based on a Japanese design, this game was set in the Second World War and included images of some Class-A Japanese war criminals, including Hideki Tojo, who appeared as "generals" and "fighters" in these games. The game also included glorified images of Japanese warships. The original game was designed in such a way that every time the Japanese side conquered a new territory, a Japanese flag would be raised, amid cheers from the Japanese army. Also programmed to be produced according to the original Japanese design were the images of Nazi figures, including Hitler, Rommel, and Himmler, as heroes: "generals" and "commanders."

Considering these images to be "emotionally unacceptable," the four young Chinese workers refused to do the job.[43] They sought the moral support of their Chinese supervisor, who, however, refused to lobby on behalf of his young colleagues, saying that the "emotional unacceptability" of the images was not a sound reason for their unwillingness to do the job. Frustrated, the workers confronted their Japanese boss, who told them that a game was just a game and was not to be confused with history; they must either do the job, or else. In defiance, the four workers took leave, during which another thirteen Chinese employees took over the job and completed the production within nine days. The finished product was subsequently shipped back to Japan.

The experience of these four young workers soon caught the attention of the urban youth media, including *Tianjin Youth News* and *Beijing Youth News*, which belong to what Yuezhi Zhao calls the "mass appeal sector within the traditional party organ structure."[44] Subsequently, national media, including Xinhua News Agency, Central Chinese Television, Central China Radio, *Liberation Daily*, and the *Economic Daily*, also covered the incident. This extensive media coverage prompted Chinese authorities to investigate the incident. Following the inquiry into the case by the Tianjin News and Publishing Bureau, the Japanese company was ordered to suspend its business operations. Bowing to both public and official pressure, the management issued a public letter of apology. However, this admission of cultural insensitivity did not seem to translate into benevolent management conduct. The company refused to reimburse the four workers for their lost wages. In anger, the workers resigned in October 1996, followed two days later by seven other Chinese colleagues.

In early 1997, responding to growing public anger at the lack of state intervention in this matter, the Tianjin News and Publishing Bureau finally expressed its official view. The "verdict" included the confiscation of the software and data for "The General's Decision," as well as the appropriation of sales profits from the game, which had been sold in China. The company was also ordered to pay a fine five times the amount of its profits on the game, and the Tianjin municipal government "extended its praise and appreciation" to the Chinese employees involved in the incident.

The support these young workers received from the state during this controversy was reactive, patchy, and ineffective. Their victory was purely moral. Although both public opinion and government legislative bodies gave their moral support, this did not translate into financial compensation. In addition, copies of "The General's Decision" continued to be sold—some of them pirate copies—on the Chinese market, and popular science and computer magazines continued to cite the product as an example of fine design and sophisticated programming, in spite of its offensive content and images. The company paid the fine and went about its business in China. Paraphernalia of "General's Verdict," including toys shaped like Japanese warships and Swastika badges, continued to circulate in the Chinese market.

The Koei Incident embodies a number of ways in which the mass-appeal media function as a barometer of the moods of urban China, as well as a creator and shaper of those moods. To start with, such expressions of resentment against the aggressive behavior of a transnational company in China would not have come to the attention of the ordinary reading public if the media—initially, urban popular media—had not decided to make an issue of it. In a time when the state has embraced transnational capitalism, and when formal regulatory measures are all but absent, the "mass appeal" media outlets have increasingly become the first and last point of contact between competing narratives of the impact of transnational corporations in urban China. In other words, the media do not merely record certain sentiments in economic life, but they have become *the* place where certain public sentiments are both initiated and promulgated.

The four young workers involved in the Koei Incident were all in their twenties and acted according to a sense of patriotism. When questioned by the media regarding their motivation in quitting the job, Qi Wei said, "Personally, I can say that if I had agreed to do the job, my conscience would never have been clear." Guo Haijing confessed that he initially wanted to work for foreign companies because of better pay and benefits, but now he realized that this also meant having to make decisions about his cultural integrity on a daily basis: "An educated Chinese should be able to figure out whether it is appropriate or not to do certain things. Making responsible decisions in one's own life means making responsible decisions for the country." Gao Yuan, the oldest of the four, was most explicit in identifying their perceived role as self-appointed custodians of Chinese national identity in the era of transnational capitalism: "Some Chinese have lost their national consciousness (*min zu yi shi*) and have only money to think of. If everyone was like this, then our country would be defeated without the enemy firing one bullet. We ordinary people cannot do much, but what we can do is to preserve national dignity by saying no to the seduction of material benefits (*wu zhi li yi*) brought by foreigners."[45]

The Koei Incident can be read as yet another example of resentment in urban China against the growing presence of transnational capitalism. The Japanese company in this case seems to have adopted an unusually aggressive posture. Iwabuchi, for instance, observes that the success of Japanese cultural production in the global market has mainly been due to a policy of producing and exporting only products that are "culturally odourless"[46]—products that do not remind people of Japan's imperialistic past and cultural particularities. What is striking in this case is that the Chinese staff in a transnational company was told to participate in the production of the offensive product. Confronted with the presence of foreign companies, the state's position is "forward-looking" and pragmatic: While it may choose to make an issue of Japan's war guilt whenever it suits China, as it did during the 1980s[47] and to some extent in the 1990s and now, the state may see it as more expedient in the current climate of global economy to forget, rather than to remember. The four young Koei workers, however, had a more "organic" sense of history. They told the press that although they were all too young to have experienced Japanese atrocities during the war, their consciousness was imbued with the evidence presented to them by older generations. Seeing the Japanese company's behavior as consistent with Japanese wartime aggression and cruelty, the young workers, and the journalists who covered their stories, operated according to a temporality that was inconsistent with that of the state.

Sina.com, Japan Airlines, and Consumer Nationalism

The Koei Incident, which took place in 1996, is by no means an isolated incident. The disjuncture between a temporality governing the state policy, which endorses global capitalism, and one inscribed in popular consciousness, which reacts against transnationalism, continues to be played out in commercial media in China. Although images of the foreign have been widely evoked to feed consumers' desire for modernity, and although many urban consumers may still prefer foreign consumer goods over home products, an antiforeign attitude to the presence of multinational companies in China has been gradually shaping the urban consciousness. Such consciousness often manifests itself in the form of consumer nationalism, whereby Chinese consumers tend to exercise citizenry rights against foreign products and services. Such trend is worth watching, since "leisure culture"—including the practices of spending money, traveling, and playing—has in fact been a state-promoted project since the 1990s.[48] In the popular Chinese consciousness, Japan embodies an irreconcilable tension between a bitter collective memory and an unstoppable contemporary transnational process; it thus becomes understandable that such consumer nationalism often has "Japan" as its target. In a widely circulated law magazine, for instance, a report details the successful legal case against Mitsubishi Motors on behalf of a Chinese passenger who was killed in a car crash as a result of the car's mechanical failure.[49]

In recent years, Chinese urban consumer nationalism has found new fermenting ground. Unlike mass-appeal papers, which are cheap and widely available, websites, though less accessible, nevertheless have the advantage of being interactive, hyperlinked, and deterritorial. Like mass-appeal papers, on the other hand, the Internet addresses readers/users in their own individuated space and time. It may be for this reason that many antitransnationalist narratives with Japan as their target find their way into this increasingly useful, albeit virtual, space. Such narratives on the Internet, like their counterparts in the mass-appeal papers, cater to an urban Chinese anxiety about the effects of the presence of multinational companies on the Chinese economy and, more important, on the Chinese psyche. This anxiety may well be a result of a lack of legislation and regulatory measures governing the operations of multinationals, as well as public disappointment in the government, whose response to the bullying behavior of foreign companies in China has been ineffectual and slow in coming.

As mentioned before, sina.com is a leading Internet media and service company for Chinese communities worldwide to publish online news and information on the Web. Since its launch in 2000, it has seemed to operate according to a set of news values that is largely independent of, if not totally alternative to, the Party journalism. It has also demonstrated a consistent interest in publishing antitransnational and antiglobalization stories. Apart from this, there are at least two other reasons why the Internet warrants careful inquiry as a serious challenge to the "unified" national space and time, and thus should be considered in juxtaposition with mass-appeal papers. Unlike newspapers in their conventional form, a news story published in cyberspace is seldom read as an isolated story. The Internet's capacity to refer the reader to other related sites means that a news story can speak to an intended audience through recourse to intertextuality. This archival dimension of the Internet journalism can be evidenced in the ways in which Japanese Airlines twice became the focal point of Chinese consumer nationalism in 2001. In January, some Chinese passengers filed a lawsuit through the Chinese Consumers Association against Japanese Airlines for its discriminatory treatment of PRC passengers during a stopover transfer due to snow. After a lengthy dispute and mediation process, the case was finally settled in July 2001, with Japanese Airlines publicly apologizing for its unfair treatment of the Chinese passengers and awarding each of the four representatives of passengers 1,500 yuan (about U.S.$200). The case was considered a triumph on the part of the Chinese consumers against Japanese Airlines, although the financial compensation was much less than anticipated. However, before the publicity related to this case had time to die down, another lawsuit by Chinese passengers against Japanese Airlines was filed. In August 2001, three Chinese passengers who were scheduled to stop over at Narita Airport were diverted to another airport, causing three days' delay and incurring additional cost on the part of the Chinese passengers.

Both incidents involving Chinese consumers against Japanese Airlines were extensively covered in the sina.com website and labeled "hot topics" (*redian huati*). What makes these Internet news stories different from other conventional forms of journalism is the possibility of hyperlink. Through links, readers were able to read, first, a cluster of news stories covering many aspects of the same incident;[50] second, the two disparate incidents in the year, both involving JAL, in juxtaposition,[51] and third, disparate news stories contributing to a general feeling of injustice done to the Chinese by Japan. Stories that contributed to this feeling, include, for instance, "Chinese Patrons Denied Entry," about a fight that erupted between some Chinese and Japanese outside a bar in Tianjin after the Chinese were told that it was a Japanese bar and only Japanese could enter.[52] They also include news stories about the activities of certain right-wing politicians in Japan,[53] as well as stories about Feng Jinhua, a Chinese national in Tokyo who was arrested by Japanese police for painting graffiti on Yasukuni Shrine and who subsequently became a heroic figure among some Chinese readers.[54] The ways in which these disparate news stories are grouped together show that sina.com does not follow the golden rule of "objectivity"—the benchmark of professional journalism—nor does the site consider it necessary to follow the Party line. Its credibility lies in effectively and efficiently catering to a palpable social sentiment and desire. However, in spite of the directed and packaged nature of these "theme tours," cyber-readers/travelers stop and start at their own pace and decide on their own itinerary; as in the ways in which the stories of the Koei Incident circulated in the press, browsing on the Internet was completely devoid of a ritualistic and ceremonial dimension. Rather than commanding a collective audience, sublime in presentation and preplanned, as in many media events, Internet usage involves a spontaneous eruption of feelings that are generated and circulated in the mundane, everyday—and sometimes virtual—space of individuals. Apart from the enhanced possibility of intertextuality, online journalism also facilitates individuated, everyday reading of news stories—in a way that is oppositional to how media events are watched—through means of interactivity. Unlike newspapers, online news and information services offer the reader the opportunity to participate, thus giving him or her the chance to change from a passive reader to an active writer/user, although not everyone takes advantage of the opportunity. The reader, as a result, feels more involved and even empowered. Cyber-readers in the online chat room or message board "speak" to the news story; post their comments, criticisms, and thoughts; support or quarrel with fellow cyber-readers; and inhabit a much more civic and pluralistic space than do viewers of media events whose only option is either to identify with or against the "author" of such event. Online interactivity also means that conversations between news users are less scripted and more subject to the moods and desires of the participating individuals. The fluid and organic nature of these cyber-conversations is evidenced in the link they made between seemingly disparate issues and topics, whose salience is obvious only to those who share a historical memory. Memory—both collective and personal—is subject to no logic, follows no rules, and needs no justification for resurfacing suddenly and making its own connections. A quick browse of the messages posted by online news readers of the JAL-related sites testifies to this: A corporate Japan in the era of globalization is condemned and denounced with the same language used more than six decades ago: "Down with the Japanese devils (*riben quizi*)!" "Jap dwarfs, get out of China!" and "Boycott Japanese goods!"

Like the Koei Incident, the reactions against JAL—and against Japan, for that matter—in the sina.com website point to the complex texture and layering of the Chinese transnational imagination. It was an instance in which transnationalism evoked feelings of anti-imperialism and national humiliation. Voluntary consumption of foreign images and things can be a liberating or even empowering experience in facilitating the formation of a broader, transnational subjectivity, but it is usually the historical memory of the nation that gets mobilized when the experience of consumption becomes unpleasant, unjust, and thus disempowering. While media events such as the Hong Kong handover or the fiftieth anniversary parade take the form of a "mandatory ritual of citizenship,"[55] Internet stories surrounding the JAL controversy point to the need to step beyond spectacles and examine the spaces of travel, leisure, and play that are inhabited by ordinary consumers, in providing new ways of imagining the nation. This may include news stories on websites, computer games, net surfing, or even e-mail communications. This is due not only to the fact that representations on the computer screen offer ephemeral, but potentially insidious, narratives of history and geopolitical reality, but also because computer technologies enable such representations to be consumed on a global scale. In fact, although the Koei Incident occurred several years ago, the memory of it is kept alive by a website of the *Beijing Youth Daily*'s coverage, making it accessible both globally and timelessly.[56] These narratives, and the meanings constructed within them—be they in the form of online news, computer games, billboard advertisements, or sports commentaries—become places that easily trigger emotional responses.

One cannot appreciate the complex texture and layering of the Chinese mediascape without looking at the juxtaposition of, and tensions between, various formats and practices, including media events, media stories, and media campaigns. Each of these formats is mobilizable, depending on the perceived nature of the occasion: While exceptional situations call for media events to present spectacles or media campaigns either to promote or to crack down on something, issues and incidents that emerge from the everyday lives of individuals tend to fall under the domain of media stories. Although media events and media stories have emerged as the dominant media formats in the Chinese mediascape in the era of globalization, both may be called into service when the state sees it necessary to launch a media campaign on a given issue or incident.

CONVERGENCE OR DIVERGENCE?

Juxtaposing media stories such as the Koei Incident and the JAL stories on sina.com with the state-orchestrated media events and news events discussed so far, we see a scenario of convergence as well as divergence, in terms of ideological position and discursive strategy. After all, nothing can stir up intense patriotic feelings among Chinese more than seeing their country and their country fellows being maltreated. As observed by many students of modern Chinese history,[57] these feelings of shame and humiliation, combined with the view that an injustice has been done, have always provided the most potent element of ferment to anti-imperialist discourses in China. Accompanying this feeling of injustice is a sense of crisis—that unless the Chinese confront the West head-on, they will face the destruction and end of Chinese civilization.[58] The spontaneous expression of patriotism from the four Koei workers may have been directed at the economic behavior of a transnational company; but it shares with the state discourse a refusal to forget the national history of shame and humiliation and a determination to "save" the country from ruins.

However, in both state-staged, live media events and media stories from the commercialized sector of the Chinese media, China's history of being colonized by imperial powers provides constant emotional resources. Both rely on mobilizing the audience by invoking the trope of "hurt feelings." Indeed, as Zhang Xudong puts it, nationalism in China in the 1990s has become a "social desire."[59] In this context, the mass-appeal media, recognizing "patriotism" as a good selling point, not only record patriotic events, but also, more important, precipitate eruptions of antiforeign sentiment and facilitate public debate on economic matters of national significance.

Let us consider the relationship between politics, spectacles, and satellite television in China, in the context of a series of "media events" staged on Chinese television during the 1990s. Here I suggest that juxtaposing imported media formats and practices such as "media events," alongside a number of other existing media formats and practices, which include "media stories," "news events," and "media campaigns," yields insight into the complexity and ambiguity of Chinese mediascape. Whereas media events are about spectacles, official time, and grand history, media stories are mostly about everyday life, unofficial time, and individual memory. Furthermore, although media events and media stories perform different spatial-temporal duties and functions in the imagining of the nation, evidence from the Chinese media suggests as much convergence—both ideologically and symbolically—as divergence between the two.

Few nations on earth have escaped the processes of globalization, convergence, and commercialization, and because of the increasing fragmentation of audiences and the multiplication of delivery modes, there is a danger in reading state-organized media events as the only actors in the construction of a nation's mediascape. National space and time are created and contingent upon media space and time; these, in turn, are constituted at the intersection of national, monopolistically staged ceremonies and rituals and "regular imaginings,"[60] which are sensitive to and expressive of the anxiety, fears, and desires of individuals in everyday life. We see the coexistence of an interruptive, but simultaneous, time brought about by the live transmission of media events, with a regular but individuated reading time. The juxtaposition of different temporalities conspires to create a heterogeneous space in which historical time is reconfigured constantly to suit the state's present agenda, while individuals' memories of their nation's past, subject to being triggered by present experience, often jar with "official time." And it is in the ongoing negotiation of these temporalities that a "nation"—what constitutes the "we" community—is constantly redefined.

Furthermore, while there is little danger of according too much significance to these state-organized spectacles, there is a temptation to overromanticize the possibility of democratization in the "banal" space of media stories in China. After all, because they operate under the logic of both Party and market,[61] the mass-appeal press sees a greater opportunity to increase circulation and generate profit if it converges with, rather than diverges from, the Party line. Although mass-appeal media may well foster the creation of a democratizing space by blurring the distinction between public and private, between state and individual, they are consistently silent on such issues as political reform and democratization, the exploitation of workers, and the growing disparities between rich and poor.

For this reason, media stories are not to be read as exclusively contradictory to, subversive of, and hence alternative to, the narratives of the nation scripted in the media events. Mass-appeal media should be given credit for registering the anxieties of the ordinary people and addressing the desires of individuals who are confronted with and are resisting the growing transnationalism in China. To think of media events and media stories dichotomously or in isolation from one another therefore runs the risk of neglecting the common cultural and emotional resources shared by these two genres, and hence turns a blind eye to the political and ideological complicity between them.

NOTES

1. The notion of "image-space" was first mentioned by cultural geographer Kevin Robins, and it refers to a symbolic space that exists independently of the traditional notion of place, which is geographically locatable. See Kevin Robins, "Reimagined Communities? European Image Spaces, beyond Fordism," *Cultural Studies* 3, no. 2 (1989): 145–65; and also David Morley and Kevin Robins, *Spaces of Identity: Global Media, Electronic Landscapes, and Cultural Boundaries* (London: Routledge, 1995), who argue that satellite television is offering a changed menu of cultural resources, by means of which audiences construct their own senses of identity.

2. Arjun Appadurai, *Modernity at Large: Cultural Dimensions of Globalization* (Minneapolis: University of Minnesota Press, 1996).

3. Shaun Moores, *Satellite Television and Everyday Life: Articulating Technology* (Bedfordshire: University of Luton Press, 1996), 26.

4. Zhao Bin, "Popular Family Television and Party Ideology: The Spring Festival Eve Happy Gathering," *Media Culture and Society* 20 (1998): 46.

5. Dai Jinhua, "Behind Global Spectacle and National Image-Making," *Positions: East Asia Culture Critique* 9, no. 1 (2001): 161–86.

6. For a good definition of "Party journalism" and its history, style, and propaganda strategies, see relevant chapters in Zhao Yuezhi, *Media, Market, and Democracy in China* (Urbana: University of Illinois Press, 1998). Also, for a recent account of the various aspects of Chinese media, using the perspective of political economy, see Lee Chin-Chuan's edited volume *Power, Money and Media: Communication Patterns and Bureaucratic Control in Cultural China* (Evanston, Ill.: Northwestern University Press, 2000); Zhao Yuezhi, *Media, Market, and Democracy in China* (Urbana: University of Illinois Press, 1998).

7. Franz Schurmann, *Ideology and Organization in Communist China* (Los Angeles: University of California Press, 1968); Yuezhi Zhao, *Media, Market, and Democracy in China* (Urbana: University of Illinois Press, 1998). This "policy" is most clearly evidenced in the Chinese media's coordination with the official celebration of the eightieth anniversary of the founding of the Chinese Communist Party in the month leading up to July 1, 2001, during which time most channels of CCTV ran programs almost exclusively related to the commemorative activities.

8. I am borrowing Hartley's notion of the "mediascape" to describe the texture and composition of the media and mediated imagination. It is useful to my analysis of the relationship between politics, consumption practices, and fragmented readership, because the concept assumes the centrality of "readership" in understanding media. It also points to the textual, meaning-making aspect of politics. See John Hartley, *Popular Reality: Journalism, Modernity, Popular Culture* (London: Arnold, 1996).

9. Some may recall that there was a large international media presence in Beijing at the time because of Gorbachev's historical visit to China.

10. See Daniel Dayan and Elihu Katz, *Media Events: The Live Broadcasting of History* (Cambridge, Mass.: Harvard University Press, 1992).

11. Dayan and Katz, *Media Events*, 7.

12. Dayan and Katz, *Media Events*, 8.

13. Dayan and Katz, *Media Events*, 9.

14. Ronald Jacobs, "Producing the News, Producing the Crisis: Narrativity, Television and Newswork," *Media Culture and Society* 18 (1996): 392.

15. Daniel Berkowitz, "Non-Routine News and Newswork: Exploring a What-a-Story," *Journal of Communication* 42, no. 1 (1992): 82–94.

16. I am making a distinction between Hartley's notion of mediasphere and Appadurai's notion of mediascape. To me, while the former refers to the texture and contours within which journalism operates and interfaces between journalism and politics, the latter denotes a fluidity of media images, formats, and practices in a given place. The dynamics and movements of such a fluid space are shaped by other "scapes," such as "technoscapes," "finance-scape," "ethno-scapes," and "ideo-scapes." See Appadura's *Modernity at Large*.

17. It is clear that the Chinese media coverage of the Hainan Incident was less subdued and sensationalized than that of the Kosovo Incident. For this reason many "ordinary people" (*lao bai xing*) in China were frustrated with the Chinese government for not taking a more aggressive stance against the United States. It is my belief, however, that the official media strategies of the Chinese government were rather shrewd and calculated: It left the people to say harsh words against the Americans, but at the same time, stood to gain the political benefits—both in terms of fostering nationalism in China and dealing with the United States in the international arena.

18. See Leslie Chang, "Beijing Struggles to Manage Information in the Internet Age: Conflicting Tales of Why a School Exploded Highlighting the Difficulties," *Wall Street Journal*, March 13, 2001.

19. McKenzie Wark, *Virtual Geography: Living with Global Media Events* (Bloomington: Indiana University Press, 1994).

20. Pan, Zhongdang, Chin-Chuan Lee, Joseph Man Chan, and Clement So, "One Event, Three Stories: Media Narratives from Cultural China of the Handover of Hong Kong," 171–187, in *Power, Money and Media: Communication Patterns and Bureaucratic Control in Cultural China*, ed. Lee Chin-Chuan. Evanston, Ill.: Northwestern University Press, 2000.

21. Dayan and Katz, *Media Events*.

22. It should be noted, however, that although officials gave lavish attention to the preparation before the event, voices of dissent were denied. The official media, for instance, were silent on the protests in Beijing in 1997 against the forced demolition of some civilian residences in preparation for the event.

23. Many media articles and some books were published prior to the media event. See, for instance, Tu Xueneng, *Zhongguo guoqing da yuebin* (China's Military Parade on the National Day) (Beijing: Dongfang Chubanshe [Orient Press], 1999).

24. Tu Xueneng, *China's Military Parade*.

25. Weekly News Bulletin in *Hua Xia Wen Zai*, October 1, 1999, no. 444, <www.cnd.org/HXWZ/CM99/cm9910a.hz8.html> (accessed May 2000).

26. In order to ensure a clear blue sky for the anniversary day, Beijing authorities apparently went to the extraordinary length of ordering smoke-emitting factories to close down for a couple of weeks beforehand (personal communication).

27. "Alienated Citizens View Celebrations as Gathering of Elites," *CND*, September 26, 1999, <www.cnd.org/CND-Global/CND-Global.99.4th/CND-Global.99-09-26.html> (accessed May 2000).

28. Eric Ma, "Re-Nationalisation and Me," *Inter-Asia Cultural Studies* 1, no. 1 (2000): 173–79.

29. John Hartley, *Uses of Television* (London: Routledge, 1999).

30. *Chinese Scholars Overseas* (*Sheng Zhou Xue Ren*), a Chinese official publication under the auspices of the state education ministry, regularly publicizes stories of how Chinese embassies overseas organize Chinese students to view media products from China, especially during times of national media events. Examples of stories like this include, for instance, "Chinese Students in Sydney and Japan Celebrate the Hong Kong Handover" (July 11, 1997), or "Overseas Chinese in Montreal and Ottawa Celebrate Hong Kong's Return" (June 27, 1997).

31. Dayan and Katz, *Media Events*.

32. Zhao Yuezhi, *Media, Market;* Zhao Bin, "Mouthpiece or Money-Spinner?: The Double Life of Chinese Television in the Late 1990s," *International Journal of Cultural Studies* 2, no. 3 (1999): 291–306; Michael Keane, "Television and Civilization: The Unity of Opposites?" *International Journal of Cultural Studies* 2, no. 2 (1999): 246–59.

33. This even applied to the highest-rated shows on CCTV, such as *Focal Point* (*jiao dian fang tan*), which for days leading up the CCP's birthday had to, as part of the commemorative activity, run monotonous interviews with Party members.

34. See Zhao Yuezhi, *Media, Market;* and Zhao Bin, "Mouthpiece or Money-Spinner?"

35. James Carey, "Political Ritual on Television: Episodes in the History of Shame, Degradation and Excommunication," in *Media Ritual and Identity*, ed. Tamar Liebes and James Curran (London: Routledge, 1998).

36. Colin Mercer, "Regular Imagining: The Newspaper and the Nation," in *Celebrating the Nation: A Study of Australia's Bicentenary*, ed. Tony Bennett, Pat Buckeridge, David Carter, and Colin Mercer (Sydney: Allen & Unwin, 1992).

37. Yu Xu, "Professionalisation without Guarantees: Changes of the Chinese Press in Post-1989 Years," *Gazette* 53 (1994): 23–44; Zha Jianying, *China Pop: How Soap Operas, Tabloids, and Bestsellers Are Transforming a Culture* (New York: New Press, 1995); Li Zunren, "Popular Journalism with Chinese Characteristics: From Revolutionary Modernity to Popular Modernity," *International Journal of Cultural Studies* 1, no. 3 (1998): 317–28.

38. Zhao Yuezhi, *Media, Market;* Geremie Barmé, *In the Red: Contemporary Chinese Culture* (New York: Columbia University Press, 1999).

39. Daniel Lynch, *After the Propaganda State: Media, Politics, and "Thought Work" in Reformed China* (Stanford, Calif.: Stanford University Press, 1999).

40. Zhao Bin, "Popular Family Television."

41. Zhao Yuezhi, "From Commercialisation to Conglomeration: The Transformation of the Chinese Press within the Orbit of the Party State," *Journal of Communication* (Spring 2000): 3–4.

42. This incident was widely covered in the popular urban media in 1996. See, for example, Liu Wu, "Tianjing guangrong gongsi shijian shimo" ("The True Account of the Tianjing Koei Incident"), *Ba Xiao Shi Yi Wai* (After Hours) 1 (1997): 12–16.

43. Prior to giving the task to the Tianjin Branch, Koei had previously requested its branches in Beijing and Shanghai to produce the program. This request was turned down by the staff for the same reason. See Liu Wu, "The Tianjing Koei Incident."

44. Zhao Yuezhi, "Commercialisation to Conglomeration," 13.

45. All quotes in this paragraph are from Liu Wu, "The Tianjing Koei Incident," 15.

46. Koichi Iwabuchi, "Marketing 'Japan': Japanese Cultural Presence under a Global Gaze," *Japanese Studies* 18, no. 2 (1998): 165–80.

47. Hidenori Ijiri, "Sino–Japanese Controversy since the 1972 Diplomatic Normalisation," *China Quarterly* 124 (1990): 639–61.

48. Wang Jing has written about the ways in which the Chinese state promotes "leisure culture" as both a material practice and discursive event. See Wang Jing, "Culture as Leisure and Culture as Capital," *Positions: East Asia Culture Critique* 9, no. 1 (2001a): 69–104; and her "Guest Editor's Introduction" to this issue.

49. For details of the story, see Zhang Hua, *"Mu zi kang zheng, gao dao riben san lin"* ("Mother and Son Taking Mitsubushi to Court"), *Mizhu Yu Fazhi* (Democracy and Law) 324 (2000): 26–29.

50. See, for instance, website <www.finance.sina.com.cn/g/20010719/84937.html> (accessed in September 2001).

51. See <www.finance.sina.com.cn/x/20010901/102868.html> (accessed September 2001).

52. See <www.news.sina.com.cn/2001-09-09/351723.html> (accessed September 2001).

53. See website <www.news.sina.com.cn/2001-09-09/351723.html> (accessed September 2001).

54. See <www.news.sina.com.cn/2001-09-11/353306.html> (accessed September 2001).

55. Jeffrey C. Alexander and Ronald N. Jacobs, "Mass Communication, Ritual and Civil Society," in *Media, Ritual and Identity*, ed. Tamar Liebes and James Curran (London: Routledge, 1998), 27.

56. See <www.sunrisesite.org/gb/?url=/forum/koei.h2.> (accessed December 1999).

57. For instance, see Lucien Pye, *The Spirit of Chinese Politics*, new ed. (Boston: Harvard University Press, 1992).

58. John Fitzgerald, "'Reports of My Death Have Been Greatly Exaggerated': The History of the Death of China," in *China Deconstructs*, ed. David S. G. Goodman and Gerald Segal (London: Routledge, 1994).

59. Zhang Xudong, "Nationalism, Mass Culture, and Intellectual Strategies in Post-Tiananmen China," *Social Text* 16, no. 2 (1998): 131.

60. Mercer, "Regular Imagining."

61. Zhao Yuezhi, *Media, Market*; Barmé, *In the Red*.

8

✦

Chinese in the Global Village: Olympics and an Electronic Nation

The discussion in the last chapter on the practice of staging *national* media events on Chinese television has allowed me to construct only half of the picture of China's electronic landscape brought about by satellite television. A reverse scenario warrants equal attention: How is a *global* media event "reproduced" by the Chinese media for its national audiences? Also, how are meanings and images of a global event "read" or interpreted by China's "national audiences" who live inside its national space? Furthermore, what goes on in the minds of diasporic audiences who are "not there" to experience the media event along with the national audience back at home?

Inspired by works on the relationship between sports media events, spectatorship, and cultural citizenship, I here want to extend and appropriate theorization about "being there"—made in the context of sports spectatorship—to consider the strategies of media production and consumption in the era of mobility, migration, and the possibility of an electronically connected "Chinese nation." In this last chapter, I will first look at the constructions of meanings of the Sydney Olympic Games from the perspectives of a Chinese domestic audience. I will then identify an array of positions adopted by a Chinese diasporic group in Australia at the time of the Sydney Games in September 2000. Finally, I will consider a number of ways in which the globalization and convergence of media and communication technologies, displacement of people, and an allegiance to a—variegated—sense of Chineseness have intersected to form a virtual global Chinese community. This community, while a result of both Chinese media images and people moving centrifugally into diasporic spaces, nevertheless has the Chinese state and the PRC exerting a centripetal force on it.

NATION, STATE, AND MEDIA EVENT

The involvement of the state-controlled Chinese media in the transmission and production of the Sydney Olympic Games was unprecedented. This was true in terms of the size of media entourage, the diversity of modes of information transmission, the ways of interactivity with spectators, and the depth and scale of coverage of specific sports media and individual athletes. Chinese Central Television (CCTV) alone sent 110 people to Sydney to cover the event.[1] Many other news organizations, including local newspapers and television stations, also sent their own reporters to Sydney. *Beijing Youth Daily* sent 11 people.

Xinhua News Agency, China's official news agency's team in Sydney, consisted of 39 people. Their contribution, however, produced only a small percentage of Xinhua's total coverage. Xinhua, for the purpose of promoting the Chinese presence in the Games, adopted two strategies. First, rather than relying on Sydney-based Xinhua reporters exclusively to supply news dispatches, photos, and stories, Xinhua's management issued its expectation to its 160 branches scattered around China and the world to contribute to the coverage of the Games from their local perspectives. This was to cater to the widespread interest in the Games, as well as to audiences' curiosity about Chinese athletes. These branches provided a large amount of coverage of Olympics-related events and individuals prior to, during, and after the Games, in a plethora of columns, in a variety of genres, including features, people's profiles, comments from the audience, and anecdotes. These materials were supplied by Xinhua to television and print media, at both national and local levels.[2]

CCTV's decision to send large numbers of people to Sydney to cover the event ensured that the media would not need to rely on syndicated materials from Western agencies. This assured the transmission of images from the event to serve the political and cultural agenda of the Chinese state. Xinhua's commitment went further. The agency maximized the reach and impact of the Games not only by transmitting the sports news, but also by generating further localized stories that related to the events themselves. This suggests that although the Olympic Games fit the category of "global media event," the production of the ideology, not just the transmission of the event, warrants closer scrutiny. In terms of presentation formats, the Chinese media coverage of the Games ensured an effective combination of live transmission and regular news updates. In terms of content, it succeeded in feeding the audience with a multicourse feast, which sandwiched live transmissions with prematch discussions and forecasts, and after-the-event discussions and retrospective analysis.

Xinhua's website was also successful in providing alternative information outlets that benefited not only domestic audiences who could not watch the Games live on Chinese television, but also diasporic Chinese who had difficulty accessing information about the performances of Chinese athletes in the Games.[3] Feeding news to the websites also meant that for the first time in covering a global media event, Xinhua staff had to work around the clock. Digitalized camera technology also facilitated quick transmission. The Xinhua website published on average more than one hundred news dispatches a day on the first day of the Games[4] and more than two hundred pictures of the opening ceremony.[5]

The argument about the close relationship between sports, state, and nation is not new. The direct intervention of the state in the working of the television markets, especially during such nationally significant sports events as the Olympics, is common in many countries, East and West, North and South. Every nation-state has a political agenda—promoting nationalism or a specific version of cultural citizenship—in the media coverage of such events. Apart from this, several other factors are at work in the case of Chinese media and the Games. Television, both national and provincial, is state-owned and state-controlled. Despite deregulation in the structure, funding, and revenue-generating mechanism, television, like Party newspapers, is expected to function as the "throat and tongue" of the Party and the government. This means that the Chinese government can expect to use television in the most direct and interventionist way when deemed necessary.[6]

It is also important to note in this context that political determination in the coverage of sports events may have occurred not in spite of, but precisely because of, economic interests in media production. While state owned and controlled media operate within the political and ideological parameters set by the Party and the government, their survival is contingent upon their capacity to generate financial sponsorship from businesses and to generate advertising dollars.[7] Unlike some of the public broadcasters in the West, which are wary of accepting sponsorship or advertising, CCTV sees no paradox in using the commercial logos of some products or companies to promote the ideology of the state. The implication of this blatant commercial dimension of the state media is clear: While media must do propaganda work, they also have to deliver their message in the most palatable and entertaining way possible. Sports, particularly the highest-rating world events like the Games, become an occasion for "commodified nationalism."[8] A good example of the happy marriage between revenue-generating and nation-building is the appearance of the Wuliangye product logo on Chinese spectators' T-shirts in the Homebush Stadium of the Sydney Olympic Games. The Chinese company that produces Wuliangye, a hard liquor, was allowed to advertise its product on the T-shirts worn by Chinese in Australia who attended the Games. In exchange for wearing the shirts, these Australian Chinese received free tickets to the stands, cheered for the Chinese athletes, and became powerful signifiers of diasporic Chinese patriotism to the domestic audiences watching the Games in China.

Apart from continuing structural and institutional factors, there are other reasons why the state wanted to get as much political mileage as possible out of covering this global sports event. One might recall the humiliating moment when the IOC President Samaranch pronounced "Sydney," rather than "Beijing." The Chinese government, anxious to repair the tarnished image to the international community following the June 4th Incident in 1989, had desperately wanted China to win the bid as the host of the 27th Olympic Games. That it had invested so heavily in its bidding campaign, only to lose to Sydney, was a blow to both the credibility of the state and the nationalist pride of its people. Acutely aware of the "dual opportunity" of hosting the Games—both external and internal[9]—China realized that to increase China's chances as a bidder for the 2008 Games, Sydney provided the single most visible international platform for China to score some points. Its competitive number of gold medalists would establish China as a major sports player in the international arena, an essential criterion for hosting such events. It would boost patriotic sentiments among the population, as well as among the Chinese communities overseas, hence generating populist support for China's intention to bid again for 2008. Ultimately, it would signal to the world that China is a globalizing nation, with political and social stability that is suitable for transnational interests. By the same sleight of hand, it would instill in its own people a national cohesion, racial pride, and faith in the government.

During the Games, Chinese television generously transmitted images of patriotic expatriate Chinese, which portrayed the centrifugal power of the PRC. One interviewee in Beijing told me that what moved her most about the Games was seeing on television the Chinese national flag hoisted on Sydney's Opera House by the Chinese communities in Sydney. Another interviewee was still visibly moved to recall the occasion when gold medals were conferred to Chinese badminton players. According to his description, the Chinese had won gold, silver, and bronze, and spectators at the stadium were mostly Chinese, many of them holding the Chinese five-starred national flag. These emotional interviews reinforced the power of televisuality: In instilling nationalistic pride in the population, images from the entertainment arena apparently proved far more effective than political sermons from the state propaganda machinery could ever be. During conversations with my parents in Beijing, my mother mentioned many times the moving scenes of the "ocean of red flags" and the drowning chorus of cheers for the Chinese at the badminton games. Obviously, these images had a profound impact on her. When I asked her what exactly had moved her, she said, "I can't help feeling emotional when I see our national flags raised and our national anthem sung again and again in a foreign country."

Although "good" patriotic overseas Chinese were sought after by camera crews, "anti-China" elements were vigorously excluded from the visual sphere, as well as from commentary. On October 27, 2000, *Beijing Youth Daily*, one of the most widely circulated newspapers in China, ran an article, "Falungong Followers Make Fools of Themselves in Sydney during the Olympics."[10] The news report was written by a reporter from Xinhua News Agency, China's official news organization, and detailed numerous attempts of Falungong followers to gain international media exposure and support during the Sydney Olympic Games. According to the news account, Falungong was the black sheep in the Chinese community. Its activities and posters appeared on a number of occasions when local Chinese in Australia held celebration parties to mark the gold medal achievements of the PRC to express moral support for Beijing's bid for the 2008 Olympic Games. The article ended by saying, "Falungong is a heretic cult organisation which has become a political weapon of the anti-China elements in the West. It seeks to disrupt the social stability and economic reform processes in China and to finally overthrow our socialist system."

"PING BO" SPIRIT, SEMIOTIC OVERDETERMINATION, AND CHINESE VIEWERS

Conversations with Chinese viewers in Beijing about watching the Games allow me to claim that there is one dimension of the Chinese television spectatorship that contributes to what I call "semiotic overdetermination"—to distinguish it from the "semiotic self-determination," in John Hartley's argument on television spectatorship.[11] This tendency is evidenced in the "spirit" (*jing sheng*) with which people watched sports events during the Games. Here I do not refer to the tendency of Chinese television to transmit only events where China was deemed likely to win medals, such as badminton, ping pong, platform diving, and weight lifting. Nor do I mean the Chinese media's practice of giving favorable and sympathetic treatment to Chinese athletes. Most countries do that to their own teams. Furthermore, as Hartley argues, television has the pedagogic function of teaching the population who "we" are.[12] In the Chinese case, television provided Chinese audiences with not just knowledge and information related to sports events, but more important, it marked out China's allies, friends, and enemies on the international stage. The overdetermination that I talk about here is the linking, almost by default, of the achievement of individual Chinese athletes with that of the nation and a collective desire to read the sports event as both a metaphor and a metonym of China's greatness and strength in the context of global politics and economy.

Most of the people I interviewed saw the Games as a platform on which China's strength as a nation was demonstrated and proved. Mr. Sun (no relation to me), a middle-aged senior public servant in Beijing, told me that he had watched most of the shows transmitted by CCTV, in spite of the fact that he himself did not participate in sports:

> What the Games displayed was a spirit and resoluteness (*zhi ji*) of the Chinese people. Many of our gold medals came when chances of winning looked really slim. Our athletes were prepared to give themselves completely to fight to the death (*ping bo*). We used to be the "sick man of Asia" but now we realized that there is nothing super-powerful about foreigners.

Many of the people I talked to in Beijing used the word *ping bo*—a word that has no ready equivalence in English—to describe the spirit of the Chinese athletes. While *ping* literally means "death-defying," *bo* means "fight to the bitter end," "fight with a very strong opponent and persevere in spite of the adversities." To Mr. Sun, it is this *ping bo* spirit that enabled the Chinese economy to boom. Pointing to the refrigerator next to him, he said:

> In the 1980s, Japanese electronic appliances filled up the Chinese household. Nowadays, they have been mostly replaced by domestic products. Our Hai'er fridge is selling so well in Europe that it has acquired the status of the inspection-free product. Some Western commentators say that China is becoming a threat to the West in the 21st century, and I think this is true, and it is really great!

This gold-medal-equals-national-strength framework was shared by Miss Wang, a young clerical staffer at Shanxi University in north China:

> This Olympic Games saw a quantum leap in the faith of the Chinese people in our country. We have never won so many gold medals, and many of these medals were not even within our expectations.

The broadcasting of the Sydney Olympic Games in China provides a perfect case to study local constructions of global events. Chinese national television produced and transmitted images directly from Sydney, hence producing materials that were "pure" and "raw." This means two things. First, the images, such as of the opening and closing ceremonies, which were globally transmitted, were broadcast with Chinese commentaries within the ideological parameters of the dominant discourses; second, the enormous Chinese media entourage, both electronic and print, ensured that the Chinese audiences were fed a continuous diet of sports events and activities that the Chinese media deemed relevant to Chinese audiences.

Having made the point that in watching the Olympic Games, Chinese audiences had received a "package deal," with meanings digested, processed, and delivered to the effect of a "semiotic overdetermination," I am anxious to emphasize that this does not mean that Chinese audiences have been duped and that the Chinese media are nothing more than a part of the state propaganda machinery. To think this way would be to fall into the trap of both the docile audience argument and the theory of the omnipotent state, hence ignoring the complexity and dynamism that mark the relationship between media consumption, cultural citizenship, commercialization, and nationalist state ideology in contemporary China. To understand this complexity, we need to consider a number of factors that conspire to ensure the semiotic overdetermination we see in the case of the Olympic Games in the Chinese media.

To start with, in China as elsewhere, sport lends itself easily as both a metonym and a metaphor in discourses of nationalism. In the absence of a battlefield during peace time, sport comes closest to acting out the dynamics of warfare,[13] with its lose-or-win inevitability, its "us-versus-them" binarism, and a "beginning-development-finish" structure. Sport, for this reason, is sometimes described as the "symbolic representation of war," and global media sports events, like the Olympic Games, have become "orgies of both nationalism and commodification."[14] The Olympics are organized precisely around nations, not around the achievements of individual athletes. Although athletes are selected on the basis of their professional excellence, they are ultimately there to "represent" the nation, wearing the national uniforms, saluting national flags, and bringing pride and glory to the nation. Olympic Games, being the most significant international sports event, naturally become the most spectacular space where nations are metaphorized, through the raising of national flags, the playing of the national anthems, and embodied—medal winners saluting the national flags and diasporic Chinese spectators singing the national anthem. It is possible and effective because it is entertainment, it consists of individuated and private activities. It addresses the spectators more as consumers than as objects of indoctrination, and sports events are presented as drama, rather than as politics.

Incidentally, the Sydney Games took place between the Chinese Mid-Autumn Festival (mid-September)—a family reunion season—and the National Day (October 1), the longest public holiday in the year, which gave the Chinese audience three weeks of nonstop, adrenaline-flowing excitement. Such high drama on a global scale, after being mediated through television, became the most palatable spiritual food (*jing sheng shi liang*), consumed in everyday familial, and very often public, settings. Many interviewees reported watching the Games in public places, such as restaurants, street stalls, or shops. This publicness refers to the spontaneously formed spaces of viewing among friends, relatives, and family members and is quite different from official spaces of organized meetings or viewings. In other words, in looking at the relationship between media spectatorship and citizenship formation, the notion of voluntary publicness is crucial. Donald's argument[15] on the centrality of cinema as a public cultural space is also useful in studying television viewership. Semiotic overdetermination—the practice of narrowing down reading possibilities—is effectively executed, not in spite of, but precisely because of, the "privatized," "mediated," and "individuated" modes of consumption.[16] What the Sydney Olympic Games on Chinese television seemed to offer was a mixture of didactic teaching and pleasurable info-tainment, in which the latter was masked, and therefore made all the more effective than the former.

In addition, a semiotic overdetermination would not be possible without the live transmission of technologized images, which depict the nation and create a spectacle-effect. This is seen, for instance, in the repetitively shown images of Chinese gold medalists kissing China's national flag and of the Chinese national flag being raised and its anthem played. Live television brought to the domestic viewers' homes the spectacle of many Chinese national flags in the stadium and sounds of cheering, infused with the patriotic sentiments of the overseas Chinese spectators during the badminton matches. This made television viewers at home feel that they were also participating in the cheering, although Sydney was across the Pacific. Writing on the power of technologized images, Rey Chow argues that an electronic medium such as film allows the entire nation to be visualized.[17] And I would add here that live transmission of important events such as the Olympic Games not only allows the entire nation, its history, culture, and people, to be visualized and spectacularized, it also contributes to the formation of a modern subjectivity that is characterized with a deterritorialized sense of cultural identity. The Chinese television spectators' identification with their counterparts in the Olympic Games Stadium points to the power of electronic images to enhance and solidify a collective cultural identity. As people in Beijing remarked to me more than once, the most effective ideological lesson of patriotism was taught outside China, and, as Chinese journalists have said, the most effective propaganda message to the international community about Beijing's suitability for the 2008 Games was delivered from the gold medal podium.[18]

Furthermore, when entering the Games, China was confident that along with Russia and the United States, it would be a strong gold medal winner. The Olympics, more than any other event, were likely to create numerous moments of glory and triumph that could easily be portrayed, even staged, and made into political spectacles to audiences both home and abroad. This, in return, would accumulate political capital for the Chinese government for its various agendas, which include promoting patriotism, increasing its political legitimacy, and scoring points for Beijing's bid for the 2008 Games. It was mainly for this reason that an unprecedented number of Chinese journalists, reporters, camera crews, and technical support teams were sent to Sydney to cover the event and ensure maximum coverage in terms of comprehensiveness, depth, and visual presentation.

Conversations with some Chinese viewers, as well as an examination of the ways in which the Games were produced and transmitted, suggest that while globalization of electronic journalism has not necessarily led to a homogenization of worldviews, a combination of political, economic, technological, and cultural factors conspired to result in an overdetermination of meaning for the Chinese viewers. In other words, global sports events such as the Olympics Games became spectacles of nationalism whereby both localization and globalization occurred. This overdetermination does not point so much to the disempowerment of the Chinese audience as it does to the growing capacity of the Chinese state to deliver propaganda while at the same time giving people what they want, a phenomenon that I call "indoctritainment," a coinage to describe the "happy marriage" between state agenda and the spectatorial desire of the population.

DIY CITIZENSHIP: WATCHING THE GAMES IN AUSTRALIA

Evidence of this semiotic overdetermination, however, is missing among the former PRC community in Australia. An obvious difference between domestic audiences in China and the Australian diaspora is "being there" versus "not being there" to watch the "sinified" version of the Games. In other words, although the Games were held in Australia, the Chinese audiences in China had far better opportunities than their diasporic counterparts to access the Chinese content of the Games. On the other hand, while they did not have access, as domestic audiences in China did, to the "sinified" reproduction of the event on national media, they could participate in the Games as stadium spectators, an option that was taken up by some. In addition, they could identify with either Australian or Chinese athletes, or both. Thus, their spectatorial practices during the Games presented an interesting case in which to study the various ways that citizenship is practiced. The different practices and positions adopted by these "absent," displaced Chinese demonstrate the increasing relevance of what Hartley calls "Do-It-Yourself" (DIY) citizenship and the role of television in constructing this notion of citizenship. According to Hartley, DIY citizenship differs from "cultural citizenship," in that the former constructs identity based on sameness, while the latter teaches difference:

> Looking at the rest of the world through television, it is inevitable that difference can be both celebrated and erased, recognised and removed, insisted upon and ignored. So there's a curious "toggle" switching between television as a teacher of "identity" among its audiences, and as a teacher of "difference" among the same population. It seems to me that this "toggle" switch is itself historical—it was set to "identity" first, promoting what I have called "cultural citizenship" and identity politics, and to "difference" more recently, promoting "DIY" citizenship and semiotic self-determination. It follows from what I've argued above that both types of citizenship may be found in social circulation simultaneously;

some groups may have moved beyond "cultural citizenship" and identity politics to "DIY citizenship" and semiotic self-determination, while others are still struggling for identity and see newer developments as irrelevant or dangerous.[19]

As implied earlier, the presence of patriotic overseas Chinese among the stadium spectators in Sydney's Homebush Stadium is seen to be significant in a number of ways. It fed into the cameras of Chinese media in Sydney, thus sending a powerful message to domestic audiences about the increasing importance that China assumes in the imagination of its "patriotic sons and daughters overseas" (*hai wan chi zi*). It also signified to the diasporic communities in Australia and other countries the desire of the overseas Chinese to continue, on one hand, to identify with the "motherland," in spite of their voluntary departure from it, and, on the other, to construct a particular Chinese identity that is suitable to their own situation. Furthermore, it portrayed the possibility of the Chinese state's vision of the "global Chinese village"—connected by new media and communication technologies and made cohesive by a common allegiance and support to the Chinese nation.

In-depth interviews with a dozen former PRC nationals who now reside in Australia, over a three-week period in October and November 2000,[20] yielded interesting results. Although I will focus on a few of these, data from other interviewees will be incorporated into the discussion where appropriate. All of them have migrated to Australia, with some holding Australian passports and others having or applying for permanent residency status (equivalent of the green card).

"MY PATRIOTISM IS INSTINCTIVE"

My first interviewee is one of the "patriotic" overseas Chinese spectators that Chinese domestic audiences saw on television. Most of the interview time with Gao was taken up with discussing his experience as a spectator, cheering for the Chinese teams in Homebush Stadium. When Gao heard that the Chinese embassy in Australia and the Australian-Chinese Sports Friendship Committee were giving out free tickets to Chinese migrants wishing to join the cheering squad for the Chinese teams, Gao took up the invitation. Residing in a university town in New South Wales and trying to complete his Ph.D. in computing, Gao is divorced and now lives alone.

Gao and his Chinese friends paid their own traveling expenses (twelve hours' driving) and for their accommodations in Sydney. When asked if he had made the trip because he wanted to support the Chinese teams or because he wanted to experience the Games firsthand, his answer was "Both." When questioned about which side he would like to win if Australia and China were competing, he said, of course, China, but if Australia was to compete with another country, he would root for Australia, as his attachment to Australia was growing. He also added that this was not the case when he first came to Australia, when he would identify with any Asian team competing against Australia. He added, as an afterthought, that he always rooted against the United States, because they were too "arrogant" (*kuang*). When I asked him if it was equally interesting to watch Chinese competing with each other, he said no, because what would give him pleasure was seeing China beat other countries. I said, half-jokingly, that his answers suggested that he was a patriotic Chinese, to which he responded:

> Maybe I am, but it is subliminal (*xia yi shi*). It never occurred to me that we over-seas China would benefit from China's becoming strong, although this is the truth. My patriotism (*aiguo*) is instinctive. It's hard to say why. There is no logic to it. It just is, like one has to eat in order to survive.

Compared with other interviewees, Gao is most explicitly patriotic, al-though he was one of the earliest to obtain Australian citizenship. However, in spite of varying responses to my question as to which side they are on, most of my respondents' answers were in favor of China. In addition, when asked if they identified with China as a "Chinese now living in Australia" or "an Australian migrant with a Chinese origin," most of them chose the former, despite some of them having already obtained Australian passports.

Gao not only considered himself a displaced Chinese, but, more important, someone with a responsibility to represent China. In relating his experience as a spectator at the badminton finals between China and Denmark and China and Indonesia, Gao made a point that individuals' behavior should be held accountable because they, once displaced from their homeland, should become the responsible representatives of their country of origin:

> On the international stage, one person is one nation. I have a theory: you can tell the quality of the people of a country (*guo min su zhi*) by looking at how spectators behave. The Danish spectators were very friendly and fair-minded, but the In-donesians were somewhat loutish or even hostile to opposing teams, although both wanted their countries to win. We have to be careful how we behave, because on international occasions such as these, a Chinese person stands for all China.

It is perhaps partly due to this sense as a custodian of Chineseness that Gao was prepared to drive to Sydney to join the cheering squad. He is the only Chinese person I know who lives far from Sydney and who volunteered to do so. Other respondents who didn't reside in Sydney, said that if they lived in Sydney, they would go, whereas many who lived in Sydney said that they were too busy to participate.

Prior to driving to Sydney, Gao watched the opening ceremony with some Chinese people in the town where he lives. Although he said that he enjoyed

the originality and novelty of the ceremony, he did not understand everything. He confessed that he understood the theme—the history, life, and
work of the Australian people—but not the details in the opening ceremony.
Yet this did not bother him, since the Games were primarily for "fun," not for
education.

In addition to being a stadium spectator in Sydney for a couple of days,
Gao, upon returning home, spent four to five hours on the Net every day
during the Games, mostly lingering on Chinese websites, looking for stories
and results that were unavailable on Australian television. He said that although his habits might have been a bit "excessive," he believed that many
overseas Chinese acquired information about Chinese teams from the Net.
When I reminded him that many Chinese in Australia have access neither to
Chinese television nor to Chinese-language websites, his answer was resigned: "It's true. It's too bad. Nothing can be done" (*mei ban fa*).

PERFORMING IDENTITY

I got in touch with Mr. Liu after reading his article in Chinese about how to
comprehend the Australianness of the Sydney Games' opening ceremony,[21]
which he had posted on *Hua Xia Wen Zai*, an online Chinese magazine based
in North America. Liu relates the opening scene, which features 120 Australian cowboys on horseback charging into the stadium, to Australian myths
that depict "swagman," "billybong," "waltzing matilda," and "the man from
the snowy river." The article traces these Australian cultural icons to a ballad
writer, Banjo Patterson, whose poem "The Man from the Snowy River" was
later made into a film. These images and music, according to Liu, came to be
closely identified as quintessentially Australian. Impressed with the display of
his intimate knowledge of Australian culture, I contacted the webmaster of
HXWZ, based in the United States, and asked for assistance in getting in
touch with the author. A few weeks later, Liu contacted me via e-mail. It
turned out that he lived in Newcastle, which was two to three hours by car
from Sydney. A series of conversations with Liu followed, initially via e-mail
and subsequently in person.[22]

Liu, together with his family, saw the opening ceremony at home, but went
to Sydney Stadium to witness a few sports events. I sensed in Liu a desire to
serve as a cultural interpreter, explaining Australian things to the Chinese. He
also seemed to be comfortable with having multiple cultural allegiances. This
intuition was confirmed by the following story:

> When I went to the Australian Stadium to watch the Games, I planned to buy
> two flags to glue on my daughter's face. Unfortunately, the Australian flags were
> sold out. So I bought one PRC flag for my daughter. Lots of people stared at her
> in the Stadium because of that. Someone approached us and asked about the flag

on her face. He was surprised that my daughter, with a Chinese flag on her face, spoke perfect Australian English.

The stadium during the Games was a truly transnational space, whereby the politics of gaze operates in both ways: Spectators go there to gaze at the athletes, but also to be gazed upon by other spectators. In many instances, gazing takes on a national dimension. Liu's self-conscious and confident behavior in this transnational space seems to imply at once both a plural and a partial subjectivity[23] and signals to me a powerful moment whereby the split identity typical of those in diaspora is articulated, communicated, and displayed in a most visual and bodily fashion. Here we have a case in which a transnational subjectivity can not only be articulated discursively, but also performed bodily. It is for this reason that I argue—continuing the discussion of the importance of the sensory and somatic experiences in chapter 6—that to trace the formation of a complex contour of a transnational imagination, one should start with the body, be it the body in front of a television set; a body sitting by a placeless computer terminal, but that nevertheless yearns for familiar food; or a body that acts sometimes self-consciously and sometimes impulsively under the gaze of the national Other in transnational spaces.

Inhabiting the space of cultural in-betweenness also means that the diasporic body in transnational space is at every juncture of its performance fraught with tension and ambiguity. Note the following account of Liu's experience in the stadium during the women's 15,000-meter long heel-and-toe walk, one of the highlights of the Games:

> We cheered for Australian athletes with the Australians, and we cheered Chinese athletes "ourselves." When Miss Wang, the Chinese athlete, first "walked" into the Stadium, I could feel the hostile audience around us, but I could not help raising my daughter on my head and rushing into the first row. Our seats were category A, just facing the Olympic Cauldron. Lots of people could see us. Unfortunately, we were the only ones who showed our excitement because since nobody expected China to win, only a few Chinese were there. It appeared that no Chinese cheering squads had been organized for this match. Later I was told even the Chinese journalists had left the Stadium before the race ended. I was rather disappointed. I took some photos of Miss Wang walking into the Stadium "alone."

Although his display of dual allegiances—on his daughter's face—was a spontaneous and uninhibited manifestation of his pluralism, his behavior following the triumphant arrival of the Chinese athlete into the stadium was an act of strategic essentialism. In the absence of official representation to mark the triumph of the Chinese athlete—an Australian contestant was anticipated to come in first—Liu felt compelled to act on China's behalf. In spite of the palpable hostility in the Australian gaze and the possibility of being ostracized by fellow spectators, Liu's reaction seemed both spontaneous and considered.

Ms. Huang, Mr. Liu's wife, behaved differently as a sports spectator. She is in her mid-thirties and works as a clerk in an accounting firm. In my separate interview with her, she told me that she had to wait a couple of hours in the queue to get three tickets for her husband, her daughter, and herself. They were hoping to buy the tickets to see the Chinese badminton and table tennis teams, but ended up buying tickets for the track and field sports, since all other tickets were sold out. Living three hours' drive from Sydney, they got up at five o'clock in the morning in order to get to the stadium on time. Nevertheless, Huang said that it was exciting to cheer for the Australian athlete, a silver medalist in pole-jumping. "I realized for the first time that I really wanted Australia to win. You could even say that I am patriotic to Australia. Yes, there are many Chinese here who couldn't care less about what's happening in Australia, but I am not one of them. I think that they lack passion in their life."

Compared with her husband, Huang had a more difficult time negotiating a dual allegiance. Talking about the heel-and-toe walking race, she said:

> I cheered for the Aussies and I cheered for the Chinese. When a couple of Australian and Chinese athletes were disqualified, one after another, only minutes before reaching the finishing line, I was equally disappointed. But what I hated most was having to make a choice between the two countries. My daughter kept asking me this question, which may sound stupid to some people: "Mum, if Australia and China are playing against each other, which side are you on?" I simply could not tell her. I didn't have an answer to this seemingly simple question. I tried to brush aside the question, hoping that it would go away.

When the Chinese athlete walked into the stadium, winning the match, Huang was excited, but much less demonstrative than her husband. She said that she was more conscious of the predominantly Australian make-up of the audience and didn't want to be singled out as supporting the opposing team— unlike her husband, who, as mentioned earlier, was ecstatic, screaming joyously, and raising their daughter high above his head.

> I couldn't do that. I am a more inhibited (ju su) person. This may also have been because we Chinese women were educated to be more gentle and moderate in our behavior. I worried more about what others would think of us. We were also brought up not to be too cocky with success.

Huang went on to tell me that she was more conscious of the possible gaze of others than her husband was, and this sensitivity sometimes took on a national or cultural dimension. She related to me the discomfort she felt when she saw former PRC nationals in Australia talk too loudly in public places or pinch fruit before buying it in the supermarket. She could imagine the gaze upon them from the Australians. Although these "country-fellows" might have been total strangers to her, she felt embarrassed on their behalf and usually walked quickly away. Here it seems that both Huang and her husband feel compelled to act as custodians of the Chinese identity, but that such a desire manifests itself in different ways. Liu seems spontaneous, demonstrative, and proud of Chinese achievements, whereas Huang seems much more sensitive to her surroundings, reflexive, and, as a result, more worried about the "undesirable" side of Chineseness. In addition, although both seem equally comfortable supporting Australia and China, Huang resorted to internalizing her dual allegiances, unlike her husband, who was happy to "wear them on his sleeve."

ACCUMULATING NATIONAL CAPITAL

Ms. Yang, formerly from Beijing, lived in Sydney for two years, prior to moving to Perth in Western Australia almost two years ago. She is pursuing her Master's of Science degree in chemical engineering, while her husband is taking an undergraduate course in computing at the local university. They are both in their thirties and have a baby of eight months. After obtaining permanent residency in Australia in 2000, they took out a mortgage and bought their first house. The grant of citizenship is still pending, because a new migrant in Australia usually has to accumulate a period of two years from the receipt of permanent residence before becoming eligible to apply for citizenship. Although their house is located in a relatively affordable suburb and has a run-down look, it occupies a decent "quarter of an acre block," the fodder of the "Australian dream." Ms. Yang told me that her husband works as a taxi driver on weekends. They sometimes attend a young Christian Bible study group, not so much because of their religious beliefs as because it gives them a regular opportunity to socialize with "Australians" and practice their English conversational skills.

At the time of the Sydney Olympic Games, Yang was five months' pregnant. Her husband, taking advantage of the discount airfare, went to Sydney to see the Games. She said that she decided not to go to Sydney with her husband, not because of her pregnancy, but due to reluctance to interrupt her studies. She did, however, watch the Games on television. Pointing to a huge, ultramodern-looking television in the lounge, she told me that she watched the opening ceremony alone at home. Then, overwhelmed by the spectacle, she drove to a Chinese friend's house, where she watched a repeat of the ceremony with her compatriots. She said that she had felt like sharing this important occasion with someone. Although it really didn't matter much to her whether they were Chinese or Australian, she had only Chinese friends. Ms. Yang told me that she preferred to watch spectacles and media events on television, rather than live, because television could transport her to more than one location spontaneously: "I wouldn't be able to see the fireworks over the Sydney Harbour Bridge if I was at the opening ceremony in the stadium, would I?" She believed that the "being there" effect—the feeling of being a participant (*canyu gan*)—could be recreated by viewing it in front of the television with friends and family.

The images of Australianness that saturated the opening ceremony were still vivid in Ms. Yang's memory when the interview took place. She recalled the horses galloping into the stadium, the lawn mowers, and the carefree sheep-shearing lads tossing coins onto the ground in a game with their mates. "They are all so ordinary, yet they are what make Australia." The ability to recognize signs of Australianness, however, is not converted, by default, into a capacity to resonate and identify with them. "I am not one of them," she stated plainly. Ms. Yang's relationship to these images of Australia—indeed, the Games were seen to be the most effective showcase of the Australian nation[24]—seem to point to the pitfalls of some of the nation-building projects in a multicultural nation-state: Certain attempts to highlight the quintessential nature of the national character to global spectators have the ramifications of including some and excluding other Australians. In other words, while they succeed in aligning and implicating a dominant sector of the Australian population by projecting images of the "true blue Aussi" on the global stage, this can be in some senses self-defeating as a nation-building project, as it fails to involve and interpellate the new Australian arrivals as national subjects.

Moving from nation-building as a state project to Ms. Yang as an individual migrant waiting to become an Australian citizen, it seems clear an institutional/political notion of citizenship does not guarantee a cultural notion of being at home for individual citizens. Indeed, a gap exists between what Hage calls "formal citizenship" or a "formal indicator of national belonging"[25] and a "practical nationality," an ability of the individual to claim national belonging in everyday life.

> Practical nationality can be understood analytically as the sum of accumulated nationally sanctioned and valued social and physical cultural styles and dispositions adopted by individuals and groups, as well as valued characteristics within a national field: looks, accent, demeanour, taste, nationally valued social and cultural preferences and behaviour, etc.[26]

Hage appropriates Bourdieu's notion of cultural capital and argues that within the nation, cultural capital takes on a "national" dimension. To have national capital, therefore, is to claim national belonging, which is achieved, according to Hage, by having one's accumulated national capital recognized as legitimately national by the dominant cultural grouping. Locating Ms. Yang according to the yardstick of Hage's "national capital" indeed reveals a rift between two forms of citizenship. Having been granted residence rights, enjoying similar rights and benefits as other Australian citizens, and waiting for their citizenship papers to come through, Ms. Yang and her husband are nevertheless not in a position to claim a sense of national belonging. This is most clearly evidenced in the disjuncture between her excitement about the *Australian* spectacle of the opening ceremony and her inability to lay any claim to such Australianness or to enjoy the spectacle of Australianness with an "Australian." By comparison, Mr. Liu (discussed earlier) seemed to have more of a sense of national belonging through his accumulated national capital, both physically—his daughter's perfect Australian accent—and culturally, with his command of Australian symbolism and imagery.

Ms. Yang told me that she would, of course, like to see those matches that the Chinese were likely to win, but few of these were shown on Australian television. As a result, she watched a lot of swimming and platform diving, which she also enjoyed immensely. Yang did not seem to worry about the lack of coverage of the Chinese athletes, nor did she go out of her way to compensate for such lack through, for instance, the Internet. In fact, she is the only one out of a dozen interviewees who told me that she put Australia above China in deciding which team to support, and she was more interested in finding out the gold medal tally for Australia than for China. "Australia has treated me well, and I want to pay it back by giving her my support." She added that she and her husband were allowed to migrate to Australia, they took an interest-free loan from the Higher Education Allowance Scheme, and they received a government subsidy when her baby was born. Ms. Yang's rationale for supporting Australia is interesting: Although it was her private decision whether to support China or Australia, and although her decision would neither bring an immediate award for her allegiance nor bear any practical consequences, it is nevertheless shaped by her perception of how much this country had done for her in the past and by her hopes for the future. "I am more concerned about the present and the future, which is here, while he [she refers to her husband] is more concerned about the past." Ms. Yang told me that her husband is much more patriotic to China than she is. In other words, Ms. Yang's support for Australia seems to be driven by an intuitive understanding of reciprocity, a sense of appreciation, and the obligation of a guest or a grateful recipient of generosity, which contrasts with what Hage describes as a "governmental" or "managerial"[27] attitude held by those Australians who feel that they have a natural claim of ownership or proprietorship on the nation. Indeed, Ms. Yang and her husband are working hard to accumulate national capital—they are obtaining degrees, improving their English, and raising a family in an "Aussie" manner. Would they eventually accumulate enough cultural capital to effect a shift from a guest mentality to a host mentality? Furthermore, could Ms. Yang's decision to root for Australia over China as a sports spectator be a sign of her internalized view, as a new Australian, of the desirability of national belonging?

"NATIONALISM IS DANGEROUS"

I interviewed Mr. Feng on a long-distance coach in northern China on an excursion that was organized by the local university, which hosted a conference that both Mr. Feng and I attended. Feng is lively, has an animated personality, and is easy to get along with. To kill time on the trip, Feng picked up a microphone and began to sing a Chinese song, karaoke style. En route to our destination he sang the *Internationale* (*Guoji Ge*, in Chinese).[28] On the way back to our hotel, he opted for a love song.

Like Gao, Feng had also received an invitation from the Chinese embassy in Sydney to participate in the cheering squad, but declined, saying that he was "too busy." Now a senior academic in Sydney, Feng told me that he was forced to watch the opening ceremonies by "the two ladies of my house" (he is married to a Chinese woman and has a daughter). His conversation with me conveyed the impression that Feng couldn't care less about the Games or about how Chinese athletes fared. He said that the lack of coverage of Chinese athletes on Australian television did not concern him and that he did not seek alternative sources of information—such as the Internet—in order to find out about the achievements of the Chinese teams. When asked to state his loyalty between Australian and Chinese teams, Feng said that he was not concerned one way or another.

Feng seemed to me unusually cosmopolitan. Perhaps he has, as Hartley says, gone beyond "identity" politics and become more tolerant of difference. When I asked him what he would do if he was given the task of arts director for the 2008 opening ceremony (should Beijing win), he said that he would like to "project the theme of globalization [or Chinese embrace of globalization] into" the ceremony. When I asked him to comment on the Sydney opening ceremony, rather than replying, he commented on how the Chinese audiences in China saw it: "My conversations with friends in China confirmed my judgment that most Chinese do not understand the importance given to the issue of Aboriginality." When I asked him what he thought of Beijing as the bidder for 2008, his answer was:

> I hope Beijing can make it and Beijing does have a good chance. The games will accelerate the pace of integration of China into the mainstream civilization.

When I asked him which side he would root for if he were a spectator at a match between Australia and China, Feng told me that he couldn't care less, and, probably as an explanation, he said (in English): "Nationalism is dangerous, mate!"

The proglobalization, antinationalistic discourse evident in Feng's responses seems to locate him squarely on the other end of the spectrum of citizenship, where he has "moved beyond identity politics" toward becoming a truly global citizen. Feng is keenly aware of cultural diversity and difference and feels at ease in both Australian and Chinese contexts. However, I could not help but detect a certain ambiguity. Later, when our conversation drifted from the Games, I learned, serendipitously, that Mr. Feng still keeps his Chinese citizenship because he hopes to join local politics in China one day, and he wishes not only eventually to retire in China, but particularly to die there.

"AUSTRALIA HAS NO CULTURE, HAS IT?"

Like Feng, Mr. Yao is also quite mobile. He told me that his job in Sydney as a research scientist requires that he be in Australia only eight months a year, so he spends on average four months in China every year. Yao's attitude toward travel is therefore quite cosmopolitan:

> I have never considered *chuguo* (leaving China and going overseas) such a big deal. It feels more like working interstate. Sydney is not that different from, say, Harbin in northeastern China. I say "hello" to my mum when I come back to Beijing and say "bye" when I head off to the airport to go to Sydney. As simple as that.

I pointed out to him that his sense of place could be different from other, less-privileged, Chinese living in Australia, who do not enjoy the same degree of financial and job security. I also mentioned that to many Chinese who lacked the technical expertise or skills to migrate to a Western country, *chuguo* is indeed a big deal. Conceding that I could be right, Yao was keen to stress to me that while he could be more privileged than other Chinese in terms of mobility, this to-and-from lifestyle is partly driven by a lack of access to Chinese cultural products in Australia and a desire to consume such products. Mr. Yao does not have access to Chinese television, because, like many Chinese living in Australia, he either rents or lives in a unit in a block of flats and hence cannot install a satellite dish. Mr. Yao said that he spends lots of time in Beijing watching television dramas and catching up with old friends. When I asked how often he consumes cultural products in Australia, he answered that there are no real cultural products in Australia, and in fact "there is no such as thing as culture in Australia." Having said this, Mr. Yao challenged me to provide a list of things that are part of Australian culture. I mentioned the pub culture, beach culture, and barbecue culture, and Mr. Yao responded, "Exactly! What has that got to do with me?"

I detect a chicken-and-egg situation with Mr. Yao, in terms of the ways he handles identity politics. Could his conundrum be easily resolved if finally he buys his own house in Sydney so that he could watch Chinese television? Or does his liminal existence—traversing Sydney and Beijing—inhibit his desire to strike roots in Sydney and hence buy a house? McKenzie Wark's well-known remark—that we do not need roots, only aerials[29]—suddenly seems a bit too glib. It seems that in order to have aerials, you need roots.

Mr. Yao did not watch the live transmission of the opening ceremony of the Games, as he was in Manila on a business trip. He later saw it on a videotape in China. Yao's comment on the lawn-mower at the opening ceremony reveals an acute cross-cultural understanding:

> Lawn mowers are a great idea. They are both evocative of Australian life, but at the same time very ordinary. As ordinary as Chinese eating watermelon seeds. But I don't think the Chinese would appreciate its significance since lawn mowers have no place in Chinese people's life. Nor do I believe that it would resonate with the Chinese living in Australia.

Mr. Yao seems equally capable of coming up with ideas on how effectively to represent Chinese cultures to the world. Should Beijing win the bid for 2008 and if he was given the chance to design the opening, he would have *chang'e* going to the moon[30] and being met there by an American astronaut. This would signify, he says, both Chinese mythology and China's capacity to integrate into the modern world. He also envisages having one thousand lamas dressed in colorful orange robes, dancing and singing. This would showcase the Chinese government's reconciliatory gesture toward Tibet and would silence Western critics on the Tibet issues. Mr. Yao's story suggests a few things: A lifestyle featuring mobility and deterritorialization does not necessarily lead to a "cosmopolitan" outlook. In fact, one can be an earthbound villager and a cosmopolitan at the same time. In addition, a conceptual or intellectual understanding of the cross-cultural difference does not necessarily translate into cultural tolerance and sensitivity. One may achieve cross-cultural media literacy at an intellectual level, but continue to practice cultural exclusion in emotional and practical terms.

Writing about the impact and implications of the globalization of electronic journalism on media consumption and research on media reception, Gurevitch[31] points to the issue of "openness": Although news materials are disseminated globally, these materials are "open texts," in the sense that they are subject to local and regional interpretation. In addition, the audiences are more likely to increase their dependency on the local decoders in making sense of the images and stories from faraway places. Because of this, there needs to be a shift, in studying the globalization of electronic journalism, from a concern with the content and flow of news and images to a concern with the activity of constructing local meaning from these globalized events and images. In other words, in looking at the intersection between media technologies, media spaces, and the local place in the increasingly globalized environment, it is important to consider both the issue of *connection*—factors contributing to openness—and the issue of *boundary*, factors preventing openness.

The former PRC nationals' identification was a deeply problematic and difficult process, since they were not only faced with a lack of access to Chinese television, but were also confronted with a "split identity" dilemma. Such a dilemma, of course, is perennial and indeed is not unique to the Chinese migrant communities. However, it was highlighted during the Sydney Olympic Games, which featured a heavy Chinese presence, in terms of both athletes and media. While the Chinese media worked around the clock to ensure that the national audiences were "taken care of," diasporic viewers, wedged between the local media, which they could not understand, resonate, and identify with, and Chinese national media, which were unavailable, had to resort to alternative strategies of identification. Consequently, media practices among diasporic communities vary, ranging from, on one end of the spectrum, a direct, active involvement and participation in the media event, to a more common pattern of settling for a mediated and, in some cases, deterritorialized identification. Although migrants uniformly profess a desire to engage in cultural production and consumption as Chinese—be it in Mr. Feng's self-styled karaoke or Mr. Yao's imagination of what Beijing (if successful) should present to the world in 2008—and although all of them express a wish for Beijing to win the bid, individuals seem to adopt different positions in identity politics.

The difference in positions expressed by migrants is articulated and negotiated in the range of ways in which the media are used: compensatory—as in Mr. Gao's use of the Internet; combative, as in Mr. Yao's oppositional reading of the symbols of opening ceremony; competitive, as in Mr. Gao's unambiguous desire to see China beat any other country, including Australia; complementary, as in Ms. Yang's preference for live transmission over "being there" and her willingness to "make do"; and nonidentifying, as in Mr. Feng's lack of interest in the Games, one way or another. It is also important to note that these strategies can be used subliminally and simultaneously. And it is in the subliminal and simultaneous deployment of sometimes competing and sometimes contradictory strategies that different forms of cultural citizenships are constructed, articulated, and formed.

The formation of those variegated and diverse ways of practicing citizenship—both cultural citizenship and "DIY" citizenship—is intrinsically linked with patterns of media consumption. If media teach the audience who "we" are and are thus inseparable from nation-building, then the lack of media products from "home" compels diasporic members to look around, "make do," and determine their own definition of who "we" are. Such negotiations are everyday practices, fluid, and subject to the specificity of the individuals' circumstances. In other words, constructing citizenship entails a variety of practices that range from "making do" in spite of the lack—as in the case of Ms. Yang staying at home to watch Australian athletes—to the pursuit of authentic Chinese experiences because of the lack, as in the case of her husband flying to Sydney to witness the Chinese victory. Constructing citizenship also involves different ways of "doing it." Some declare their loyalty and preference publicly and performatively, as Mr. Liu did; others make a private decision and keep their preference to themselves, as did Ms. Huang and Ms. Yang. The ways in which citizenship is understood and practiced also differ greatly. For some, it is about compartmentalizing two notions of citizenship, both cultural and DIY. It is also about compartmentalizing two forms of citizenship, both literal and cultural. Mr. Gao and Ms. Yang's husband both hold Australian passports and assert their citizen's rights as Australians, but their cultural and emotional identification is unambiguously with China. For others, it is about the juxtaposing and linking of these two forms of citizenship. Both Ms. Yang's wish to do something in return for Australia and Ms. Huang's reluctance to take sides between Australia and China point to the possibility of such juxtaposition.

TOWARD AN ELECTRONIC CHINESE NATION?

Consider the following complaint from a mainland Chinese who now lives in the United States:[32]

Unfortunately, I live in the States and there is little coverage of the Chinese athletes from the American television network. They go on and on about an American gymnast who came in 6th while making fun of the Chinese athlete who won the gold medal. It's ridiculous.

This article, posted in one of the Chinese-language websites that is maintained by former mainland Chinese now living in diaspora, is about not being able to watch the Games. What exactly does this disgruntled and displaced Chinese person get out of posting an article on the Internet? What does it say about the strategies of a group of viewers, who, due to displacement, fall through the crevice of globalized electronic journalism and hence do not belong to any of the "national semiosis"?[33] When it comes to viewing national transmissions of global media event such as the Games, the former PRC Chinese find themselves largely inhabiting a "no man's land." Since audience participation, the crucial component of what defines a media event[34] is missing, communication about that media event takes the form of talking about the missing, rather than the witnessing, of the event or the event per se. In this sense, as an articulation of one's regret at "not being there," the narrative about missing the event is as important as one about witnessing the event, and indeed, what better place than the Internet to express this feeling of regret?

I implied in the last chapter that Dayan and Katz's work on media events says little about how to read media events staged in non-Western systems.

Due to the relatively late entry of television into domestic space in many developing and/or non–liberal/democratic countries, where the governments nevertheless want to exploit the power of technology, the notion of media events needs to be revisited and revamped in order to provide theoretical relevance to the phenomenon of semiotic overdetermination. Here I would add that unless the theory of the media event can adequately account for absence—a want-to-be witness wishing to "be there," but in fact not "being there"—it has limited use in the study of the consumption practices of increasingly deterritorialized and fragmented audiences. The discussion so far in this chapter of the ways in which the meaning of the Olympics as a global media event became overdetermined, after global images were processed, transmitted, and relayed into the "national semiosis," suggests the power of interpellation: the national spectators willingly subjecting themselves to being hailed as "we," "the Chinese." In chapter 4, I have pointed to, in the context of former PRC nationals watching television dramas on videotape, a process of voluntary interpellation, whereby the displaced Chinese willingly subject themselves to possible media propaganda of the Chinese state. I implied that this process is strategic and political, in that it allows a racially othered community to carve out its own symbolic and representational space. In the case of watching the Games, the process of interpellation of the Chinese media allows the Chinese athletes, the Chinese television sports commentators, and the Chinese spectators to be conflated under the category of "we." Though this is not unique to the Chinese case—and, indeed, the combination of prepared scripts and spontaneous utterances of "we have won" is capable of evoking the deepest national pride[35]—Chinese sports commentators during the Games were seen to be primarily in the business of "making it national."[36]

In this light, the complaint of the Chinese migrant quoted earlier can be read as an inchoate articulation of loss brought about by his migration. Existing between two systems of meaning—embodied by the American television network, which he can access, but does not identify with—and Chinese television, which he identifies with, but has no access to, what the migrant laments is the loss of the privilege of "voluntary interpellation," the opportunity to be hailed as one of "us." A general preliminary inquiry into the availability of Chinese-language television programs shows that SBS[37] (Special Broadcasting Service) is the only channel in Australia that supplies a small dose of news from home.[38] The CCTV Channel 4 is devoted to broadcasting overseas, but viewers need satellite dishes to access it. Some Chinese migrants have installed the satellite dish, which allows them access to television from China, but the high cost has discouraged others from following suit. Apart from the cost of installation, many other people live in rented accommodations or flats in multistory buildings, both of which prohibit or discourage viewers from installing satellite dishes. CCTV's programs are also accessible via the Internet.[39] However, though this gives the diasporic body that is not "there" unprecedented access to television programs from "home," the accessibility is nevertheless limited to those who have a high-capacity computer and a reliable online environment. More important, what online television offers is merely the content, not the familial, public, and collective viewing environment that marks the way that media events are watched in China.

Theorizations in media events also fail to consider the increasingly important role that the diasporic body plays in "messing up" the global/local delineation. This role is best evidenced in the celebrated incident that involved NBC's commentary on Chinese athletes during the 1996 Olympic Games in Atlanta. When athletes from the People's Republic of China marched into the Atlanta stadium during the opening ceremony, NBC reporter Bob Costas's running comment included an attack on China's human rights record, its abuse of intellectual property rights, and his suggestion that many Chinese athletes at the Games were taking performance-enhancing drugs. Costas's commentary initially eluded Chinese authorities and media, but greatly enraged Chinese expatriates, including students, academic, engineers, and entrepreneurs living in the United States. They wrote to American and Chinese newspapers, citing Costas's commentary as a typical example of America's patronizing attitude toward China. They also made use of the Internet to publicize Costas's comments, gathering e-mail petitions and protest letters. The Chinese Foreign Ministry subsequently took issue with NBC, demanding an official apology from Costas. This campaign was so effective that Costas quickly became an American whom Chinese love to hate.[40]

Interestingly, the Chinese intervention in the American media's attempt to construct meanings in an imperialistic fashion first took the form of Chinese communities in America protesting against the media's unfair and distorted treatment of subject matter relating to China and subsequently demanding apologies from American media organizations. These protests often became catalysts that aroused latent anti-American sentiments. In many cases, the sentiments of diasporic Chinese were taken up by mainland Chinese, and individuals' spontaneous reactions became organized expressions. The diasporic members' resistance to the dominant meanings of the host culture, their capacity to interrogate and intervene against imperial voices, and their willingness to assume a role as cultural custodians of Chineseness, in spite of not "being there," had profound implications in reworking the assumptions behind the media event argument. First, the construction of the meaning of media events is not limited to the "script" prepared to explain the event per se; it is necessary to take into account the utterances outside of, and subsequent to, the media event. Second, since the diasporic condition is premised upon absence, it is crucial to examine the alternative strategies of "being there" that are adopted by migrants in times of global media events.

One important way of being there is made possible by the widespread use of the Internet, which increasingly is providing an irreplaceable forum for de- territorialized members of the community to maintain some kind of pres- ence. The proliferation of Chinese-language websites that are maintained by former mainland Chinese now living in diaspora attests to this. These (non)places are virtual "saloons," "coffee bars"—places of public sphere— where conversations about being Chinese, ranging from remembering the most traumatic national tragedies, such as the Nanjing Massacre (see chapter 5), to reminiscing about the simple pleasures of eating food in China (see chapter 6) continue to occur, not in spite of, but precisely because of, the par- ticipants' geographic and physical absence. These conversations mix politics with everyday life experience and range from debates on the governance of the Chinese regime to personal accounts of living in diaspora. They function both to include those who share the cultural memory, history, and experience of being Chinese and to exclude those who do not. Through virtual trips to these sites, one's strategy of maintaining some kind of relationship to the PRC—including its official positions—is articulated, one's allegiances to the "motherland" are reclaimed/renounced, and one's sense of self as a Chinese, albeit displaced, is renewed and reconfirmed.

The most powerful evidence of this diasporic group's desire to maintain a strong relationship to the PRC lies in the tenacity of the discourse on patriot- ism and the constant and earnest debates on the Internet over the meaning of patriotism. For someone who has decided to leave China and has taken up cit- izenship in the United States, Canada, or Australia, what does "being patri- otic" mean and entail? As I discussed earlier, the meaning of patriotism is overdetermined for Chinese citizens living in the PRC, over the question of whether one should support Beijing's bid to host the Games in 2008. Because of this consensus, voices of dissent and dissonance are either marginalized or suppressed. In contrast to the Chinese in the PRC, diasporic members are not subject to the politics of coercive consensus. Instead, the meaning of patriot- ism is contested and constantly reworked, according to the logic of "semiotic self-determination." A good example is the debate that has taken place on the Internet about whether patriotism means "supporting" or "opposing" Beijing's bid. Wang Dan, the well-known student political dissident now in exile, al- legedly expressed his support for Beijing and explained his position in terms of his patriotism. Wang's public statement seems to have had a polarizing effect on the diasporic community. One writer posted an article on a Chinese web- site, denouncing Wang's behavior as "opportunistic" and calling those who share Wang's view "traitors" (*mai guo*—betraying the country), rather than pa- triots (*ai guo*—loving one's country). This writer also argued vehemently against China's official position on the issue of the Olympics. This issue was taken up by another writer, who argued that patriotism means different things to different people and should not be judged by one's position for or against Beijing. This writer said that for this reason, Wang Dan was entitled to his own view.

> On the issue of Beijing's bid, I concur with you. I am not a keen supporter. The difference between you and me is while I do not support Beijing's bid, I do not want to criticise those who do. One can both support and oppose Beijing's bid in the name of patriotism. I believe Wang Dan when he says that his support for Beijing's bid was motivated by his patriotism. After all, Wang does not try to monopolise patriotism, nor does he call those opposing the bid unpatriotic. Your problem is that you do.[41]

The problem confronting this diasporic group, as consumers of a global media event, is that although some members are not capable of "being there" to witness and participate as a "national audience," others nevertheless inherit a cultural mapping of "we-dom" versus "they-dom."[42] While the Internet presents itself as a substitute "place" for them to be on important occasions such as the Games, it operates in a somewhat decontextualized way, in that watching and talking about the Games on the Net is not public, communal, and familial, as would be viewing it on television in China. Falling through the crevices of global electronic journalism, belonging to the system of meaning of neither the motherland nor the host country, the diasporic body claims virtual space and practices being Chinese in a "do-it-yourself" fashion. The diasporic subject is, and begs to be, different from the Chinese now living in China, as well as from other diasporic members, while at the same time it constructs its own meaning of patriotism in relation to the "motherland." Although the meaning of "patriotism"—*aiguo*—is subject to interpretation and contestation, it proves to be enduring the inhabitants of an electronically connected Chinese nation. Consisting of both PRC media audiences and those former PRC nationals now living outside China, this virtual community is made possible not in spite of, but precisely because of, the power of the Chinese state and the strength of a collective memory of the Chinese nation.

NOTES

1. Information from *Focal Point* (*Jiaodian Fangtan*), CCTV's highest-rating show, September 2000.
2. Xu Jiren, *"Yong chuang xin siwei baodao aoyun"* ("Innovative Ways of Reporting Olympic Games"), *Chinese Journalist* 10 (2000): 34–35.
3. See Xinhua websites: <aoyun.xinhuanet.com> (accessed October 2001).
4. Xu, "Innovative Ways," 35.
5. Pu Renren, *"Aoyu tupian, jiewang gaofei"* ("Olympic Images Flying across the Net"), *Chinese Journalist* 10 (2000): 37.

6. A good example of the use of media for political mobilization in China is in the ways that media events are televised on the Chinese television. See chapter 7 in this book.

7. Zhao Yuezhi, *Media, Market and Democracy in China* (Urbana: University of Illinois Press, 1998); and "From Commercialisation to Conglomeration: The Transformation of the Chinese Press within the Orbit of the Party State," *Journal of Communication* (Spring 2000): 3–25.

8. David Rowe, *Sport, Culture and the Media* (Buckingham: Open University Press, 1999), 23.

9. John Sinclair, "More Than an Old Flame: National Symbolism and the Media in the Torch Ceremony of the Olympics," *Media International Australia* 97 (2000): 37.

10. Li Shufeng, *"Fanlungong xini yan chouqu"* (Falungong Followers Make Fools of Themselves in Sydney during the Olympics), *Beijing Youth Daily*, October 27, 2000, 7.

11. John Hartley, *Uses of Television* (London: Routledge, 1999), 159.

12. Hartley, *Uses of Television*.

13. Norbert Elias and Eric Dunning, *Quest for Excitement: Sport and Leisure in the Civilising Process* (Oxford: Basil Blackwell, 1986).

14. Rowe, *Sport, Culture*, 22–23.

15. Stephanie Donald, *Public Secrets, Public Spaces: Cinema and Civility in China* (Lanham, Md.: Rowman & Littlefield, 2000). Donald argues that before we settle on the "national" or "transnational" dimension of cinema, it is crucial to acknowledge the publicness of cinema.

16. Hartley, *Uses of Television*.

17. See Rey Chow, *Primitive Passions* (New York: Columbia University Press, 1995).

18. Yang Taoyuan, *"Zuei hao de sheng ao zuan chuan zai ling jiang dan shang"* ("The Best Propaganda for Beijing 2008 Lies on the Medal Podium"), *Liangwang Magazine* 40 (2000): 4–6.

19. Hartley, *Uses of Television*, 159.

20. These interviews usually took the form of extensive conversations, often followed by more focused questions in in-depth interviews. Some communications were in person, while others were on the phone. They were mostly conducted in Chinese, and the dialogues cited in this article are my translation.

21. Jingyuan Liu's article "Aozhu bentu shiren pideseng de liangshou shi" (Two poems by Australian native poet Patterson) is available on <www.cnd.org/HXWZ/CM01/cm0101a.hz8.html#6> (accessed October 2001).

22. Liu and his family have become good friends with me, since a job transfer to Western Australia resulted in them moving across the continent and settling in Perth, where I live. It is an instance whereby personal contact, which is usually location-contingent, was made possible by the enabling technology of cyberspace.

23. Hamid Naficy, *The Making of Exile Culture: Iranian Television in Los Angeles* (Minneapolis: University of Minnesota Press, 1993).

24. John Sinclair, "More Than an Old Flame"; David Rowe, "Global Media Events and the Positioning of Presence," *Media International Australia* 97 (2000): 11–22.

25. Ghassan Hage, *White Nation: Fantasies of White Supremacy in a Multicultural Society* (Sydney: Pluto, 1998), 49.

26. Hage, *White Nation*, 53.

27. Hage, *White Nation*, 46.

28. One cannot appreciate the humor of the occasion without understanding that "Internationale," to the mainland Chinese, evokes the past collective era of communism and socialism. It was also appropriated and sung by the prodemocracy students in Tiananmen Square at the June 4th Incident in 1989.

29. McKenzie Wark, *Virtual Geography: Living with Global Media Events* (Bloomington: Indiana University Press, 1994).

30. *"Chang'e bengyue"* (*"Chang'e* Going to the Moon") is the story of a beautiful lady going to the moon. It is the most romantic and imaginative story in Chinese folklore.

31. Michael Gurevitch, "The Globalization of Electronic Journalism," in *Mass Media and Society*, 2d ed., ed. James Curran and Michael Gurevitch (London: Arnold, 1996), 204–23.

32. See <www2.fhy.net.GBF/2000.fhy0009d.gbf> (accessed October 2000)

33. Hartley, *Uses of Television*.

34. Daniel Dayan and Elihu Katz, *Media Events: The Live Broadcasting of History* (Cambridge, Mass.: Harvard University Press, 1992).

35. Alec McHoul, "On Doing We's: Where Sport Leaks into Everyday Life," *Journal of Sport and Social Issues* 21, no. 3 (1997): 315–20; Rowe, "Global Media Events."

36. Graeme Turner, *Making It National: Nationalism and Australian Popular Culture*, (St. Leonard, NSW: Allen & Unwin, 1994).

37. SBS is a public broadcaster that caters to the multicultural audiences of Australia. It transmits half an hour's news from some of the countries in their own languages. Chinese television news in Mandarin is available in the morning.

38. Sinclair et al., "Chinese Cosmopolitanism and Media Use," in *Floating Lives: The Media and Asian Diasporas*, ed. Stuart Cunningham and John Sinclair (University of Queensland Press, 2000).

39. See <www.backchina.com/tv/index.html> (accessed October 2001).

40. See "Chinese Organizations Demand Costas Apology," *USA Today*, September 3, 1996, 3C.

41. See <www.creaders.org/forums/politics/messages/171867.html> (accessed October 2001).

42. John Hartley, *Tele-Ology: Studies in Television* (London: Routledge, 1992).

Conclusion: Toward a Transnational China?

Around 9:00 P.M., July 13, 2001, in Moscow, Juan Samaranch, the soon-to-retire chairman of the International Olympics Committee and the man who in 1993 announced "Sydney" instead of "Beijing," spoke again: "The IOC has decided that the city to host the 2008 Olympic Games is *Beijing*."

"Beijing." That word electrified China—literally, overnight. Flashing its earliest news bulletin with a screaming headline "We Have Won!" (*women yinle*), China's Central Television devoted itself that day to the coverage of this news. The much-awaited announcement in Moscow threw the nation into instant ecstasy and euphoria. Again and again, the camera showed people weeping with joy and relief. On television, Jiang Zemin, the party secretary of the CCP, and the other members of the Politburo attended the prearranged celebration gala held at *Shiji Tan* in Beijing. Breathing with excitement into the microphone Jiang made three points. First, congratulations, Beijing!; second, a big thank-you to the Chinese people, IOC, and Beijing supporters all over the world; and third, the entire Chinese population should work hard together with Beijing people to make the Games a success. After the speech, Jiang and his colleagues went to Tiananmen Square, where celebrations were already in full swing. Accompanying the images of mass euphoria, a hysterical journalist shouted into the microphone: "Tiananmen has witnessed many historical events. Tonight, 1.3 billion people's dream has finally come true."

Television cameras then zoomed in on overseas Chinese communities. The Chinese Commerce Association of Canada displayed a huge list of online signatures of worldwide supporters for Beijing. A number of overseas Chinese looked overwhelmed with joy. One shouted, "Long live the Chinese nation" (*zhonghua minzu wansui*) and "Long live the motherland" (*zuguo wansui*).

211

While the Chinese media sought images of patriotic overseas Chinese, this community also seemed to be seeking the Chinese media. Twelve hours before Samaranch was due to make his announcement, the Chinese Students and Scholars Association of Louisiana State University wrote to Xinhua—China's official news agency—expressing their best wishes: "Over the last few days, we have organized many activities supporting Beijing. This is because we wanted to simulate an environment of excitement and expectation so that our hearts can beat in tandem with the people of the motherland" (*he zuguo renmin de xin yiqi tiaodong*).[1] Following the overseas Chinese, CCTV's camera then focused on crowds of Chinese university students—all wearing T-shirts with their university logos. A university student, apparently in his late teens, said to the camera: "I am scheduled to go abroad to study by the end of this month. But I am still Chinese, and I will definitely come back to see the Games in 2008."

Celebration seemed to be underway everywhere. Fireworks lit the sky. On the Great Wall, 2008 torches were lit. Following the story about the celebrations in Beijing—entitled "Sleepless in Beijing" (Beijing *wuren rushui*)—the bulletin ended with generous footage of other Chinese cities and provinces, including Taiwan, partying to midnight.

The viewing of this mass euphoria did not just take place in the living rooms of Chinese viewers in China. As mentioned earlier, through satellite transmission, CCTV now has footprints in many countries in North America, Europe, Australasia, and Asia, including Japan. The diasporic communities watched the same Chinese news bulletin, albeit in a delayed and dispersed fashion. It may not have occurred to the diasporic body, swept by joy and triumph brought to them by the television sets in their living rooms, to give thought to the question of who the "We" were in the "We Have Won!" headline: Was it Beijing, the Chinese state, the Chinese population? Did it include themselves, who are no longer "there" or are no longer Chinese citizens? From the perspective of the Chinese state, winning could be a godsend for purposes of political legitimization and nation-building; from the point of view of television viewers—dispersed and displaced individuals—it was a moment when being recruited into the "we" community may have been quite sweet. According to the Voice of America, Chinese communities of former PRC nationals took to the streets in the Chinatown of Toronto, celebrating Beijing's victory. That same evening, CBS, Canada's national broadcaster, received numerous calls from angry listeners complaining about the Chinese community's display of disloyalty to Canada. To them, it was plainly wrong that while enjoying the benefits of living in Canada, the Chinese there were on China's side.[2]

The media euphoria in July 2001 following the IOC's announcement of Beijing as the winner of the 2008 Games is a classic media event: It was transmitted live, preplanned, and well-orchestrated; it was about "contest, conquest and coronation"[3]—note the headline "We Have Won!"; it was certainly ritualistic and ceremonial, displaying national strengths and commanding, though not demanding, the participation of a national audience; and, above all, it was hegemonic: The opponents of Beijing were nowhere to be seen and heard, and the obvious political and economic conflicts of interest between Beijing and other cities and provinces were elided.[4]

Like many other Chinese living in Australia, I watched CCTV Channel 4's news bulletin that day from 6:30 A.M. to 7:00 A.M. on the SBS channel, a special national broadcaster for ethnic communities, partly because I wanted to know, like many other Chinese people overseas, if Beijing had won; and partly because my parents, retired from decades of high school teaching and living in Anhui Province China, but at the time visiting me in Australia, were eager to hear the result. Their joy was palpable. The happy tears glistening in their eyes brought home to me again the complex ways in which the nationalist agenda of the Chinese state converged with the "gut feelings" of ordinary Chinese people. When media technologies, the state, and mobility—both virtual and real—intersect, as they did here, it marks a powerful moment in the transformation of China's transnational imaginary. The contour and shape of such an imaginary is a culmination of important moments such as this. They also include, as I have described in this book, the time when television first arrived in the homes of Chinese villagers; when images of the global cities, coupled with stories of Chinese who had just arrived in them, began to beam into the living rooms of urban residents in China; when PRC nationals living overseas were finally able to tell their stories in their own way to friends, families, and audiences back at home; and when this group of Chinese, many having left China resolutely and in a somewhat hurried fashion, realized that they were still besieged with homesickness and nostalgia and started to reconnect with China in their own—and often cyber—ways. These moments also include the Chinese state's realization of the power of live satellite transmission.

These are moments of both departures and returns and represent different stages in the process of China's journey to modernity. Like all other previously examined moments, the media euphoria following the IOC's announcement both results from and contributes to the ongoing process of forming transnational imagination. More important, these moments both result from and further contribute to the intersection between media technologies, the flow of people and images, and the desire of the Chinese state. Above all, each of these moments was possible either because of, or in spite of, the Chinese state. In every possible crevice and intersection connecting the body, home, community, city, nation, and the globe, the Chinese state marks its strong and firm presence. Upon winning the bid, Liu Jingmin, vice mayor of Beijing and the executive vice president of the Beijing Olympic Games Bid Committee, announced that Beijing would do its best to connect China to the world. It would, according to him, expand its fiber-optic networks to cover all Olympic sites, providing a secure broadband network to deliver the Games to the world; it would introduce a mobile communication network capable of handling 500,000 calls in the Olympic site area; and it would establish a digital cable TV network that was capable of HDTV transmission for all Olympic venues.

As someone who left China more than a dozen years ago, I watched the euphoria of Chinese people from my home in the diaspora. The young Chinese university student's declaration on national television of his intention to both love his country (*aiguo*) and leave it (*chuguo*) resonated with me. I could not help but construct a hypothetical account of this aspiring young man: He might be one of the privileged people who came from a well-to-do home in Shanghai or Beijing, with a father who has money and/or power; he may be endowed with many familial connections overseas. Alternatively, he could have come from a home in a rural village like Ermo's—Ermo did have a son, didn't she, who went to the university, thanks to his hard work and family expectations? His education might have been supported either by his parents selling crops from their land; by his mother selling noodles, if he was Ermo's son; or by his *dagongmei* sisters, now working away from their village home. He may have seen stories about the "Chinese in the New World"—stories that made him restless and filled him with an irresistible urge to see the world outside with his own eyes. He could also be somewhere in-between the two scenarios I conjure up here. In either case, he must have jumped through the hoop of TOEFL. I still have vivid memories of the long queues that camped overnight, waiting to secure TOEFL test application forms, outside my university in Shanghai a decade and a half ago. The student may also have been to the American embassy, to both protest against U.S. imperialism and apply for a visa. About to leave and already talking about return, he is one of the many and most recent embodiments of the ambiguity and ambivalence that mark the transnational imagination in contemporary China. His declaration on national television brings home to me, the author of a book called *Leaving China*, that "leaving" may never be complete, just as "return" may never be total. An electronic landscape, a virtual Chinese nation has been created, connecting—rather than separating—"China" and a paradiasporic Chinese community, to the consequence of inhibiting, rather than facilitating, this paradiasporic group's entry into the diasporic public sphere.

English media scholar James Lull, writing about television in China in the 1980s, has this to say:

> The simplistic and condemning impression of the West that China's government has promoted for so many years backfires now that everyone watches television

and makes their own interpretations of life outside the country. The restrictive Chinese television system still leaks powerful images that fuel alternative visions of the West.[5]

Although this may no longer be—if it ever was—an accurate description of how the Chinese see the world, Lull nevertheless alludes to the capacity of ordinary viewers to engage in imagination, as well as the power of such imagination. As the previous chapters suggest, the media do not simply reflect the imagination of life outside China; they are constitutive of it. In other words, television dramas, films, news and magazines, websites and homepages, and global media events are not only the places through which transnational imagination is recorded; more important, the media are also the sites and acts whereby people participate in the very process of imagining.

Although the adoption of global media formats and practices, complemented by occasional but regular media campaigns, afford the Chinese state a promising prospect of concocting a relatively unified national time and space, such a template for (trans)national imagining is constantly challenged, undermined, and fragmented by a more quotidian, decentralized, and individuated way of imagining the national self/otherness. On the other hand, however, this scenario, while fraught with tension and contradiction, also suggests the determination and, dare I say, the capacity of the Chinese state to make its influence felt in spite of the fragmentation and fluidity of the Chinese mediascape. This capacity further manifests itself in the state media's strategy to, in times of media events, deliver entertainment and indoctrination within a single package, as well as its capacity to effectively interpellate the "absent" national audiences. A central paradox presented in these findings has emerged: In spite of the fragmentation and proliferation of a sense of the nation's place and time, a reworked transnational imagination nevertheless continues to privilege the national history and the concept of a sovereign state.

However, as I have also shown, it is not simply the media that should be credited with effecting the transformation of a transnational imagination. Mobility and the changed—and changing—translocal practices of the Chinese population are other dynamic forces. The demise of the *hukou* system and the routinization of passport application have accelerated movements of people from the village to the city, from the hinterland to the coast, and from China to overseas, exposing more and more Chinese to variegated experiences of becoming modern. As borders are traversed and boundaries blur, a memory of the Chinese nation, which is time-specific and location-bound, is having to jostle with a mobile and deterritorialized understanding of time, space, and selfhood.

Those who want to leave China, either vicariously or bodily, look forward and outward and partake of an endless cycle of reproduction of fantasies, desires, and yearnings for the foreign and the modern; others who want to return to China—culturally, if not physically—look backward and inward toward China's collective history and memory for continuous cultural nourishment. Ermo and television viewers in the village "go" to exotic places without leaving home, thanks to the arrival of television in their homes, and former PRC residents now living outside China practice virtual homecoming, courtesy of new video technologies and the Internet. In both cases, a certain degree of ambiguity, ambivalence, and even contradiction mark the process of their transnational imagining: inferiority complex mixes with superiority complex, desire goes with fear, and national pride often is sustained by a hatred for the imperialist Other and a collective sense of pride and humiliation.

It has not been my intention to compare and assess which force—media or mobility—has a more profound impact on the formation of transnational imagination. In fact, media, mobility, and the power of the Chinese state have conspired to produce and reproduce uneven and unequal processes of transnational imagination. Central to these processes is not only the mobility of media images, but also media images of mobility. It is therefore not surprising by now that the contour and the shape of the Chinese transnational imagination are indeed intricate. These processes are fluid, sometimes confusing, and always complex. They are marked with, first of all, an interface between the material—the flow of people—and the symbolic, the flow of images; second, a convergence between the private and the public; third, a coalition of popular sentiments and state desire; fourth, an overlap between the national and the diasporic; fifth, a fusion of looking toward the future (imagination) and looking toward the past (memory and identity); and sixth (which is related to the fifth), a conflation of space (here or there) and time (now or then). These processes are about creating openness and building—which includes virtual and mediated—connections. They are also about dissolving, maintaining, negotiating, and contesting boundaries—again, both real and symbolic. To understand the complexity of these processes, we need to consider at all times "the mutually constitutive relationship between transnationalism and nationstatism."[6] And, above all, these processes are invariably linked to the new possibilities—brought about by new media technologies—of conceiving place and space. None of these processes is unique or specific to China, but the contiguous and combinatory relationship among these processes is the consequence of Communist China opening itself up in response to the forces of globalization, global media, and communication and technological convergence since the economic reforms. If I may finish this book by making a prediction, it will be that the 2008 Olympic Games in Beijing will be the most spectacular occasion to showcase the outcome of these processes of the Chinese transnational imagination.

NOTES

1. See <www.news.xinhuanet.com/zhibo/20010713/709917.htm> (accessed October 2001).

2. See <www.bbsland.com/bcchinese/messages/919.html> (accessed October 2001).

3. Daniel Dayan and Elihu Katz, *Media Events: The Live Broadcasting of History* (Cambridge, Mass.: Harvard University Press, 1992).

4. A quick browse on some of the Chinese-language websites, both mainland and diasporic, tells a more sobering and balanced story. Some Shanghai residents, for instance, were not impressed with the fact that, again, Shanghai may be expected to make sacrifices to help Beijing. For another example, a factory worker said bluntly that he did not share the feeling of euphoria. "I still have to get up early in the morning for my shift work. Otherwise, I will not be able to sustain a meagre living." See <www.org.HXWZexpress> (accessed July 15, 2001).

5. James Lull, *China Turned On: Television, Reform and Resistance* (London: Routledge, 1991), 174.

6. Wang Jing, "The State Question in Chinese Popular Cultural Studies," *Inter-Asia Cultural Studies* 2, no. 1 (2001): 37.

Bibliography

Alexander, Jeffrey C., and Ronald N. Jacobs. "Mass Communication, Ritual and Civil Society." Pp. 23–41, in *Media, Ritual and Identity*, ed. Tamar Liebes and James Curran. London: Routledge, 1998.

"Alienated Citizens View Celebrations as Gathering of Elite." *CND* (September 26, 1999). <www.cnd.org/CND-Global/CND-Global.99.4th/CND-Global.99-09-26.html> (accessed May 2000).

Althusser, Louis. *Lenin and Philosophy and Other Essays*. London: New Left Books, 1971.

"American Enterprises Online." See <www.findarticles.com/> (accessed August 2001).

Anderson, Benedict. *Imagined Communities: Reflections on the Origins and Spread of Nationalism*. London: Verso, 1983.

Appadurai, Arjun. *Modernity at Large: Cultural Dimensions of Globalization*. Minneapolis: University of Minnesota Press, 1996.

Asian Economic News, February 15, 1999–September 18, 2000.

Bailey, Cameron. "Virtual Skin: Articulating Race in Cyberspace." Pp. 29–45, in *Immersed in Technology*, ed. Mary Anne Moser. Cambridge, Mass.: MIT Press, 1996.

Barmé, Geremie. *In the Red: Contemporary Chinese Culture*. New York: Columbia University Press, 1999.

———. "To Screw Foreigners Is Patriotic: China's Avant-Garde Nationalists." *The China Journal* 34 (1995): 209–34.

Barthes, Roland. *Mythologies*. London: Paladin, 1973.

Becker, Jasper. *Hungry Ghost: China's Secret Famine*. London: John Murray, 1996.

Befu, Harumi. "Introduction." Pp. 1–5, in *Cultural Nationalism in East Asia: Representation and Identity*, ed. Harumi Befu. Berkeley: University of California Press, 1993.

Bell, David, and Gill Valentine. *Consuming Geographies: We Are Where We Eat*. London and New York: Routledge, 1997.

Berkowitz, Daniel. "Non-Routine News and Newswork: Exploring a What-a-Story." *Journal of Communication* 42, no. 1 (1992): 82–94.

Bhabha, Homi. "Arrivals and Departures." Pp. 1–16, in *Home, Exile, Homeland: Film, Media, and the Politics of Place*, ed. Hamid Naficy. New York: Routledge, 1999.

———. "Dissemination: Time, Narrative, and the Margin of the Modern Nation." Pp. 291–322, in *Nation and Narration*, ed. Homi Bhabha. London: Routledge, 1990.

Bourdieu, Pierre. *Distinction: A Social Critique of the Judgement of Taste*. London: Routledge & Kegan Paul, 1984.

Brooks, Timothy. *Documents on the Rape of Nanking*. Ann Arbor: University of Michigan Press, 2000.

Cao Guilin. *The Green Card: A Beijing Girl in New York (Luka: Beijing Guniang Zai Nuyue)*. <www.shuku.net/dblx/html.01/4-2-1.html> (accessed November 2001).

Carey, James. "Political Ritual on Television: Episodes in the History of Shame, Degradation and Excommunication." Pp. 42–70, in *Media Ritual and Identity*, ed. Tamar Liebes and James Curran. London: Routledge, 1998.

Chan, Stephan. "What Is This Thing Called Chinese Diaspora?" *Contemporary Review* 1 (February 1999): <www.findarticles.com> (accessed November 2001).

Chang, Iris. *The Rape of Nanking: The Forgotten Holocaust of World War II*. New York: Basic Books, 1997.

Chang, Lesley. "Beijing Struggles to Manage Information in the Internet Age: Conflicting Tales of Why a School Exploded Highlight the Difficulties." *Wall Street Journal*, March 13, 2001.

Chen Xiaomei. *Occidentalism: A Theory of Counter-Discourse in Post-Mao China*. New York and Oxford: Oxford University Press, 1995.

"China Urges Japan to Release Feng Jinhua Who Threw Paint over Yasukuni Shrine." *Australian Chinese Times* (August 29, 2001): 20.

"Chinese Students Rally at US Embassy in Tokyo." *Asian Political News* (May 17, 1999). See <www.findarticles.com> (accessed August 2001).

Chow, Rey. "King Kong in Hong Kong: Watching the 'Handover' from the USA." *Social Text* 16, no. 2 (1998): 93–108.

———. *Primitive Passions*. New York: Columbia University Press, 1995.

———. *Writing Diaspora: Tactics of Intervention in Contemporary Cultural Studies*. Bloomington and Indianapolis: Indiana University Press, 1993.

Ciecko, Anne, and Sheldon Hsiao-peng Lu. "Televisuality, Capital and the Global Village." *Jump Cut* 42 (1999): 77–83.

Clifford, James. "Diasporas." *Cultural Anthropology* 9, no. 3 (1994): 308.

———. "Traveling Cultures." Pp. 96–116, in *Cultural Studies*, ed. Larry Grossberg, Carry Nelson, and Paula Treicher. New York: Routledge, 1992.

Dai Jinhua. "Behind Global Spectacle and National Image-Making." *Positions: East Asia Culture Critique* 9, no. 1 (2001): 161–86.

———. *Wu Zhong Feng Jing (Sceneries in the Fog: Chinese Cinema 1978–1998)*. Beijing: Beijing University Press, 2000.

———. "Redemption and Consumption: Depicting Culture in the 1990s." *Positions: East Asia Culture Critique* 4, no. 1 (1996): 127–43.

Davin, Delia. *Internal Migration in Contemporary China*. London: Macmillan, 1999.

Dayan, Daniel, and Elihu Katz. *Media Events: The Live Broadcasting of History*. Cambridge, Mass.: Harvard University Press, 1992.

de Certeau, Michel. *The Practice of Everyday Life*. Berkeley: University of California Press, 1984.

"Dilin liuxue, chongshuo fenyun" ("The Pros and Cons of Young Children Studying Abroad"). *Chinese Scholars Abroad* 6 (June 2001): 9.

Donald, James. *Imagining the Modern City.* London: Athlone, 1999.

———. ed. *Fantasy and Cinema.* London: BFI, 1989.

Donald, Stephanie. *Public Secrets, Public Spaces: Cinema and Civility in China.* Lanham, Md.: Rowman & Littlefield, 2000.

Donald, Stephanie, and Wanning Sun. "Going Home: History, Nation, and the Mournful Landscapes of Home." *Metro* 129–30 (September 2001): 140–51.

Duara, Presanjit. *Rescuing History from the Nation: Questioning Narratives of Modern China.* Chicago: University of Chicago Press, 1995.

Dutton, Michael. *Streetlife China.* Melbourne: Cambridge University Press, 1998.

Eagleton, Terry. "Edible Ecriture." Pp. 203–8, in *Consuming Passions: Food in the Age of Anxiety,* ed. Sian Griffiths and Jennifer Wallace. Manchester and New York: Manchester University Press, 1998.

Elias, Norbert, and Eric Dunning. *Quest for Excitement: Sport and Leisure in the Civilising Process.* Oxford: Basil Blackwell, 1986.

Elsaesser, Thomas. "Social Mobility and the Fantastic: German Silent Cinema." Pp. 23–38, in *Fantasy and Cinema,* ed. James Donald. London: BFI, 1989.

Featherstone, Mike, ed. *Global Culture: Nationalism, Globalism and Modernity.* London: Sage, 1990.

Fitzgerald, John. "'Reports of My Death Have Been Greatly Exaggerated': The History of the Death of China." Pp. 21–58, in *China Deconstructs: Politics, Trade, and Regionalism,* ed. David S. G. Goodman and Gerald Segal. London: Routledge, 1994.

Fogel, Joshua, ed. *The Nanjing Massacre in History and Historiography.* Berkeley: University of California Press, 2000.

Fregoso, Rosa Linda. "Recycling Colonialist Fantasies on the Texas Borderlands." Pp. 169–92, in *Home, Exile, Homeland: Film, Media, and the Politics of Place,* ed. Hamid Naficy. New York: Routledge, 1999.

Gabaccia, Donna. *We Are What We Eat: Ethnic Food and the Making of Americans.* Cambridge, Mass.: Harvard University Press, 1998.

Gillespie, Marie. *Television, Ethnicity and Cultural Change.* London: Routledge, 1995.

Gries, Peter Hays. "'A China Threat?' Power and Passion in Chinese Face Nationalism." *World Affairs* (Fall 1999). See <http: www.findarticles.com> (accessed October 2001).

Gunew, Sneja. "Feminism in the Politics of Irreducible Differences: Multiculturalism/Ethnicity/Race." Pp. 1–19, in *Feminism and the Politics of Difference,* ed. Sneja Gunew and Anna Yetman. Boulder, Colo.: Westview, 1993.

Gurevitch, Michael. "The Globalization of Electronic Journalism." Pp. 204–23, in *Mass Media and Society,* ed. James Curran and Michael Gurevitch. 2d ed. London: Arnold, 1986.

Hage, Ghassan. *White Nation: Fantasies of White Supremacy in a Multicultural Society.* Sydney: Pluto, 1998.

Hall, Stuart. "Introduction: Who Needs 'Identity'?" Pp. 1–17, in *Questions of Cultural Identity,* ed. Stuart Hall and Paul du Gay. London: Sage, 1996.

———. "Cultural Identity and Diaspora." Pp. 231–42, in *Undoing Place? A Geographical Reader,* ed. Linda McDowell. London: Arnold, 1995.

Han Xuan. *Shi Zhile* (The Joy of Food) (*shi zhi le*, my translation). <http://www.cnd.org/HXWZ/CM99/cm9908a.hz8.html#3> (accessed October 2000).

Hannerz, Ulf. *Transnational Connections: Culture, People, Places.* London: Routledge, 1996.

Haraway, Dona. *Simians, Cyborgs, Women: The Reinvention of Nature.* New York: Routledge, 1991.

Hartley, John. *Uses of Television.* London: Routledge, 1999.

——. *Popular Reality: Journalism, Modernity, Popular Culture.* London: Arnold, 1996.

——. *Tele-Ology: Studies in Television.* London: Routledge, 1992.

Harvey, David. *The Condition of Postmodernity.* Oxford: Blackwell, 1989.

He Chunhui. *"Kan jiao dian fang tan"* ("Looking at the Focal Point"). Pp. 305–15, in *Ju jiao jiao dian fang tan* (Focusing on the Focal Point), ed. Yuan Zhengmin and Liang Jianzhen. Beijing: China Encyclopaedia Press, 1999.

He Guimei. "The Appropriation of Socialist Classics at the Turn of the Century" ("*Shehui zhuyi jingdian huayu zai shiji zhijia de nuoyong*"). Paper presented to *Locating China: Space, Place and Popular Culture.* Hangzhou, June 18–21, 2001.

Hein, Laura, and Mark Selden, eds. *Citizenship and Memory in Japan, Germany, and the United States.* Armonk, N.Y.: M. E. Sharpe, 2000.

Hidenori, Ijiri. "Sino-Japanese Controversy since the 1972 Diplomatic Normalisation." *China Quarterly* 124 (1990): 639–61.

Hong Junhao. *The Internationalization of Television in China: The Evolution of Ideology, Society, and Media since the Reform.* Westport, Conn.: Praeger, 1998.

Honig, Bonnie. "How Foreignness 'Solves' Democracy's Problems." *Social Text* 16, no. 3 (1998): 1–27.

Huaren. See <www.huaren.org/> (October 2001).

Hua Xia Wen Zai, 444 (1 October 1999). See <www.cnd.org/HXWZ/CM99/cm9910a.hz8.html> (accessed May 2000).

Iwabuchi, Koichi. "Marketing 'Japan': Japanese Cultural Presence under a Global Gaze." *Japanese Studies* 18, no. 2 (1998): 165–80.

Jacka, Tamara. "My Life as a Migrant Worker." *Intersections* 4 (September 2000). See <wwwsshe.murdoch.edu.au/intersections/issue4/> (accessed November 2001).

Jacka, Tamara, and Arianne Gaetano, ed. *On the Move: Women in Rural–Urban Migration in Contemporary China.* New York: Columbia University Press, in press.

Jacobs, Ronald. "Producing the News, Producing the Crisis: Narrativity, Television and Newswork." *Media Culture and Society* 18 (1996): 373–77.

Jameson, Frederic. "Remapping Taipei." P. 148, in *New Chinese Cinemas: Forms, Identities, Politics,* ed. Nick Browne, Paul G. Pickowicz, Vivian Sobshack, and Esther Yau. New York: Cambridge University Press, 1994.

Jess, Pat, and Doreen Massey. "The Contestation of Place." Pp. 133–74, in *A Place in the World?* ed. Doreen Massey and Pat Jess. London: Open University Press and Oxford University Press, 1995.

Juchau, Meirelle. "Forgetful Memory: The Holocaust, History and Representation." *The UTS Review: Cultural Studies and New Writing* 2, no. 2 (1996): 70.

Katshichi Honda, *The Nanjing Massacre: A Japanese Journalist Confronts Japan's National Shame.* Armonk, N.Y.: M. E. Sharpe, 1999.

Keane, Michael. "Television and Civilization: The Unity of Opposites?" *International Journal of Cultural Studies* 2, no. 2 (1999): 246–59.

———. "Ethics and Pragmatics: China's Television Products Confront the Cultural Market." *Media International Australia* 89 (1998): 75–86.

Keane, Michael, and Tao Dongfeng. "Interview with Feng Xiaogang." *Positions* 7, no. 1 (1999): 193–99.

Kingston, Beverley. "Are We What We Eat?" In *The Abundant Culture*, ed. David Headon, Joy Hooton, and Donald Horne. Sydney: Allen & Unwin, 1995.

Knight, Alan. "Washing Away One Hundred Years of Shame." Pp. 72–92, in *Reporting Hong Kong: Foreign Media and the Handover*, ed. Alan Knight and Yoshiko Nakano. Surrey: Curzon, 1999.

Kolar-Panov, Dana. *Video, War and the Diasporic Imagination*. London: Routledge, 1997.

———. "Video as the Diasporic Imagination of Selfhood: A Case Study of the Croatians in Australia." *Cultural Studies* 10, no. 2 (1996): 288–314.

Kundera, Milan. *The Unbearable Lightness of Being*. New York: Harper and Row, 1984.

Law, Clara. Interview with Julia Rigg on Radio National, Australia, April 28, 2001.

Lee Chin-Chuan, ed. *Power, Money and Media: Communication Patterns and Bureaucratic Control in Cultural China*. Evanston, Ill.: Northwestern University Press, 2000.

Lefebvre, Henri. *The Production of Space*. Oxford: Blackwell, 1991.

Li Shufeng. "Falungong Followers Make Fools of Themselves in Sydney during the Olympics." *Beijing Youth Daily*, October 27, 2000, 7.

Li Zunren. "Popular Journalism with Chinese Characteristics: From Revolutionary Modernity to Popular Modernity." *International Journal of Cultural Studies* 1, no. 3 (1998): 317–28.

Liu Fang, Liu Lishen, and Wang Wanping. *The Woman Who Chased a Dream (Zuei Meng Nuren)*. Beijing: Guangming Daily Press, 2000.

Liu Jianzi. *"Tao guan tian guan de qi shi"* ("Inspirations from Clay Pots and Iron Pots"). *Dushu* (Readings) 258, no. 9 (2000): 72–80.

Liu, Jing-Yuan. "Aozhou bentu shiren pideseng de liangshou shi" (Two poems by Australian native poet Patterson), on www.cnd.org/HXWZ/CM01/cm0101a.hz8. html#6 (accessed October 2001).

Liu, Lydia. "Beijing Sojourners in New York: Postsocialism and the Question of Ideology in Global Media Culture." *Positions: East Asia Culture Critique* 7, no. 3 (1999): 763–96.

———. "The Female Body and Nationalist Discourse: Manchuria in Xiao Hong's *Field of Life and Death*." Pp. 157–80, in *Body, Subject, and Power in China*, ed. Angela Zito and Tani Barlow. Chicago: University of Chicago Press, 1994.

Liu Wu. *"Tianjin guangrong gongsi shijian shimo"* ("The True Account of the Tianjin Koei Incident"). *Ba Xiao Shi Yi Wai* (After Hours) 1 (1997): 12–16.

Liu Xin. "Space, Mobility, and Flexibility: Chinese Villagers and Scholars Negotiate Power at Home and Abroad." Pp. 91–114, in *Ungrounded Empires: The Cultural Politics of Modern Chinese Transnationalism*, ed. Aihwa Ong and Donald M. Nonini. New York and London: Routledge, 1997.

Loshitzky, Yosefa. "Travelling Culture/Travelling Television." *Screen* 37, no. 4 (1996): 323–35.

Lu, Sheldon Hsiao-peng, ed. *Transnational Chinese Cinemas: Identity, Nationhood, Gender*. Honolulu: University of Hawaii Press, 1997.

Lull, James. *China Turned On: Television, Reform and Resistance*. London: Routledge, 1991.

Lupton, Deborah. *The Food, the Body and the Self.* London: Sage, 1996.

Lynch, Daniel. *After the Propaganda State: Media, Politics, and "Thought Work" in Reformed China.* Stanford, Calif.: Stanford University Press, 1999.

Ma, Eric. "Re-Nationalisation and Me." *Inter-Asia Cultural Studies* 1, no. 1 (2000): 173–79.

Ma Ya. "On Eating a Donkey." Trans. Wanning Sun. <www.cnd.org/HXWZ/CM00/cm0004c.hz8.html#7> (accessed August 2000).

Mackie, Vera. "The Metropolitan Gaze: Travelers, Bodies, Spaces." *Intersections* 4 (September 2000): <wwwsshe.murdoch.edu.au/intersections/issue4/> (accessed October 2000).

Massey, Doreen. "Imagining the World." Pp. 5–52, in *Geographical Worlds*, ed. John Allen and Doreen Massey. Oxford: Open University Press and Oxford University Press, 1995.

Massey, Doreen, and Pat Jess, eds. *A Place in the World?* London: Open University Press and Oxford University Press, 1995.

McClintock, Anne. *Imperial Leather: Race, Gender, and Sexuality in the Colonial Conquest.* New York: Routledge, 1995.

McHoul, Alec. "On Doing We's: Where Sport Leaks into Everyday Life," *Journal of Sport and Social Issues* 21, no. 3 (1997): 315–20.

Meng Yue. *"Nuxin biaoxiang yu minzhu shenghua"* ("Representations of the Female and National Myths"). *Er shi yi shi ji* (The 21st Century) (April 1991): 103–12.

Mercer, Colin. "Regular Imagining: The Newspaper and the Nation." Pp. 24–26, in *Celebrating the Nation: A Study of Australia's Bicentenary*, ed. Tony Bennett, Pat Buckeridge, David Carter, and Colin Mercer. Sydney: Allen & Unwin, 1992.

Mitchell, Tony. "Boxing the Roo: Clara Law's Floating Life and Transnational Hong Kong-Australian Identities." *UTS Review* 6, no. 2 (2000): 103–14.

Mitra, Ananda. "Diasporic Websites: Ingroup and Outgroup Discourse." *Critical Studies in Mass Communication* 14, no. 2 (1997): 158–81.

———. "'Nations and the Internet': The Case of a National Newsgroup, 'soc.cult. indian.'" *Convergence: Journal of Research in New Technologies* 2, no. 1 (1996): 44–75.

———. "Marginal Voices in Cyberspace," *New Media & Society* 3, no. 1 (2001): 29–48.

Moores, Shaun. *Satellite Television and Everyday Life: Articulating Technology.* Bedfordshire: University of Luton Press, 1996.

———. "Television, Geography and 'Mobile Privatization.'" *European Journal of Communication* 8 (1993): 365–79.

Morley, David. "Bounded Realms: Household, Family, Community, and Nation." Pp. 151–68, in *Home, Exile, Homeland: Film, Media, and the Politics of Place*, ed. Hamid Naficy. New York: Routledge, 1999.

Morley, David, and Kevin Robins. *Spaces of Identity: Global Media, Electronic Landscapes, and Cultural Boundaries.* London: Routledge, 1995.

Morse, Margaret. "Home: Smell, Taste, Posture, Gleam." Pp. 63–74, in *Home, Exile, Homeland: Film, Media, and the Politics of Place*, ed. Hamid Naficy. New York: Routledge, 1999.

———. *Virtualities: Television, Media Art, and Cyberculture.* Bloomington: Indiana University Press, 1998.

Mulvey, Laura. "Visual Pleasure and Narrative Cinema." Pp. 303–15, in *Movies and Methods*, vol. 2, ed. Bill Nichols. Berkeley: University of California Press, 1985.

Naficy, Hamid. "'Between Rocks and Hard Places': The Interstitial Mode of Product in Exilic Cinema." Pp. 125–50, in *Home, Exile, Homeland: Film, Media, and the Politics of Place*, ed. Hamid Naficy. New York: Routledge, 1999a.

———. "Framing Exile." Pp. 1–16, in *Home, Exile, Homeland: Film, Media, and the Politics of Place*, ed. Hamid Naficy. New York: Routledge, 1999b.

———. "Theorising 'Third World' Film Spectatorship." *Wide Angle* 18, no. 4 (1996): 3–26.

———. "Phobic Spaces and Liminal Panics: Independent Transnational Film Genre." *East/West Film Journal* 8, no. 2 (1994): 1.

———. *The Making of Exile Culture: Iranian Television in Los Angeles*. Minneapolis: University of Minnesota Press, 1993.

Naficy, Hamid, ed. *Home, Exile, Homeland: Film, Media, and the Politics of Place*. London and New York: Routledge, 1999.

Nanjing Massacre Site. <www.cnd.org/njmassacre/njm-tran-ch14.htm> (accessed September 2001).

Narayan, Uma. *Dislocating Cultures: Identity, Traditions, and Third-World Feminism*. New York: Routledge, 1997.

Nonini, Donald M., and Aihwa Ong. "Chinese Transnationalism as an Alternative Modernity." Pp. 3–36, in *Ungrounded Empire: The Cultural Politics of Modern Chinese Transnationalism*, ed. Aihwa Ong and Donald M. Nonini. London: Routledge, 1997.

Ong, Aihwa. "On the Edge of Empires: Flexible Citizenship among Chinese in Diaspora." *Positions: East Asia Culture Critique* 1, no. 3 (1993): 745–77.

Ong, Aihwa, and Donald M. Nonini, ed. *Ungrounded Empires: The Cultural Politics of Modern Chinese Transnationalism*. New York and London: Routledge, 1997.

Pan Zhongdang, Chin-Chuan Lee, Joseph Man Chan, Clement Y. K. So. "One Event, Three Stories: Media Narratives from Cultural China of the Handover of Hong Kong." Pp. 171–87, in *Power, Money and Media: Communication Patterns and Bureaucratic Control in Cultural China*, ed. Lee Chin-Chuan. Evanston, Ill.: Northwestern University Press, 2000.

Peckham, Shannan. "Consuming Nations." Pp. 171–82, in *Consuming Passions: Food in the Age of Anxiety*, ed. Sian Griffiths and Jennifer Wallace. Manchester and New York: Manchester University Press, 1998.

Peters, John Durham. "Exile, Nomadism, and the Diaspora: The Stakes of Mobility in the Western Canon." Pp. 17–44, in *Home, Exile, Homeland: Film, Media, and the Politics of Place*, ed. Hamid Naficy. New York: Routledge, 1999.

Powdermaker, Hortense. *Hollywood the Dream Factory: An Anthropologist Looks at the Movie Makers*. London: Secker & Warburg, 1950.

Pu, Renren. *"Aoyu tupian, jiewang gaofei"* ("Olympic Images Flying across the Net"). *Chinese Journalist* 10 (2000): 37.

Pye, Lucien. *The Spirit of Chinese Politics*, new ed. Boston: Harvard University Press, 1992.

Qian Ning. *Liuxue Meiguo* (Studying in the U.S.). Nanjing: Jiangsu Wenyi Chubanshe, 1996, or <www.shuku.net/novels/oversea/usa/usa.html> (accessed January 2000).

Radway, Janice. "Reading the Romance." Pp. 449–65, in *The Communication Theory Reader*, ed. Paul Cobley. London: Routledge, 1996.

Ripe, Cherry. *Goodbye Culinary Cringe*. St. Leonards: Allen & Unwin, 1993.

Robins, Kevin. "Reimagined Communities? European Image Spaces, beyond Fordism." *Cultural Studies* 3, no. 2 (1989): 145–65.

Rose, Gillian. "Place and Identity: A Sense of Place." Pp. 87–132, in *A Place in the World*, ed. Doreen Massey and Pat Jess. Oxford: Open University Press, 1995.

Rowe, David. "Global Media Events and the Positioning of Presence." *Media International Australia* 97 (2000): 11–22.

——. *Sport, Culture and the Media*. Buckingham: Open University Press, 1999.

Ryans, Tony. "'Goldfish,' Dragons and Tigers: The Cinema of East Asia," Vancouver Asian Film Festival Film Catalogue, 1995, n.p.

Sarup, Madan. "Home and Identity." Pp. 93–104, in *Travellers' Tales: Narratives of Home and Displacement*, ed. George Robertson, Melinda Mash, Lias Tickner, Jon Bird, Barry Curtis, and Tim Putnam. London and New York: Routledge, 1994.

Scannell, Paddy. "Media Events." *Media, Culture and Society* 17 (1995): 151–57.

Schein, Louisa. "Performing Modernity." *Cultural Anthropology* 14, no. 3 (1999): 361–95.

——. "Gender and Internal Orientalism in China." *Modern China* 23, no. 1 (1997): 69–98.

Schudson, Michael. "Deadlines, Datelines, and History." Pp. 79–108, in *Reading the News*, ed. Robert Karl Manoff and Michael Schudson. New York: Pantheon, 1986.

Schurmann, Franz. *Ideology and Organization in Communist China*. Los Angeles: University of California Press, 1968.

Selden, Mark. "The United States, Japan and the Noncombatant in Twentieth Century Wars in Asia: Reflections on Responsibility, Reparations and Reconciliation." Keynote speech delivered at University of Toronto on September 28, 2001.

Sheng Zhou Xue Ren (Chinese Scholars Abroad) 134, no. 4 (2001), <www.chisa.edu.cn> (accessed August 2001).

Sheridan, Susan. "Eating the Other: Food and Cultural Difference in the Australian *Women's Weekly* in the 1960s." *Journal of International Studies* 21, no. 3 (2000): 320–29.

Shohat, Ella. "By the Bitstream of Babylon: Cyberfrontiers and Diasporic Vistas." Pp. 213–32, in *Home, Exile, Homeland: Film, Media, and the Politics of Place*, ed. Hamid Naficy. New York: Routledge, 1999.

Sinclair, John. "More Than an Old Flame: National Symbolism and the Media in the Torch Ceremony of the Olympics." *Media International Australia* 97 (2000): 35–46.

Sinclair, John, Audrey Yue, Gay Hawkins, Kee Pookong, and Josephine Fox. "Chinese Cosmopolitanism and Media Use." Pp. 1–34, in *Floating Lives: The Media and Asian Diasporas*, ed. Stuart Cunningham and John Sinclair. St. Lucia: University of Queensland Press, 2000.

Skribis, Zatko, "Making It Tradable: Videotapes, Cultural Technologies and Diasporas." *Cultural Studies* 12, no. 2 (1998): 265–73.

Smith, Anthony. "Towards Global Culture?" Pp. 171–92, in *Global Culture: Nationalism, Globalisation and Modernity*, ed. Mike Featherstone. London: Sage, 1990.

Smith, Neil. "Homeless/Global: Scaling Places." Pp. 87–119, in *Mapping the Futures: Local Cultures, Global Change*, ed. Jon Bird, Barry Curtis, Tim Putnam, George Robertson, and Lias Tickner. London: Routledge, 1993.

"Snakeheads Seen Linked to Truck Holding 58 Dead Immigrants." *Asian Economic News*, June 28, 2000, <www.findarticles.com> (accessed August 2001).

Soja, Edward. *Thirdspace: Journeys to Los Angeles and Other Real-and-Imagined Places.* Oxford and Cambridge, Mass.: Blackwell, 1996.

Solinger, Dorothy. *Contesting Citizenship in Urban China: Peasant Migration, the State, and the Logic of the Market.* Berkeley: University of California Press, 1999.

Song Qiang, Zhang Zangzang, and Qiao Bian. *Zhongguo Keyi Shuobu* (China Can Say No). Beijing: Zhonghua Gongshangliang Chubanshe, 1996.

Sun, Wanning. "Indoctrination, Fetishization and Compassion: Media, Mobility and the Constructions of the Working Girl." In *On the Move: Women in Rural–Urban Migration in Contemporary China,* ed. Tamara Jacka and Arianne Gaetano. New York: Columbia University Press, in press.

———. "A Chinese in the New World: Television Dramas, Global Cities, and Travels to Modernity." *Inter-Asia Cultural Studies* 2, no. 1 (2001a): 81–94.

———. "Anhui Working Girls in Shanghai: Gender, Class and a Sense of Place." Paper presented to the workshop on "Space and Place: Popular Culture in China." Hangzhou, China, June 18–21, 2001b.

———. "Media Events or Media Stories? Time, Space and Chinese (Trans)nationalism." *International Journal of Cultural Studies* 4, no. 1 (2001c): 25–43.

———. "Love Your Country in Your Own Way: Chinese Nationalism, Media and Public Culture." *Social Semiotics* 8, no. 1 (1998): 297–308.

———. "People's Daily, China and Japan: A Narrative Analysis." *Gazette: The International Journal for Mass Communication Studies* 54, no. 1 (1995): 198–207.

Tang Xiaobing, "Configuring the Modern Space: Cinematic Representation of Beijing and Its Politics." *East-West Film Journal* 8, no. 2 (1994): 47–69.

Teo, Stephen. *Hong Kong Cinema: The Extra Dimensions.* London: BFI, 1997.

"Tokyo's New Overseas Chinese Community Thriving." *Asian Economic News,* March 22, 1999. <www.findarticles.com/cf_0/m0WDP> (accessed August 2001).

"Tragedy and Technology Makes Overseas Chinese Unite." *The Straits Times,* August 8, 1998. <www.straitstimes.asia1.com/pages/cyb1_0820.html> (accessed August 1999).

Trinh T. Minh-Ha. "Other Than Myself/My Other Self." Pp. 9–26, in *Travellers' Tales: Narratives of Home and Displacement,* ed. George Robertson, Melinda Mash, Lias Tickner, Jon Bird, Barry Curtis, and Tim Putnam. London and New York: Routledge, 1994.

Tu Weiming. *The Living Tree: The Changing Meaning of Being Chinese Today,* ed. Tu Wei-ming. Stanford, Calif.: Stanford University Press, 1994.

Tu Xueneng, *Zhongguo guoqing da yuebin* (China's Military Parade on the National Day) Beijing: Dongfang Chubanshe, 1999.

Turkle, Sherry. *Life on the Screen: Identity in the Age of Internet.* London: Phoenix, 1995.

Turner, Graeme. *Making It National: Nationalism and Australian Popular Culture.* St. Leonard, NSW: Allen & Unwin, 1994.

Wang, Jing. "Culture as Leisure and Culture as Capital." *Positions: East Asia Culture Critique* 9, no. 1 (2001a): 69–104.

———. "Guest Editor's Introduction." *Positions: East Asia Culture Critique* 9, no. 1 (2001b): 1–27.

———. "The State Question in Chinese Popular Cultural Studies." *Inter-Asia Cultural Studies* 2, no. 1 (2001c): 35–52.

———. *High Culture Fever: Politics, Aesthetics and Ideology in Deng's Era*. Berkeley: University of California Press, 1996.

Wang Xiaomin. "Preface." Pp. 1–26, in *Zai Xin Yishixingtai De Longzhao Xia* (Under the Dominance of the New Ideology), ed. Wang Xiaomin. Nanjing: Jiangsu People's Press, 2000.

Wang Yi. "Intellectuals and Popular Television in China." *International Journal of Cultural Studies* 2, no. 2 (1999): 222–45.

Wark, McKenzie. *Virtual Geography: Living with Global Media Events*. Bloomington: Indiana University Press, 1994.

Werbner, Pnina. "Diasporic Political Imaginaries: A Sphere of Freedom or a Sphere of Illusions?" *Communal/Plural: Journal of Transnational and Cross-Cultural Studies* 6, no. 1 (1998): 11–32.

Williams, Raymond. *Television: Technology and Cultural Form*. London: Fontana, 1974.

Wilson, Elizabeth. *Sphinx in the City*. London: Virago, 1991.

Wilson, Tony. *Watching Television: Hermeneutics, Reception and Popular Culture*. Cambridge: Polity, 1993.

Wolff, Janet. "On the Road Again: Metaphors of Travel in Cultural Criticism" (reprinted from 1992). Pp. 180–94, in *Undoing Place?: A Geographical Reader*, ed. Linda McDowell. London: Arnold, 1995.

———. *Feminine Sentences: Essays on Women and Culture*. Cambridge: Polity, 1990.

Wollen, Paul. "The World City and the Global Village." *Emergences: Journal for the Study of Media and Composite Cultures* 9, no. 1 (1999): 69–78.

Xu Jiren. "*Yong chuang xin siwei baodao aoyun*" ("Innovative Ways of Reporting Olympic Games"). *Chinese Journalist* 10 (2000): 34–35.

Yang, Mayfair. "Mass Media and Transnational Subjectivity in Shanghai: Notes on (Re)Cosmopolitanism in a Chinese Metropolis." Pp. 287–322, in *Ungrounded Empire: The Cultural Politics of Modern Chinese Transnationalism*, ed. Aihwa Ong and Donald M. Nonini. London: Routledge, 1997.

———, ed., *Spaces of Their Own: Women's Public Sphere in Transnational China*. Minneapolis: University of Minnesota, 1999.

Yang Taoyuan. "*Zuei hao de sheng ao xuan chuan zai ling jiang dan shang*" ("The Best Propaganda for Beijing 2008 Lies on the Medal Podium"). *Liangwang Magazine* 40 (2000): 4–6.

Yang Xiaohong. "Eating All the Way." Trans. Wanning Sun. <www.cnd.org/HXWZ/CM00/cm0005c.hz8.html#9> (accessed October 2001).

Yi Min. "Going to the Funeral: The Untold Sadness of Chinese in America." Originally published in *Beijing Youth Daily*. <www.clibrary.com> (accessed August 2001).

Yu Hongmei. "*Zhebi yu kejian: Xinwen he wenxue zhongde xiagang nugong xinxiang fengxi*" ("Hidden versus Visible: Images of the Sacked Female Workers in News and Literature"). Luce Project on Media and Cultural Production Seminar, Beijing, December 1999.

Yu Xu. "Professionalisation without Guarantees: Changes of the Chinese Press in Post-1989 Years." *Gazette* 53 (1994): 23–44.

Yue, Audrey. "Migration as Transition: Clara Law's Autumn Moon." *Intersections* 4 (September 2000). <wwwsshe.murdoch.edu.au/intersections/issue4/yue.html> (accessed October 2000).

Yue Gang. *The Mouth That Begs: Hunger, Cannibalism, and the Politics of Eating in Modern China*. Durham, N.C.: Duke University Press, 1999.

Zhang Hua. *"Mu zi kang zheng, gao dao riben san lin"* ("Mother and Son Taking Mitsubushi to Court"). *Mizhu Yu Fazhi* (Democracy and Law) 324 (2000): 26–29.

Zha Jianying. *China Pop: How Soap Operas, Tabloids, and Bestsellers Are Transforming a Culture*. New York: New Press, 1995.

Zhang Youxue. *"Liuxue renyuan huiguo chuangye xianzhang fengxi"* ("An Analysis of the Chinese Students Who Have Returned from Overseas Study"). *Sheng Zhou Xue Ren* (Chinese Scholars Abroad) 134, no. 4 (2001). <www.chisa.edu.cn.> (accessed August 2001).

Zhang Xudong. "Nationalism, Mass Culture, and Intellectual Strategies in Post-Tiananmen China." *Social Text* 16, no. 2 (1998): 118.

Zhao Bin. "Mouthpiece or Money-Spinner?: The Double Life of Chinese Television in the Late 1990s." *International Journal of Cultural Studies* 2, no. 3 (1999): 291–306.

——. "Popular Family Television and Party Ideology: The Spring Festival Eve Happy Gathering." *Media Culture and Society* 20 (1998): 43–58.

Zhao Yuezhi. "From Commercialisation to Conglomeration: The Transformation of the Chinese Press within the Orbit of the Party State." *Journal of Communication* (Spring 2000): 3–25.

——. *Media, Market, and Democracy in China*. Urbana: University of Illinois Press, 1998.

WEBSITES

<www.aoyun.xinhuanet.com> (accessed October 2001).

<www.backchina.com/tv/index.html> (accessed October 2001).

<www.bbsland.com/bcchinese/messages/919.html> (accessed October 2001).

<www.cctvbase.net/data_center/data_content.asp?id=186> (accessed September 2001).

<www.clibrary.com/digest/0108/13026.html> (accessed October 2001).

<www.cnd.org> (accessed October 2001).

<www.cnd.org/huazhao> (accessed October 2001).

<www.creaders.org/forums/politics/messages/171867.html> (accessed October 2001).

(accessed October 2001).

<www2.fhy.net.GBF/2000/fhy0009d.gbf> (accessed October 2001).

<www.jiyuu-shikan.org/nanjing/contents.html> (accessed October 2001).

<www.org.HXWZexpress> (accessed July 15, 2001).

<www.sunrisesite.org/gb/?url=/forum/koei.h2.> (accessed December 1999).

<www.members.tripod.com/~funkytomoya/massacre/sample01.htm> (accessed October 2001).

<www.meltingpot.fortunecity.com/sudan/47/> (accessed October 2001).

(accessed October 2001).

<www.news.xinhuanet.com/zhibo/20010713/709917.htm> (accessed October 2001).

Index

"eating bitterness," 81
Economic Daily (newspaper), 170
"educated youth literature," 80–81
education: overseas, 3; role of television in, 32; rural, 35–36
electronic journalism. *See* Internet; television; video technology
Elsaesser, Thomas, 44
e-mail, 12, 13, 159, 161, 175
embarrassment, over news coverage of China, 98–99
Ermo (Zhou Xiaowen), 21–34; comparison with *Not One Less* (television program), 22; and effects of city life, 30–34; endings for, 24–25; negative aspects of modernity in, 24, 25, 26; overview of, 21; positive aspects of television in, 28–30; social status issues of, 25–27; summary of, 23–24
Erzi (television program), 82
ethnographer, Chinese migrant as, 70
ethnographic self-writing, 54
ethnography, focus of, 87, 107
ethnoscapes, 82
exile: in a cultural and epistemological sense, 140; and filmmakers, 48; gastronomic, 140; meaning of, 8; self-, 95; willing and voluntary, 80
exotica, 52, 73, 74

Falungong cult, 166–67, 187
famine of 1958–1962, 144–45
fantasies: of China, 114–15, 116–18; and film, 44; and television, 21–22, 44
fan yu yan. See antiallegorical films
Farewell China (film): border in, 47; comparison with *Goldfish* (film), 55; overview of, 45–46; phobic spaces in, 49–50
fear, in films, 48–50, 56, 59
Feng Hua Yuan (periodical), 119–20
Feng Jinhua, 1, 127, 174
Feng Xiaogang, 60. *See also Be There or Be Square*
fetish for Chinese things, 97–98, 99, 100, 106, 117

films: antiallegorical, 54; antimodernity and, 31, 39; and "border cinema," 47–48; comparison with television, 44, 71; fifth-generation, 54; influence on transnational imagination of, 43–45, 62; "migrant worker" narratives in, 81–82; music in, 50, 79; phobic spaces in, 48–50, 55, 56, 78–79; portrayal of village life in, 39; publicness of cinema, 44; spectatorship, 39; women's pursuit of modernity, 39–40. *See also Chinese in the New World* narratives; *names of specific films*; video technology, and viewing by migrant community
Floating Life (Law) (film), 49
Flower, Kathy, 72
Follow Me (television program), 72
food consumption, 137–57; adjusting to non-Chinese food, 140; cooking methods, 148; dissociation from cultural calendar, 151; in East versus West, importance of, 153; effect of having experienced food scarcity on, 143–44, 147; ethnic restaurants, 140–41, 148–49; experiences, 142–43, 145, 148–51; and memories of home, 145–46; in "other" cultures, 152–53; and relationship to languages, 153–54; role in transnational subjectivity formation of, 138; social-symbolic value of, 138–39; and transnational liminality, 146; vocabulary of, 144; websites about, 147; when traveling back to China, 149–50, 151–52
foreigners, blonde, 27
foreign languages, 27
foreign products and services, 172–76
Fregoso, Rosa Linda, 47
Fuji TV, 108
funerals, returning to China for, 92

Gao Yuan, 171–72
gastronomization, 144
gender. *See* women

About the Author

Wanning Sun is a native of Anhui Province, People's Republic of China. She studied, practiced, and taught journalism in Beijing and Shanghai for several years prior to moving to Australia. She is now a lecturer in media and communication studies at Curtin University of Technology, Western Australia.